YOUNG STUDENTS

Learning Library®

VOLUME 16

Panama—Pottery and China

NEWFIELD
PUBLICATIONS

MIDDLETOWN · CONNECTICUT

PHOTO CREDITS

A-Z BOTANICAL COLLECTION page 1949(center); HEATHER ANGEL page 1942(top left); 1948(center left); 1949(bottom); ASSOCIATED PRESS page 1887(top right); BIOPHOTOS page 1876(top left); 1949(bottom right); BRITISH MUSEUM page 1916(top left); 1970(bottom left); 1971(top left); 1988(bottom left); CERN page 1881(bottom left and center right); J. ALAN CASH page 1868(top left); 1874(center left); 1878(bottom left); 1964(top left); MICHAEL CHINERY page 1939(bottom); 1942(bottom); 1949(top right); 1974(top right); BRUCE COLEMAN LIMITED page 1919(top left); 1928(bottom left); DEPT. OF COMMERCE (BUREAU OF PUBLIC ROADS) page 1975(bottom right); GENE COX page 1871(bottom right); ARMANDO CURCIO EDITORE SPA page 1869(top right); 1870(top left); 1872(center left); 1876(bottom right); 1884(bottom left); 1885(both pics); 1886(top left); 1887(bottom center); 1908(bottom right); 1910(top left); 1911(top & center right); 1912(both pics); 1914(all pics); 1920(top left); 1922(center left); 1926(top & center left); 1927(bottom left); 1943(bottom right); 1950(top right); 1951(bottom right); 1956(bottom left); 1959(both pics); 1961(top right); 1969(top left); 1973(bottom right); 1975(top right); 1985(bottom right); 1988(center left); 1989(top left & bottom right); DERBY MUSEUM & ART GALLERY page 1937(top right); DESIGN COUNCIL page 1954(top left); EMI page 1987(bottom left); EPA/NYPL page 1987(top & bottom right); MARY EVANS PICTURE LIBRARY page 1936(bottom left); FOTOMAS page 1898(top left); GENERAL DYNAMICS page 1874(bottom left); GEO-SCIENCE page 1948(top left); STANLEY GIBBONS page 1983(top right); SONIA HALLIDAY page 1918(bottom left); 1919(top right); 1988(bottom right); BY GRACIOUS PERMISSION OF HER MAJESTY THE QUEEN page 1879(top right); RUSSELL F. HOGELAND page 1873(top right); 1907(top right); 1962(bottom left); HENRY HOLT page 1960(bottom left); KIT HOUGHTON page 1906(bottom left); LIBRARY OF CONGRESS page 1932(bottom left); 1933 (top right); 1968(top left); 1969(top right); MANSELL COLLECTION page 1883 (bottom right); 1911(bottom right); 1922 (bottom right); MINISTRY OF AGRICULTURE, FISHERIES & FOOD page 1943(top left); B. MONK page 1917(bottom right); 1918(top left & bottom right); PAT MORRIS page 1866; 1876(bottom left); 1929(top right); TONY MORRISON page 1904(top left); MUSEUM NATIONAL PARIS page 1903(top right); NHPA page 1880(top left); 1892(top right); 1929(bottom left); 1939(top right); 1946(top left); NATIONAL FILM BOARD OF OTTAWA page 1889(top right); NATURE PHOTOGRAPHERS page 1880(bottom left); 1962(bottom right); NEW YORK PUBLIC LIBRARY page 1931(top right); PETER NEWARK'S WESTERN AMERICANA page 1886(bottom left); DANIEL OCKO page 1981(top right); OKLAHOMA PLANNING & RESOURCES BOARD page 1933(center right); PANAMA CANAL COMPANY page 1867(top right); 1868(bottom right); PARFUMS LAGERFELD LIMITED page 1899(top right); PENNSYLVANIA DEPT. OF COMMERCE page 1893(top right); PICASSO MUSEUM page 1926(bottom right); POPPERFOTO page 1925(bottom right); 1977(top right); REX FEATURES page 1978(top left); SARN STUDIOS page 1898(bottom left); G. R. ROBERTS page 1922(top left); SCIENCE MUSEUM page 1919(bottom right); SPECTRUM COLOUR LIBRARY page 1967(top right); 1986(top left); STEDELIJIK MUSEUM, AMSTERDAM page 1981(bottom left); TENNESSEE TOURIST DEVELOPMENT page 1878(top left); ENRICO TRICARICA page 1973(top right); USDA PHOTO page 1963(top right); UNITED STATES CAPITOL HISTORICAL SOCIETY page 1930(top right); 1958(bottom left); UNITED STATES ENVIRONMENTAL PROTECTION AGENCY page 1970(top left); M. VAITIER page 1968(bottom left); DAVID & JILL WRIGHT page 1982(bottom left); ZEFA page 1875(bottom right); 1877(top right); 1888(top left); 1890(bottom left); 1896(top left); 1908(top left); 1909(top left & bottom right); 1910(bottom right); 1913(top right); 1924(top left); 1934(top left); 1950(top & bottom left); 1951(top right); 1966(both pics); 1967(bottom left & right); 1972(both pics; 1976(all pics); 1977(bottom right); 1983(bottom left); 1985(top left).

Copyright © 1992 by Newfield Publications, Inc.; 1974, 1972 by Funk &Wagnalls, Inc., & Newfield Publications, Inc.

ISBN 0-8374-0486-X

1993 Edition

Contents

PANAMA The Republic of Panama occupies the isthmus (narrow piece of land) that connects Central and South America. The Caribbean Sea (a part of the Atlantic Ocean) lies to the north, and the Pacific Ocean lies to the south. Panama's eastern border with the South American nation of Colombia is in the jungles of the province of Darien. Its western border is high in the mountains touching the Central American nation of Costa Rica. Panama is slightly smaller in area than South Carolina. (See the map with the article on CENTRAL AMERICA.)

Panama has a damp, tropical climate; the wettest region is on the northern side of the isthmus. The Panama Canal bisects (cuts into two parts) the country. From the western bank of the canal, the land rises from the low-lying canal area to the *Ilanos* (plains) of the central provinces, where much rice (Panama's chief crop) and sugarcane are grown. The land rises gradually to a level of more than 11,000 feet (3,350 m) at the extinct volcano, El Baru, near the Costa Rican border. Here, coffee *fincas* (farms) lie on the mountainsides and orange groves in the valleys. Cattle ranches are in the lower land. The center of the cattle industry is the city of David, on the Pacific side of Pan-

ama, where modern meat-packing facilities are located. Near the Costa Rican border on both the Atlantic and Pacific coasts lie the banana plantations.

East of the Panama Canal lie the coastal ranges and swampy interior plain of Darien province. This land is chiefly inhabited by two groups of Indians, the Choco and the Cuna. Off Panama's Atlantic Darien coast is the San Blas archipelago, a string of a thousand little islands. The San Blas Indians have lived there since fleeing from the Spanish on the Darien mainland in the 1500's.

Panama's largest city and capital is Panama City, on the Pacific Ocean near the Pacific entrance to the Panama Canal. Tourism has become an important business. The location of the canal has brought shipping business to the city and has made it a small international finance center. Many ships are registered in Panama and fly its flag.

▲ *Boquete is a town in a beautiful green valley in the Chiriqui Mountains of Panama. Coffee farms border this lovely area.*

◀ *A group of pelicans at the edge of a lake. Behind them is a flock of flamingos. See* PELICAN.

PANAMA

Capital City: Panama City (448,000 people).
Area: 9,211 square miles (75,650 sq. km).
Population: 2,450,000.
Government: Republic.
Natural Resources: Copper.
Export Products: Bananas, shrimp, coffee, sugar, clothing.
Unit of Money: Balboa.
Official Language: Spanish.

▲ *The Panama Canal is the world's busiest ship canal. A series of locks raises ships 85 feet (26 m) above sea level.*

Most of the Panamanians are of mixed Spanish, Indian, and black ancestry. Spanish is the main language, but English is also widely spoken.

Panama was ruled by Spain from about 1519 to 1821, when it became a province of Colombia. Panama later tried to break away from Colombian rule. In 1903, with U.S. help, it gained its independence. Panama then signed a treaty with the United States, giving permission for the construction, maintenance, and defense of an interoceanic canal within an area of Panama (the Panama Canal Zone).

Panama has usually had an unstable government. Since gaining its independence in 1903, the country has had more presidents than the United States has had in all its history. In 1978, two treaties were signed by the United States and Panama, providing for Panamanian control of the canal after December 31, 1999. In 1989, U.S. troops landed in Panama and arrested the Panamanian ruler General Noriega. He was taken to the United States on drug smuggling charges.

ALSO READ: CENTRAL AMERICA, PANAMA CANAL, SOUTH AMERICA.

pilot comes aboard and takes over the ship from the captain. Only a canal pilot with years of experience can safely guide today's huge fast ships through the narrow channels, locks, and tricky currents of the canal that was built for small, slower ships of the early 1900's. The canal is 50 miles (80 km) long and at least 300 feet (91 m) wide. One or more pilots (four in the case of huge supertankers) guide the ship through the three sets of Gatun Locks, raising the ship a 28-foot (8.5-m) step at a time up to 85 feet (26 m) above sea level—the height of Gatun Lake. The ship sails through Gatun Lake in two or three hours. From Gatun Lake the ship proceeds into Gaillard Cut—the most hazardous part of the journey. The cut is wide enough here for ships to pass each other. The cut goes through the highest part of the isthmus.

At the end of the Gaillard Cut the ship enters the Pedro Miguel Locks and goes down one 30-foot (9-m) step. Then it passes through the Miraflores Lake and into the Miraflores Locks. There, two sets of locks take the ship down to sea level in the Pacific Ocean, at the port of Balboa.

▼ *During the 1960's the Panama Canal was widened at Gaillard Cut so that two large ships could pass each other without danger. This put an end to most one-way traffic in the cut.*

In times past, mules were used to pull ships through canals. The powerful electric locomotives that pull ships through the locks of the Panama Canal are still called "mules."

PANAMA CANAL By cutting through the Isthmus of Panama, the Panama Canal connects the Atlantic and Pacific oceans. It also divides North and South America.

The ships of the world depend on this artificial waterway to save them traveling a distance of more than 13,000 miles (21,000 km) around the continent of South America. This was even more true when the Suez Canal in Egypt was closed to shipping from 1967 to 1975. Ships from Europe that once went east to Suez had to sail west to the Panama Canal to reach the Orient.

As a ship approaches the Panama Canal from the Atlantic Ocean at the town of Cristóbal, a Panama Canal

From 1881 to 1889, Ferdinand de Lesseps's French company (which had dug the Suez Canal) tried and failed to build a sea-level canal across the Isthmus of Panama. The United States later acquired the French rights and built the Panama Canal from 1904 to 1914. Colonel George Goethals of the U.S. Corps of Engineers headed the project. His ideas for simple, gravity-operated water systems have proved long-lasting in this tropical climate where heat and rust destroy complicated machinery. Colonel William Crawford Gorgas of the U.S. Army Medical Corps led the forces that controlled the yellow fever and malarial mosquitoes that had earlier caused the deaths of many French canal workers.

The Panama Canal is run by the Panama Canal Commission, a joint U.S. and Panamian authority. In 1903, the United States signed a treaty with Panama and acquired *sovereignty* (full control), for an annual payment to Panama, over the canal and the ten-mile-wide (16-km-wide) Panama Canal Zone. The zone was returned to Panamian control in 1979, though the U.S. retains access to vital areas of canal operation. Full control of the canal will be given to Panama after December 31, 1999.

ALSO READ: PANAMA.

PANDA Two kinds of bearlike mammals that live in Asia are named panda. They are related to the raccoon family. The panda most often seen in pictures is the giant panda. It looks like a big black-and-white teddy bear, with white fur and black rings around its body and a black spot around each eye. It grows to be about five feet (1.5 m) tall and can weigh more than 200 pounds (90 kg). The giant panda is a rare animal. It lives in the bamboo forests in the mountains of China and eats chiefly bamboo shoots.

In 1972, the People's Republic of China gave the United States two giant pandas, which were housed in the National Zoo in Washington, D.C. Zoos around the world have begun breeding programs to raise pandas in captivity. In China, wild pandas and their bamboo forest habitats are protected by law.

The other kind of panda, called the lesser panda, resembles the raccoon. The lesser panda is about two or three feet (60 to 90 cm) long. It looks like a large, furry cat with a long, bushy tail. The tail has rings around it like a raccoon's tail. The lesser panda has white fur on its face and reddish fur on its body. It lives in the Himalaya Mountains and climbs trees, sleeping in a hollow tree trunk. It eats bamboo shoots and leaves.

ALSO READ: BEAR, MAMMAL, RACCOON.

▲ *The giant panda feeds on bamboo. Because of its selective diet, it is a rare animal and not easy to keep in captivity.*

▲ *The lesser panda looks like a friendly little animal, but it does not like to be handled and has a ferocious bite.*

▲ *The cover of a program from an 1875 performance of the Christmas pantomime* Cinderella.

PANDORA To open a Pandora's box is an expression meaning to let troubles out into the world. In Greek mythology, Pandora was the first mortal (human) woman. Her name means "all-gifted." Zeus, ruler of the gods, was angry with Prometheus, who had stolen fire from the gods. So he had the god of fire create Pandora. She was given a box and told never to open it. Zeus wanted her to bring misery to mankind. She was married to Prometheus's brother, Epimetheus, who allowed her to satisfy her curiosity and open the box. All the evils that afflict mankind flew out. Pandora slammed the box shut, saving one blessing—hope.

ALSO READ: MYTHOLOGY.

PANTOMIME Pantomime is a kind of entertainment in which actors perform without words. Ancient Roman audiences understood what was going on when the actors made broad gestures. The word "pantomime" comes from the Greek words *panto*, meaning "all," and *mime*, meaning "imitate."

In the 1500's, a form of pantomime called *commedia dell'arte* was developed in Italy. It featured delightful characters named Harlequin, a clown; Columbine, a young maid; and Pantaloon, a father. Pantomime came to England in the 1700's and became enormously popular. It included dancing and music and had clever machinery that made magic seem to happen right on stage. Lavish pantomimes of fairy tales are performed at Christmastime in England today.

Some of the greatest actors began their careers in pantomime. Charlie Chaplin, Bert Lahr, and Buster Keaton were superb American pantomimists. The world's best known pantomimist is a Frenchman, Marcel Marceau. He and other mimes often play sad, gentle little people who are constantly victimized, or "picked on," by others.

Many people enjoy playing a pantomime game called *charades*. A player silently acts out a word while the others try to guess what it is. Can you act out "pantomime"?

ALSO READ: ACTORS AND ACTING.

PAPER The world's first maker of paper was the wasp. The wasp chews tiny pieces of wood into a pulp. The pulp mixes with the saliva in the wasp's mouth. The wasp then spits out the wet pulp and smooths it into a thin sheet. When the pulp dries, it becomes paper. It is used by certain kinds of wasps to build their nests.

Today, we use paper for writing on, but thousands of years ago, our

The Chinese invented paper in about A.D. 105. In the 8th century, the Arabs captured some Chinese papermakers and took them off to Baghdad. There they started several state-owned paper mills. It was not until 1590 that the first paper mill was founded in England.

1. Rags, mixed with water, were shredded to pulp.

2. Pulp was stirred in a vat. A wire screen or sieve was dipped into the pulp, lifted out, shaken, and laid on felt.

3. The wet sheets were screw-pressed to compress and dry the fibers.

4. Paper sheets were peeled off the felt and dried.

ancestors communicated by drawing pictures on stones or animal horns. Later, people wrote on strips of bark from trees, on silk, or on skins of sheep or goats. Animal skins prepared for writing were called *parchment*.

Parchment and silk were costly. Tree bark was easily torn or cracked. People searched for something better to write on. They found it in the plant called *papyrus*, which grew along the banks of the Nile River in Egypt.

Papyrus is a reed, a kind of grass that grows in wet places. The Egyptians crisscrossed strips of papyrus to make small woven mats. Each mat was soaked in the river to soften the reeds. Then it was taken out, placed on a flat stone, and pounded with another stone. This pounding broke up the fibers in the wet reeds and mashed them together so that they made a flat sheet. The sheet was dried in the sun. It could then be used instead of parchment or silk as a writing surface. But the first paper, as we know it, was produced in China about A.D. 105. It was made by the same process as that used by the wasp. The Chinese mashed tree bark into a wet pulp, squeezed out the water, and pressed the pulp into flat sheets, which dried into paper. The Arabs brought the secret of papermaking to Europe in the 1100's.

Today, paper is made by machines, but the basic process is the same as the one the Chinese used. Most paper is made on the Fourdrinier machine. This machine is named after the two Fourdrinier brothers who built the first one in 1803. It consists of a belt of wire mesh on which watery pulp is spread. The belt passes through a series of rollers, which press the water out of the pulp. The belt then passes under a turning cylinder, called a dandy roll. The dandy roll gives the paper a woven or flat surface. Near the end of the machine, the belt passes through two felt-covered couching rolls, which press out more

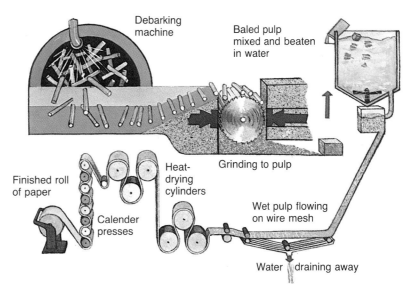

water. It then goes through two sets of smooth metal press rolls. The press rolls give the paper a smooth finish. The last step before cutting is calendering, or pressing the paper between chilled rollers. Calendering gives the paper an even smoother finish, called a machine finish. At the end of the Fourdrinier machine, the paper is wound on spools into large rolls. The paper is slit into strips and cut into sheets.

The cheapest paper is made from wood pulp. Better quality paper is made from a pulp mixture of wood and cloth. The finest stationery is made entirely of cloth pulp, or rag fibers, usually cotton or linen. Paper containing rag fibers usually has a watermark. A watermark is a design pressed into the wet pulp by the dandy roll. When the pulp dries, the watermark becomes translucent; that is, the watermark can be seen clearly only when the paper is held to the light. The watermark may be a picture of some kind and may include the words "rag content."

Paper is used for many purposes besides writing. Money is made from paper. Groceries and other goods are carried in paper bags. Paper cups are used for drinking. Paper labels tell customers what cans of food contain. Books are made of paper. Paper is used as a base for roofing and as a lining for wooden walls. Paper is used

Debarking machine

Baled pulp mixed and beaten in water

Finished roll of paper

Heat-drying cylinders

Grinding to pulp

Calender presses

Wet pulp flowing on wire mesh

Water draining away

▲ *How paper is made from wood pulp. The pulped wood is mixed with water and poured onto a wire mesh belt. The water is squeezed out, leaving a web of fibers that are then dried and rolled.*

▲ *The torn edge of a piece of colorful wrapping paper seen through a magnifying glass. The wood fibers are easy to see under these conditions.*

PAPER SCULPTURE

▲ *These huge figures on a parade float are made of papier-mâché, a form of paper sculpture.*

for wrapping and packaging many industrial items. Tissue paper and wax paper are used in homes and offices every day. Even clothing is sometimes made of paper. Nearly everyone reads newspapers and magazines. Artists draw and paint pictures on paper. Many goods come in cardboard boxes, which are paper products; in fact almost half the paper we use is in the form of boxes and packaging.

ALSO READ: LUMBER AND LUMBERING.

PAPER SCULPTURE At Christmastime, many people make colorful paper chains to hang on Christmas trees. In hot weather, people often make fans of folded sheets of paper. Airplanes or gliders can be made from paper. All these are examples of paper sculpture. They are all made by changing flat paper into forms or shapes. The art of paper sculpture is hundreds of years old. Japanese children learn *origami*—the art of folding paper in special ways to make flowers and animals.

Experimenting with Paper Sculpture
You will need strong glue, tape, scissors, and paper for making sculptures. The paper may be construction or poster paper in all colors, typing paper, wallpaper, or brown paper from paper bags. Whichever paper you use, it must be stiff enough to

keep the shapes you are folding.

Before making anything very complicated, you should experiment with paper to find out what you can do with it. Try bending and folding the paper in various ways. Try pleating it (making folds back and forth, like a fan). You can curl paper by pulling it along the edge of your scissors or wrapping it around a pencil. You can cut spirals from circles or squares by starting at the edge and cutting around and around in a circular or square pattern until you reach the center. Experiment with making springs and spirals, cylinders and cones, using glue where necessary. You can also weave paper strips together to form mats.

Papier-Mâché Papier-mâché is a way of making solid sculpture out of wet paper and paste. Papier-mâché is a French term meaning "chewed paper." In France during the 1700's, old paper posters were ripped up and mixed with glue and paste to make boxes, trays, figurines, and other things.

■ LEARN BY DOING
You can make papier-mâché sculpture by tearing newspaper into strips an inch (2.5 cm) wide and about a foot (30 cm) long. Lay the strips in a large pan and cover them with water. Put a cup of flour into another pan and add enough cool water to make it heavy and thick. Then slowly add boiling water until the mixture becomes a creamy paste. Dip strips of wet newspaper into the paste and mold them together into an animal, a person, or whatever shape you want. You can make a papier-mâché bowl or dish by wetting the inside of a regular bowl or dish and then molding several layers of the papier-mâché to the moistened surface. Trim the edges of your sculpture and let it stand in a warm, dry place for two days to harden. (If you are making a bowl or dish, leave the papier-mâché

in the bowl while hardening.) After it has dried, you can decorate your sculpture with paints. ■

ALSO READ: MASK, PAPER, SCULPTURE.

PAPUA NEW GUINEA Papua New Guinea occupies the eastern half of the island of New Guinea. It borders on the Indonesian province of Irian Jaya on the west. The country has lowlands along the coasts and dense forests and mountains inland. Until recently much of the country was unexplored by outsiders. Papua New Guinea is a little larger than California.

Papua New Guinea has high temperatures and heavy rainfall all year round. Many of the people live in isolated villages. They grow crops of sweet potatoes, bananas, rice, and fruits, and they also keep pigs. Beef cattle are now being raised on grassland areas.

Agricultural products include coconuts, cocoa, and coffee. Timber and prawns (similar to shrimps) are also important. Copper is the principal mineral export, and some natural gas has been discovered.

The population of Papua New Guinea comes from many native Melanesian tribes, Australians, Europeans, and Chinese. Some 600 local languages are spoken, but Pidgin (simplified) English is the principal means of communication.

Britain first claimed the southern half in 1884 and then gave it to Australia in 1905. Germany claimed the northern half in 1884, but Australia seized it in World War I. Much of Papua New Guinea was then administered by Australia, first under a League of Nations mandate and later through a U.N. trusteeship. The two parts of the country were given self-government in 1973 and complete independence in 1975.

The country is governed through a national parliament that meets in the capital, Port Moresby. The leader of the government is the prime minister. Papua New Guinea is a member of the Commonwealth of Nations, and Queen Elizabeth II is represented by a governor-general.

ALSO READ: MELANESIA, NEW GUINEA, PACIFIC ISLANDS.

PARACHUTE The word "parachute" is a combination of an Italian word *parare* (to protect) and a French word *chute* (fall). The use of the parachute was first suggested by Leonardo da Vinci, but the first practical parachute was not invented until the 1780's. A Frenchman, André Jacques Garnerin, succeeded in parachuting from a balloon in 1797. After that, parachutes became a part of the regular equipment of balloonists. By the end of World War I, parachutes were adopted as lifesaving devices for all

▲ *Paper sculpture is fun to make. This is a horse's head made from paper that has been cut, folded, and curled in various ways. Children made this hanging paper sculpture for a school project.*

PAPUA NEW GUINEA

Capital City: Port Moresby (145,000 people).
Area: 178,273 square miles (461,691 sq. km).
Population: 3,885,000.
Government: Parliamentary state.
Natural Resources: Copper, gold, silver, natural gas, potential for oil.
Export Products: Gold, copra, coffee, copper, palm oil, lobster.
Unit of Money: Kina.
Official Language: English.

▲ *A drawing of Leonardo da Vinci's original design for a parachute.*

▲ *When a parachute opens, the large canopy pulls against the air and slows the fall. The parachutist pulls on control lines attached to the canopy to steer the parachute. Holes in the canopy make for greater control.*

▼ *This Air Force fighter has a drogue parachute that opens as the plane lands and helps to slow it down.*

pilots and passengers of military airplanes.

During World War II, all the fighting nations transported troops behind enemy lines by plane, landing the soldiers from low altitudes by parachute. In the Korean War, the U.S. Air Force also used parachutes to drop heavy equipment, such as tanks, trucks, and field guns. Paratroopers were often dropped into the jungles of Southeast Asia during the Vietnam War.

The modern-day parachute is a canopy about 30 feet (9 m) across, made of panels of silk or nylon. A small hole in the center of the canopy lessens the jolt when the parachute opens. A series of shroud lines are sewn into the seams between the panels. The lines pass over the canopy and are connected at the ends by two metal rings. A harness, which fits around the shoulders and body and between the legs, attaches to the rings. The parachute is carefully folded in a canvas container on the jumper's back when not in use. The jumper pulls a small *ripcord* to release the folded parachute. A smaller parachute pulls the main parachute out of the container.

A parachute jumper dives from a plane and pulls the ripcord after about three seconds. The slight delay enables the jumper to fall far enough to be sure the opened parachute does not get entangled in the plane. Once the parachute opens, the jumper descends at a rate of about 17 feet (5 m) a second. The jumper hits the ground with about the same force as if he or she had jumped freely from a height of ten feet (3 m). Paratroopers usually jump with their parachutes attached to a static line that opens the parachute automatically.

Parachutes are often used to drop supplies and rescue crews at the sites of accidents, forest fires, and other disasters, where there is no available road or where land travel would take too much time. Spacecraft, manned or unmanned, have been lowered to the ground or into the sea by parachute—or several parachutes. Supersonic fighter planes release parachutes from their tails to slow their speed when landing.

The exciting sports of "parachute jumping" and "sky diving" have been popular since the 1950's. Sports parachutists aim for pinpoint landings on targets. They often use parachutes having holes in them, so they can control the direction of their descent and landing point. During "free fall," a sky diver delays opening the parachute and makes planned movements. The jumpers are in free fall between the time when they jump from the plane to the time when they pull their ripcords. Highly skilled sky divers can control their movements during more than 60 seconds of free fall and can perform all kinds of "acrobatics" at more than 12,000 feet (3,500 m) above the ground.

ALSO READ: AIRPLANE, AIRSHIP, BALLOON, HANG GLIDING.

PARAGUAY Paraguay is a South American country surrounded by other countries, so it has no seacoast. Brazil on the east, Bolivia on the north, and Argentina on the south and west border Paraguay. (See the map with the article on SOUTH AMERICA.) The country is about the same size as California, but it has less then one-seventh of California's population.

Asunción, the country's capital city, is a busy port on the Paraguay River. The river flows into the Paraná

PARAGUAY

Capital City: Asunción (490,000 people).
Area: 157,048 square miles (406,752 sq. km).
Population: 4,780,000.
Government: Republic.
Natural Resources: Iron ore, manganese, limestone, hydroelectric potential.
Export Products: Cotton, soybeans, lumber, vegetable oils, coffee, tung oil, meat products.
Unit of Money: Guarani.
Official Language: Spanish.

River and into the Río de la Plata (the large estuary that separates Argentina and Uruguay).

The Paraguay River divides the country into two regions. Eastern Paraguay is made up of a high, forested plateau and wooded hills and plains. Many crops are grown in the fertile eastern grasslands.

Few people live in western Paraguay, called the Chaco, a low plain covered with scrub forest and marshes. Oil and minerals have been found in the Chaco, but much of the land is unexplored. Rivers often overflow their banks in the eastern Chaco, but in the west, the land becomes drier, and water is scarce. Jaguars, carpinchos (large rodents), and tapirs live in the Chaco.

Most Paraguayans are *mestizos* (a people of mixed Spanish and Guaraní Indian ancestry) who are farmers. Cotton, soybeans, corn, sugarcane, tobacco, rice, and fruits are grown. Cattle raising is done on large plantations. Some people work in the forests, cutting down hardwood trees for export. Paraguay is one of Latin America's poorest and least industrialized countries.

The Spanish explorer, Juan de Salazar, founded the city of Asunción in 1537. Paraguay was ruled by Spain until independence was won in 1811. A major political figure was Solano Lopez, Paraguay's most famous hero. Several dictators have ruled Paraguay. Alfredo Stroessner became president in 1954. He was reelected

six times, but was overthrown by General Andrés Rodriguez in 1989.

ALSO READ: CONQUISTADOR, SOUTH AMERICA, SPANISH HISTORY.

PARASITE A parasite is an animal or plant that lives off another animal or plant, called a *host*. The parasite gets its nourishment either by taking some of the host's nourishment or by slowly eating the host. Most parasites are harmful to their hosts, but they do not usually kill them. If a parasite kills its host, then it must find another host. Many parasites cannot move on their own, so they die if the host dies.

Two kinds of parasites are *external* parasites and *internal* parasites. External means "outside." External parasites live on the outside of their host. Externally parasitic plants, such as mistletoe, send tubes through a host tree's bark to get nourishment. Animals pierce (poke holes in) the host's skin and suck out nourishment. Fleas, mosquitoes, lice, ticks, and bedbugs are external parasites. They are often not too different from their relatives that are not parasites.

Internal parasites live inside the host. They are very different from their nonparasitic relatives. Internal parasites have very complicated life cycles. A fairly typical internal parasite is the tapeworm. A tapeworm living in a person's digestive tract

The forests of Paraguay produce quebracho, one of the hardest woods in the world. (The name *quebracho* comes from the Spanish language and means *ax-breaker*.) The wood is much used in building. The bark of the tree also produces tannin, a substance used in tanning leather.

▼ *Asunción is Paraguay's capital, largest city, and cultural center. It is also a busy river port (the Paraguay River is in the background.*

1875

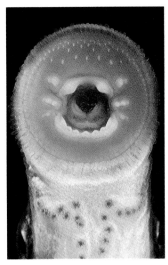

▲ *The lamprey's mouth is a sucker armed with horny teeth. With its mouth, the lamprey clings to a fish and sucks its victim's blood.*

▲ *Ticks are common parasites. This tick is gorged with blood sucked from its host, a European hedgehog.*

It is estimated that plant parasites cause several billion dollars worth of damage to crops each year in the United States.

(stomach and intestines) lays eggs that pass out of the body with wastes. If the eggs end up in water, they develop into a larva (young tapeworm) that can swim around. In order to develop further, the larva must be eaten by a certain kind of shrimp. Then the shrimp must be eaten by a fish. The larva moves from the shrimp to the muscles of the fish, where it *encysts* itself (covers itself with a hard coating). If a person eats the fish without cooking it well, the larva goes into the person's digestive tract, where it changes into an adult tapeworm. To avoid getting tapeworms, or any of the many other parasitic worms, you should always cook foods well, especially meat and fish.

Although an internal parasite has a very complicated life cycle, it has a very simple body. An adult tapeworm has a head, or *scolex*, with hooks and suckers to hold onto the host. Behind the scolex grows a long chain of segments, which absorb food from the host's stomach. Each segment has male and female sex organs. Eggs are fertilized by sperm from the same tapeworm. When the segments are completely filled with fertilized eggs, they drop off and pass out of the host's body. The eggs grow as parasites.

The tapeworm has close relatives that have eyes, brains, and digestive cavities (stomachs). But the tapeworm has no eyes, brain, or stomach. It does not need them to live the kind of parasitic life it leads. Most internal parasites have lost almost everything but the ability to hook onto their host, absorb nourishment, and reproduce.

Some internal parasites are *microscopic*—too small to be seen except through a microscope. Malaria and sleeping sickness are caused by microscopic parasitic animals that are carried to their hosts by flies and mosquitoes. Nest parasites don't attach themselves to the host. They just take food from the host.

Many fungi, bacteria, and viruses are parasitic. Fungi can be internal or external parasites. Athlete's foot is a common disease caused by an external fungus.

Bacteria are microscopic plants that can cause disease and damage body tissue. Viruses are so small that they cannot be seen under an ordinary microscope and so primitive (simple) that biologists are not sure if they are living things at all. But viruses can cause a wide variety of diseases, including chicken pox.

Parasites are both very simple and very complicated. They have usually lost the ability to do certain things for themselves, but to make up for this loss, they have developed very complicated ways of getting other animals to do things for them.

ALSO READ: ANIMAL, ANIMAL KINGDOM, BACTERIA, EVOLUTION, VIRUS.

PARASITIC PLANT Plants that live on and get their food from other live plants or animals are called parasitic plants. Almost all parasitic plants lack *chlorophyll*. Chlorophyll is the green coloring matter that makes it possible for most plants to make their own food. Because they cannot make their own food, parasitic plants get their nourishment by taking it from other plants and animals. These plants and animals are referred to as *hosts*. Almost all bacteria are parasitic plants. So are some kinds of fungi. One parasitic fungus is wheat rust, which kills wheat plants. Dodder is a wiry, leafless plant parasite that destroys alfalfa, clover, and flax.

Mistletoe has some chlorophyll. It makes some of its own food but also grows as a parasite on many kinds of trees. Mistletoe has no true roots. It twines around the host tree. Thin tubes, called *haustoria*, grow from the mistletoe into the bark of the host. The haustoria anchor the mistletoe, and through them, the mistletoe

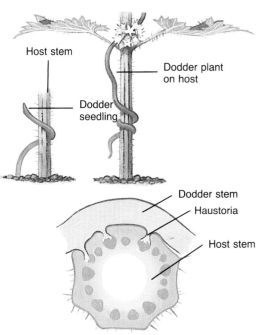

▲ *Dodder is a parasitic plant. It twines around the host's stem for support and takes food from the host through tubes called haustoria. Dodder destroys alfalfa and clover in particular.*

draws sap from the host. The dodder also uses haustoria to feed from its host.

ALSO READ: PARASITE.

PARIS Paris is the beautiful capital city of France. It is the artistic, commercial, scientific, and theatrical center of the country. Located on the Seine River, Paris is also a transportation center. A great network of rivers, canals, roads, and railroads meets in the city. More than two and a half million people live in the central city of Paris, but about 10 million people live in the entire metropolitan area.

Paris is often called the "City of Light," because so many great ideas and cultural achievements began there. The headquarters of UNES-CO, the United Nations Educational, Scientific, and Cultural Organization, is in the city. Paris is also an international center of fashion.

The Seine River divides the city of Paris in two. Thirty-two bridges cross the river. The oldest, and perhaps the most famous, of these is the Pont Neuf. It was built in the 1500's, but its name means "New Bridge." On the Île de la Cité (Island of the City) in the middle of the Seine is the Gothic cathedral of Notre Dame. The Left (south) Bank of the river is popular with artists and students. The Sorbonne, one of the world's oldest universities, is located there. So is the old Luxembourg Palace, now the meeting place of the French senate. The Right (north) Bank is the business center. The white-domed church of Sacré Coeur (Sacred Heart) is a landmark there. It stands atop Montmartre, the tallest hill in Paris and a beautiful part of the city.

Perhaps the most famous landmark in Paris is the Eiffel Tower. The massive Arc de Triomphe (Arch of Triumph) celebrates French military victories. The Louvre, once a palace for French kings, is now one of the greatest art museums in the world.

Paris is named after a small tribe of Gauls called the Parisii, who built a village on Île de la Cité in the Seine about 2,000 years ago. The Romans conquered the area and called the village "Lutetia Parisiorum," or "the muddy place of the Parisians." By the 13th century Paris had become a great medieval center of learning.

ALSO READ: CATHEDRAL, FRANCE, GOTHIC ARCHITECTURE, LOUVRE.

▲ *The Eiffel Tower was designed by the French engineer Alexandre Gustave Eiffel (1832–1923). It was built in 1889, entirely of iron. At 985 feet (300 m), it was the world's tallest structure at the time.*

▼ *This hand-tinted postcard shows the Champs-Élysées (Elysian Fields), one of the most beautiful avenues in Paris. At one end of the avenue (top left) stands the Arc de Triomphe (Arch of Triumph).*

▲ *Knotts Berry Farm is an Amusement Park in California. This exciting ride is "The Corkscrew".*

A single tree has been named a state park in Wye Mills, Maryland. The Wye Oak was made a state park in 1940. It is the oldest oak in Maryland—over 400 years old.

▼ *A tame elephant greets visitors to Tsavo National Park in Kenya, Africa.*

PARK Parks are places set aside for public recreation. They offer many things to see and do. Parks may have playgrounds, baseball or football fields, flower gardens, lakes, swimming pools, or even zoos. Most parks have green lawns and trees, paths, and open places where people can take walks, have picnics, or just relax in the sunshine.

The first parks were forests that belonged only to the king. The king hunted antelope, deer, and other animals in his park. Ordinary people could not go into the park at all. In the 1600's and 1700's, nobles and other rich people had laid out different kinds of parks next to their castles and palaces. These parks were landscaped with trees, lakes, and broad lawns and had large flower gardens surrounded by walls or fences. The kings of Prussia had a very lovely park called Sans Souci, which means "without care." The kings of France had large, beautiful parks next to their palaces in Versailles and in Paris. Some of the large public parks in London, England, were once private parks owned by wealthy nobles. Today, most of these gardens and parks are open to the public. Anyone can visit them and enjoy their beauty.

Parks made especially as places of recreation for ordinary people were first built only about 150 years ago.

The best-known public park in the United States is Central Park in New York City. Originally, this land was used for farming. But as the city grew larger, people began to see the need for a public park. The city bought the land in the 1850's and two men, Calvert Vaux and Frederick Law Olmsted, designed the park. They laid out walks and drives, lakes and gardens, great lawns and playing fields, and a band shell, where people could listen to music. Central Park was such a success that soon many other cities in the United States began to build large parks.

Today, parks are found in almost every city and town. Most of them are owned and operated by local governments. The Federal Government and state governments have also set aside parks. These are often located in unusually scenic spots or in places of historic significance.

ALSO READ: NATIONAL PARK.

PARLIAMENT A parliament is the highest *legislative*, or lawmaking, body in a country. The word "parliament" comes from the French word *parler*, which means "to talk." Thus "parliament" means a place to talk or debate. The British Parliament dates from 1295 and is one of the oldest. Known as the "Mother of Parliaments," it has been a model for lawmaking bodies the world over. Australia, Canada, New Zealand, and many other countries also use the term "parliament" for their legislatures.

The British Parliament is housed in the area of London called Westminster. It consists of two chambers, the House of Lords and the House of Commons. The House of Lords is made up of British *peers*, people who hold titles of nobility. Some titles are inherited or passed down from generation to generation. Others are granted for life, as a special honor.

Important clergy also sit in the House of Lords. So do senior judges, called law lords. They hear cases appealed to the House of Lords, the highest court.

Members of the House of Commons are elected by the people of Great Britain. Each member represents a different district, or *constituency*. General elections are held at least every five years. Voters are usually offered a choice of representatives from several political parties.

The leader of the party with the most representatives, or *seats*, in Parliament usually becomes prime minister. The prime minister is the most powerful government leader in the nation, but he or she is bound by law to follow the advice of Parliament. (In this way the parliamentary system differs from the United States's *separation of powers*. Each of three bodies—the President and executive staff, the Congress, and the Supreme Court—has well-defined limits of power, according to the U.S. Constitution.)

New laws and matters of national policy are discussed by both Houses. A vote is taken, and the legislation is passed if a majority of members favors it. The Lords seldom disagree with decisions made by the Commons. If they do disagree, they can

only delay legislation for a period of six months. The Commons is by far the more powerful House. The king or queen of Great Britain must approve all laws before they can be put into practice. In modern times, however, this has become only a formality, and the monarch is always expected to agree with Parliament.

ALSO READ: CONGRESS, UNITED STATES; GOVERNMENT, LEGISLATURE.

PARROTS AND PARAKEETS

Parrots are brightly colored birds that live in the warmer parts of the world. There are more than 310 kinds of parrots. They range in size from the pygmy parrot, only three inches (7.5 cm) long, to the macaws, which are more than three feet (90 cm) long.

Parrots have large beaks. Both the upper and lower parts of their beaks are hinged and can be moved up and down. Parrots use their beaks for cracking nuts and seeds, for smoothing their feathers, and for climbing. Some parrots hang by their beaks. Parrots have four-toed feet. The two front toes and the two rear toes can be closed like fingers of a hand. Parrots often use their feet like hands to hold

▲ *Queen Elizabeth I sits at the head of Parliament in the late 1500's. This was the old House of Lords—the members of the Commons stood at the end of the room.*

▼ *In the wild, budgerigars are green, with yellow and black markings. The fancy colors of pet parakeets have been obtained by selective breeding.*

▼ *The House of Commons, the legislative assembly of the British Parliament.*

▲ *The crimson rosella is an Australian parakeet. It is an agile climber, using its curved beak as well as its claws to scramble about in trees.*

▲ *A yellow-bellied parrot from West Africa.*

their food when eating. Parrots also use their feet when climbing. They are among the best climbing birds. Most parrots are good fliers, and they walk easily on the ground.

Parrots have loud, harsh voices. The gray parrot of Africa and the green Amazon parrot can easily be taught to "talk." Parrots cannot understand what they say; they simply mimic, or imitate, the sounds of words.

Parakeets are middle-sized parrots that live in Australia, Asia, Africa, and the Polynesian islands of the Pacific Ocean. There were once large numbers of parakeets in the southern and eastern United States. But they were killed for their bright feathers, and because they ate fruit crops. The last of these parakeets was seen in 1910. The shell parakeet, or budgerigar ("budgie"), of Australia is a popular cage bird and also a good "talker." Lorikeets are similar to parakeets but are smaller.

Cockatoos are large, crested parrots of Australia and nearby islands. Cockatiels are similar but smaller. The pink cockatoo and the white cockatoo (which has yellow and red markings) are kept as pets. Macaws, which live in Central and South America, are the largest and most brightly colored par-

rots. Macaws can be scarlet and blue; red, yellow, and blue; and yellow and blue. Lovebirds are small, plump African parrots. They choose a mate for life and stay together in pairs.

■ LEARN BY DOING

If you want to keep a parrot or parakeet as a pet, make sure you provide the bird with a cage big enough to allow it to move about freely and spread its wings. The cage should have perches and water and food cups. Make friends with your pet by talking to it softly. Remember that sudden noises or movement startle birds. Once your bird is tame, you can let it out of the cage, but make sure all doors and windows in the room are closed before you do so.

Parrots can give a painful bite, so do not poke your finger into a parrot's cage unless you know it is friendly. ■

ALSO READ: BIRD, PETS

PARTHENON   see ACROPOLIS.

PARTICLE ACCELERATOR

All matter is made up of atoms. Scientists used to think that the atom was the smallest particle of all, but now they know that the atom itself is made up of even smaller particles. These are called *subatomic particles*.

Atoms are so small that they cannot be seen, even under a microscope. Subatomic particles are very much smaller! The only way that scientists can study them is to break up atoms. They do this using a machine called a particle accelerator. This speeds up subatomic particles until they are traveling close to the velocity of light. When an atom is hit by a particle traveling at this speed, it disintegrates. The subatomic particles fly off in different directions. From the way in which they do this, physicists can tell a great deal about those particles. Today, for example, scientists believe that all matter is made of subatomic particles called *quarks*. Quarks are believed to come together to form subatomic particles such as *protons*, *neutrons*, and *electrons*.

Particle accelerators were first made in the 1920's and 1930's. Modern ones are very big and expensive to build. The simplest type is the *linear accelerator*, or *linac*. The linac belonging to Stanford University in California is two miles (3.2 km) long.

Linacs accelerate particles in a straight line. Most big-particle accelerators, however, are ring-shaped. In them, particles are accelerated to very high speeds as they travel around the ring. Accelerators of this type are called *proton* synchrotrons. The most important is at work near Geneva, in Switzerland.

ALSO READ: ANTIMATTER, ATOM, MATTER.

PARTS OF SPEECH In a play, actors take the parts of characters. Together, all the characters tell the story as the play is acted out. Each character or role is different from every other. In language, words are like actors. Each word takes a different part to help tell the story of the sentence. And just as in a play, each part is different.

There are eight main parts to our language—nouns, pronouns, verbs, adjectives, adverbs, prepositions, conjunctions, and interjections. These groups are called parts of speech. Every word belongs to one or more of these groups. Which part of speech a word belongs to depends on how the word is used in the sentence. A dictionary will tell you if a word is a noun, adjective, or some other part of speech.

A *noun* is a word that names. The name of everything in the world is a noun. It may be the name of a particular person (Frederick Douglass); a place (America); a thing (encyclopedia); a quality (thoughtfulness); an idea (patriotism); or a unit of measure (inch). The subject of a sentence (what a sentence is *about*) is always a noun—or a pronoun.

A *pronoun* is a word that can be used in place of a noun to mean the same thing as the noun it replaces. The name *pronoun* means "for a noun." The most common pronouns are called *personal pronouns*. They show whether the pronoun stands for the person or persons speaking, or first person (I, we); the person spoken to, or second person (you); or a person or thing being talked about, or third person (he, she, it, they).

A *verb* is a word that expresses some action or a state of being.

It *was* a warm morning.

LeRoy *threw* the ball.

He *was playing* in the yard.

A verb may be one word, as in the first and second sentences. A verb may also be more than one word, as in the third sentence. If it is more than one, it is called a *verb phrase*. The verb is a word that tells you what happens in a sentence.

We have small particle accelerators in our homes. The picture on your TV screen is made by a beam of tiny electrons striking the inside of the television tube. These negatively charged atomic particles are given a high speed by being attracted by a high positive voltage.

▲ *The Irish physicist Ernest Walton who, with another physicist, Sir John Cockcroft, developed the first nuclear particle accelerator in 1931. They were both awarded the Nobel Prize for Physics.*

▼ *Particle accelerators have enabled scientists to discover more about the atom and subatomic particles.*

An *adjective* is a word that says something about a noun or pronoun. The adjective may describe or define the noun or pronoun in some way.

> A *good* player needs a lot of energy.
>
> His *dusty* car screeched to a stop.

There are many different types of adjectives. Among those used most often are words called *articles*. *A*, *an*, and *the* are the most common articles.

An *adverb* modifies (limits the meaning of) a verb, an adjective, or another adverb. An adverb indicates such things as *how*, *when*, *where*, or *why* something happened.

> Frances arrived *late* (modifies the verb *arrived*).
>
> Chocolate pudding is an *extremely* sweet dessert (modifies the adjective *sweet*).
>
> Jim whistled *quite* softly (modifies the adverb *softly*).
>
> Put your books *down* (modifies the verb *put*).

A *preposition* is a word or group of words whose purpose is to show the relationship between a noun and another word in the sentence. Ideas about direction, position, source, and time are expressed by prepositions.

> The plane flew *into* the sunset.
>
> The lamp hangs low *over* the table.
>
> The children can hardly wait *until* Christmas.

A *conjunction* is a word or group of words that join other words or groups of words called *phrases* or *clauses*. The most familiar are the conjunctions *and*, *but*, *for*, *or*, and *nor*.

> You *and* I can walk the dog.
>
> I wanted to watch the late news, *but* I was too sleepy.
>
> She doesn't know whether to stay *or* to go.
>
> March seems like neither winter *nor* spring.

An *interjection* is a word or group of words used to express emotion.

> *Wow!* What a game!
>
> *Oh*, do you have to go already?

> *For goodness sake!* I thought you'd never get here!

Prepositions, conjunctions, and interjections never change in their form (spelling). All other parts of speech change to show such things as how many are or who is (or was, or will be) talking, and about whom or what. These changes in the form of words are called *inflections*. The inflection of nouns and pronouns is called *declension*. (For example, *boy* is singular, and *boys* is plural.) The change or inflection of a verb is known as *conjugation*. (For example, I *sing*, but he *sings*.) And *comparison* is the word used to describe the inflection of adjectives and adverbs. (Tom is *tall*. His brother is *taller*. But his father is *tallest* of the three.) These terms are used for inflections in foreign languages, as well as in the English language.

ALSO READ: GRAMMAR, LANGUAGES.

PASCAL, BLAISE (1623–1662) Blaise Pascal's father wanted him to be a student of ancient languages. However, the boy, born in Clermont-Ferrand, France, proved to be so brilliant at mathematics that his father abandoned his early hopes.

Pascal was a genius. He was only 16 when he published his first math book, on geometry. It was so good that the great French scientist René Descartes refused at first to believe it had been written by someone only 16 years old. Before he was 21 Pascal built a mechanical calculator, or adding machine.

Pascal asked his brother-in-law to help with various experiments on the Earth's atmosphere. These involved climbing high mountains to see if the weight of the atmosphere was less the higher they went. This proved to be the case. An Italian scientist, Evangelista Torricelli, had done this experiment using a mercury barometer. Pascal did the same, but he used

The calculating machine that Blaise Pascal developed between 1642–44, to help his father in his tax assessing job, is often considered to be the world's first digital calculator.

red wine instead of mercury. The barometer he built was 46 feet (14 m) long!

Pascal also worked out that if a fluid (liquid or gas) is in a container, the pressure that it exerts on the inside walls of the container should be the same in all directions. Again, he was proved correct.

ALSO READ: BAROMETER, FLUID.

PASSOVER The joyful Jewish holiday of Passover (*Pesach*) celebrates the exodus (leaving) of the Hebrews from Egypt and their safe flight across the Red Sea.

Passover gets its name from an incident described in the Bible. According to the Old Testament, the Israelites, or Jews, were slaves in Egypt. Moses, a Hebrew prophet, was sent by God to ask the Egyptian pharoah to free the Hebrews. When the pharoah refused, God sent ten plagues (disasters) against Egypt. The tenth plague was the killing of the eldest son of each family. Through Moses, God instructed the Jews to mark their doorposts with lamb's blood, so that the angel of death would *pass over* their houses.

Passover is celebrated for eight days, beginning at sundown on the fourteenth day of the Jewish month of Nisan. This is usually about the same time as the Christian Holy Week before Easter. In Israel, Passover is celebrated for seven days. Before the first day of Passover, the home must be cleaned thoroughly to remove every crumb of "non-Passover" food. All meals during the holiday must be prepared and served in pots and dishes that are used only at Passover.

On the first two nights of Passover, a special service and meal, a *seder*, is held in the home. Various special dishes are served, each one symbolizing some hardship undergone by the slaves in Egypt. For instance, a mix-

ture of apples, nuts, and spices represents *mortar*, a building material used in labor for the Egyptians. Squares of *Matzo*, or unleavened bread, are eaten instead of leavened bread throughout the holiday. This is to recall that when the Jews fled from Egypt, they did not have time to put leaven in their bread to make it rise. It also recalls the unleavened bread they ate for 40 years after leaving Egypt.

The head of the family leads the others in giving thanks to the Lord and in reading from the *Haggadah*, which tells the story of the Jews in Egypt and their journey to the "Promised Land." The youngest person at the seder asks "Four Questions" about the meaning of Passover. The questions are answered by the person conducting the seder—usually the head of the family. The seder ends with joyous songs, extolling the exodus from Egypt.

ALSO READ: EASTER, JEWISH HISTORY.

PASTEUR, LOUIS (1822–1895) Not much more than a century ago, no one knew what caused diseases such as cholera, anthrax, and rabies. Louis Pasteur, a French chemist, discovered that these diseases and many others are caused by germs, or *bacteria*. Because his work launched the science of *bacteriology* (the study of

▲ *The first calculating machine was invented and completed by Blaise Pascal in 1642. It could add and subtract numbers.*

▲ *Louis Pasteur, French chemist and bacteriologist.*

PATENTS AND COPYRIGHTS

At 17, Louis Pasteur gained the lowly job of school usher. His task was just keeping order. But one pupil had a microscope that Louis borrowed to study insects. This sparked his interest in tiny life forms, a hobby that became a career and eventually made him famous.

In 60 years the great inventor Thomas Alva Edison patented no fewer than 1,000 inventions, yet he said that genius was "1 percent inspiration and 99 percent perspiration." It took him two years and thousands of experiments to find an effective filament for the incandescent light bulb.

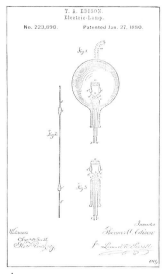

▲ *A copy of the original patent drawing of Thomas Edison's light bulb.*

bacteria), Pasteur is called the "Father of Bacteriology."

Pasteur was born in Dole in eastern France. He studied chemistry at a college called the École Normale in Paris. Within a year after his graduation, Pasteur made some very important discoveries about the structure of crystals. Shortly afterward, some French winemakers asked him to find out why their wines were turning sour. Pasteur found that a certain kind of bacteria was the cause. He showed the winemakers how to heat wines gently to kill the bacteria. This process, called *pasteurization*, is also used to kill harmful bacteria in milk.

Pasteur then began to battle disease. He proved that bacteria are living things and that they cause disease. He believed that people could be protected from certain diseases by receiving small injections of the bacteria that cause the diseases. In 1885, Pasteur proved his theory by saving the life of a small boy who had been bitten by a rabid dog. Pasteur prevented the boy from getting rabies by injecting weakened rabies bacteria into him. This method is still used to treat rabies.

ALSO READ: BACTERIA, IMMUNITY, MEDICINE.

PATENTS AND COPYRIGHTS
Patents and copyrights are legal protection against theft. Just as you would not want anyone to steal your belongings, you would not want anyone to claim credit for a song you wrote or a soft drink you invented. Patents and copyrights protect writers, artists, composers, and inventors from people who would use their work without paying for it.

A patent is a grant (like a contract) issued by the government of a country to protect someone's invention from being copied and used by others. Newly manufactured products, machines, designs, and processes can

be patented. Even new kinds of plants can be patented! The government must make sure that everything being patented is both useful and brand new, so the granting of a patent may take several years. A patent that is awarded in the United States protects against misuse only in this country. If inventors want to protect their inventions in other countries, they must get patents there.

A U.S. patent is granted to an inventor for 17 years. During that time, all others in the country cannot make, use, or sell his or her invention. (Patents on designs run for no more than 14 years.) In the United States, only an act of Congress can extend the term of a patent. The term "patent pending" is used to inform the public that an application for a patent is on file in the Patent Office for a certain item. Anyone using these terms falsely to deceive other people can be fined by the government.

Just as a patent is a form of protection for an inventor, a copyright protects an author of a literary, dramatic, musical, or other artistic work. The owner of a copyright is granted by law certain exclusive rights to the work. He or she is given the right to print, reprint, and copy the work; the right to transform and revise the work; the right to perform and record the work. The copyright owner can sue anyone who violates one of these rights without his or her permission.

Most countries have copyright laws protecting works published by their own citizens. Treaties between some countries provide for copyright protection in all of the countries involved. No one but the author, or those receiving the right from him or her, can legally claim copyright. (Publishers, rather than authors, often obtain copyrights.) Just owning a manuscript, screenplay or painting is not enough to obtain a copyright. To obtain a copyright for a published work, the author must publish the work and fill out a copyright application. When registering a claim in the Copyright Office of the Library of Congress after publication, he or she must supply two printed copies of the work.

The term of copyright in the United States begins on the day the work is published with the notice of copyright and runs for the duration of the author's life, plus 50 years.

ALSO READ: BOOK, INVENTION.

PATRICK, SAINT (about 389–about 461)

Saint Patrick was the man who brought Christianity to Ireland about 1,500 years ago. Today, Saint Patrick is the patron, or special, saint of Ireland. March 17 is Saint Patrick's feast day. This day is a special holiday for Irish people all over the world, when they celebrate the memory of Saint Patrick.

Saint Patrick's family were Christians who lived in ancient Britain. When Patrick was about 16 years old, he was taken prisoner by bandits and sold as a slave in Ireland. He escaped after six years and had many adventures before he returned home. He then had a dream in which the poor people he had known in Ireland asked him to come back to them.

Saint Patrick decided to become a priest and return to Ireland. Most of the Irish were pagans at that time. They believed in magic, magicians, and spirits. Saint Patrick spent the rest of his life in Ireland. He taught the Irish about Christianity and founded many churches and monasteries. A legend tells that Saint Patrick destroyed all the snakes in Ireland by driving them into the sea. A few of his writings still exist.

ALSO READ: IRELAND, SAINT.

PAUL, SAINT (about A.D. 3–about 67)

Saint Paul was born in Tarsus, Cilicia (now Turkey). His name was originally Saul. His family was Jewish, and Saul studied in Jerusalem to become a teacher of religion. As a young man, he persecuted the followers of Jesus Christ. One day, as told in the New Testament of the Bible, he was traveling to Damascus, Syria. As he came near the city, a light from the sky suddenly flashed around him. He fell to the ground and heard a voice say, "Saul, Saul! Why do you persecute me?" The voice was that of Jesus Christ. This vision made him decide to be a Christian. He changed his name to Paul, and became one of the greatest *apostles*, or witnesses of Christ. Paul is called the "Apostle to the Gentiles" (non-Jews). He preached about Jesus Christ to many different peoples on three long journeys through the eastern Roman Empire. Everywhere he went, new communities of Christians sprang up. Paul wrote letters called *epistles* to the new communities. These epistles are in the New Testament of the Bible. The letters told the new churches how to carry on their work.

Paul's teachings angered some of the Jews, who did not agree with his ideas. The Roman governors were afraid that he would stir up a rebellion. Paul was put into prison for two years in Jerusalem, and then two more years in Rome. He was set free, but then was arrested again. In his second trial, Paul was condemned to die. He was beheaded (not crucified) because he was a Roman citizen.

ALSO READ: APOSTLES, CHRISTIANITY, MISSIONARY, SAINT.

PAVLOV, IVAN (1849–1936)

Ivan Petrovich Pavlov was a Russian scientist who won the Nobel Prize in 1903 for his study of the digestion of food. He is better known, however, for his discovery of the conditioned reflex.

Pavlov studied medicine at the Military Medical Academy in St. Petersburg (now Leningrad). He became a

St. Patrick is said to have driven all the snakes out of Ireland. He did this by standing on a seashore cliff. Every time the saint rang his service bell, he threw it over the cliff. With it went an avalanche of snakes. And every time the bell was returned to him miraculously.

▲ *Saint Paul, shown in a fresco in a church at Barcelona, Spain.*

▲ *Ivan Pavlov, Russian scientist.*

▲ *A painting of Anna Pavlova, the great Russian ballerina.*

▲ *Pawnee Indians once raised crops and hunted buffalo.*

professor at the Academy of Medicine and Surgery in St. Petersburg in 1895 and did his most important research there.

In his most famous experiments, Pavlov showed food to a hungry dog. The dog drooled saliva. The saliva flowed in the dog's mouth because it was needed to moisten and digest the food the dog was about to eat. The flow of saliva in the dog's mouth was a kind of *reflex*. Every time Pavlov gave food to the dog, he rang a bell. After Pavlov had done this a number of times, saliva flowed in the dog's mouth whenever it heard the bell— even though no food was in sight. The dog's saliva-producing reflex had been *conditioned* by the sound of the bell. Pavlov's discovery of the conditioned reflex had much influence on the developing science of psychology and the study of behavior.

ALSO READ: CIRCULATORY SYSTEM, DIGESTION, NERVOUS SYSTEM, NOBEL PRIZE, PSYCHOLOGY.

PAVLOVA, ANNA (1882–1931)
Anna Pavlova was so weak as a child that her parents feared she might not live. But she grew up to become one of the world's greatest ballet dancers.

Pavlova was born in St. Petersburg (now Leningrad), Russia, the child of poor parents. She was taken to see a ballet when she was eight, and from then on she dreamed only of dancing. At age ten, she was accepted at the Imperial Ballet School of the Russian Court, where she spent seven years in training. After graduation she danced small parts at the Imperial Theater. Her dancing was so brilliant that she became a *prima ballerina* (leading dancer).

When Sergei Diaghilev, the great ballet producer, took the Russian Ballet to Paris, Pavlova danced leading parts with his company. Often she was paired with the great dancer, Vaslav Nijinsky. After a time, she

formed her own ballet company. Her performances in the United States brought knowledge of ballet to thousands of people who had never before seen that kind of dancing.

Pavlova was unable to return to Russia after the Soviet revolution of 1917. When not on tour with a dance company, she spent her vacations in England. She died of pneumonia while on tour in Holland. Her desire for perfection, her great skill and precise body control, as well as her graceful beauty made her dancing unforgettable. Perhaps the most famous of all her dances was "The Dying Swan," which was choreographed (arranged) for her by Michel Fokine. In that dance, she enacted the death of a swan.

ALSO READ: BALLET; DANCE; NIJINSKY, VASLAV.

PAWNEE INDIANS
The Pawnee were a group of tribes originally from the area of what is now Texas. From there they moved about, living throughout the Great Plains, especially in what is now Kansas and the Platte River valley of Nebraska. The Pawnee were both hunters and farmers, raising crops such as corn, tobacco, squash, and beans in the fertile fields along the rivers. They hunted deer and buffalo. The houses of the Pawnee were made of wooden frames covered with earth and animal skins. They used buckskin (the skin of deer) to make clothes.

About 10,000 Pawnee lived on the plains during the 1700's. They were organized in small village groups. Children were named according to the mother's family, rather than the father's. The positions of chief and priest were passed on from father to son. Their main gods were the Sun, the Earth Mother, and the Morning Star.

Through a series of treaties, the U.S. Government took over Pawnee land. Although the Pawnee fought with other Indian tribes, they were friendly with white settlers. Many Pawnee men served as scouts for the U.S. Army during the numerous Indian wars of the 1800's. They also served as guards on the Union Pacific Railroad.

The Pawnee population got smaller as the result of tribal wars, mostly battling against the Sioux. Many Pawnee died from epidemics of cholera and smallpox—diseases of the white people. In 1876, the Federal Government moved the remaining Pawnee to a reservation in Oklahoma.

ALSO READ: INDIANS, AMERICAN.

PEACE CORPS The Peace Corps is a United States government agency founded for the purpose of promoting world peace and friendship. The Peace Corps furnishes personnel to aid developing countries. The volunteers are given the opportunity to find out about life in less affluent countries, and the program also helps people in those poorer countries get to know and understand Americans.

Peace Corps members must be at least 18 years old and U.S. citizens. The Peace Corps matches the talents and skills of its volunteers with requests for aid from foreign countries. For example, if an African nation needs a medical technician to give vaccinations, the Peace Corps will send one. Peace Corps volunteers work in over 60 countries, mainly in agriculture, rural development, health, and education.

A person joining the Peace Corps starts a three-month training program. The volunteers learn to adapt their skills to the particular jobs they will have to do. They also learn about the countries they will work in and the language they will need to speak. The training period prepares them for life in the countries where they will work for two years.

The Peace Corps was founded by President John F. Kennedy in 1961. It proved so popular with Americans that in 1964 the Federal Government set up a similar program to help poor people in the United States. This program is called VISTA, for Volunteers in Service to America. The Peace Corps, VISTA, and other government volunteer programs became part of an independent Federal Government agency called ACTION in 1971. The Peace Corps was formerly part of the Department of State.

ALSO READ: KENNEDY, JOHN FITZGERALD.

PEARL Pearls form inside the shells of certain oysters and other kinds of mollusks. The pearl begins

▼ *Japanese workers grading and sorting cultured pearls.*

▲ *Helping children like these in a crowded Bombay slum is a difficult task for this U.S. Peace Corp worker.*

The oysters we eat do not produce valuable pearls. The pearls of edible oysters are dull and do not gleam.

The ancient Romans prized pearls so highly that their rulers allowed only people of a certain rank to wear them. Only a special group of traders were permitted to deal in pearls. They were known as *margaritarii*—from the Latin word *margarita*, meaning pearl.

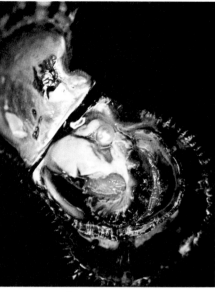

▲ *A pearl forms inside an oyster. By placing a tiny bead inside an oyster's shell, a cultured pearl can be grown. The oyster coats the bead with mother-of-pearl.*

▼ *The attack by the Japanese naval air forces on Pearl Harbor brought the United States into World War II. Today the U.S.S.* Arizona *Memorial, built over the wreck of the battleships destroyed in the attack, honors those who died at Pearl Harbor.*

to form when a tiny particle, such as a grain of sand or a living parasite, gets inside the shell. The oyster coats the particle with a layer of smooth material called *nacre*, or *mother-of-pearl*. The nacre protects the body of the oyster from being irritated by the parasite or grain of sand. As time goes by, more layers of nacre are added, and gradually a pearl is formed.

Many mollusks besides oysters form pearls. The conch produces pink pearls. Pearls from some mollusks are a silvery black color. Cultured pearls are produced when a person places a tiny bead inside the oyster shell. The oyster covers the bead with nacre, and a large, round pearl results. Cultured pearls have been produced since the early 1900's, especially in Japan, where culturing pearls has become a major industry. There are still some pearl divers, people who dive underwater to gather oyster pearls. Natural pearls are pearls produced without any help from people. River pearls are produced by freshwater mussels.

ALSO READ: CLAMS AND OYSTERS, GEM, JEWELRY, MOLLUSK.

PEARL HARBOR It was Sunday on December 7, 1941. The bluegreen waters of Pearl Harbor on the island of Oahu, Hawaii, were peaceful in the bright sunlight. The powerful battleships and cruisers of the U.S. Pacific Fleet floated at anchor. Headlines in the Sunday newspaper told about Japanese occupation of areas in Indochina, but no one expected trouble in Hawaii.

Suddenly, sirens wailed. Japanese torpedo planes screeched over the fleet. In a surprise attack that lasted less than two hours, about 360 Japanese aircraft pounded five battleships into useless hulks. Japanese submarines also attacked. The attacks severely damaged 13 other vessels and destroyed 188 U.S. airplanes.

The Japanese attack came as a complete surprise. People who lived in Honolulu thought at first that the smoke and noise came from make-believe war games. But when the smoke cleared, 2,280 Americans were dead, and nearly 1,200 wounded.

December 7 marked Japan's entrance into World War II on the side of Germany and Italy. On December 8, the United States declared that a state of war had existed with Japan since the attack. "Remember Pearl Harbor" became a slogan during World War II.

ALSO READ: HAWAII, JAPAN, WORLD WAR II.

PEARSON, LESTER (1897–1972) The Canadian statesman, Lester Bowles Pearson, served as prime minister of Canada from 1963 to 1968. As an international diplomat, he worked for world peace.

Lester Pearson was born in Toronto, Canada. He joined the Canadian army at the outbreak of World War I in 1914. After the war, he studied at the University of Toronto and won a scholarship to Oxford University, in England.

In 1928, Pearson joined the Canadian Department of External Affairs, which is similar to the U.S. Department of State. He served as ambassa-

dor to the United States from 1945 to 1946. Two years later, Pearson was elected a member of the Canadian parliament and appointed secretary of state for external affairs.

Pearson played a major part in the creation of the United Nations organization. He served as president of the United Nations General Assembly from 1952 to 1953. He also helped to found the North Atlantic Treaty Organization (NATO). Pearson was responsible for the United Nations settlement of the Suez Canal crisis in 1956, after Israel, Great Britain, and France had invaded Egypt. For this, he was awarded the Nobel Peace Prize.

Pearson worked to build Canada's friendship with the United States, Great Britain, and other countries. He resigned as prime minister and as head of Canada's Liberal Party in 1968. He was succeeded by Pierre Trudeau.

ALSO READ: CANADA; TRUDEAU, PIERRE.

PEARY, ROBERT (1856–1920) Robert Peary had one great aim in life. He wanted to be the first person to reach the North Pole. He succeeded on his third attempt.

Robert Edwin Peary was born in Cresson Springs, Pennsylvania. In 1881, he became a lieutenant in the U.S. Navy, working with the civil engineer corps. Between 1886 and 1897, Peary led several expeditions to Greenland. Among the valuable contributions he made to science were the proof that Greenland was an island and the discovery on Melville Bay of large meteorites. He tried unsuccessfully to reach the North Pole in 1902 and 1906.

On July 17, 1908, Peary sailed from New York City on his final expedition to the North Pole. The ship sailed northward for two months before the ice prevented it from going

further. The crew lived on the ice-bound ship through the long Arctic winter. On March 1, 1909, Peary set out for the North Pole, about 450 miles (720 km) away. With him were 24 persons on 19 sledges (sleds), pulled by 133 huskies (Eskimo dogs).

The entire route lay across floating ice, or ice floes. When they came to lanes of open water, they had to wait until the lanes closed up or froze over. If the ice cracked while they were on it, they might be stranded on ice floes. One of Peary's men did fall into the icy water and died before the others could reach him. Most members of the expedition went only a part of the way, clearing a path, building igloos, and storing supplies to be used by the returning explorers.

On March 31, Peary and his fellow explorer, Matthew Henson, started the final march to the Pole. With them were four Eskimos and their dogs. On April 6, 1909, after taking readings from various instruments, Peary discovered that he had reached the North Pole. The next day, he planted the U.S. flag at the top of the world.

When he returned, Peary found that another explorer, Frederick Cook, claimed to have reached the Pole before him. The records of both men were studied. In 1910, the U.S. Congress decided by a special vote that Peary's claim was the real one. He was promoted to the rank of rear admiral in 1911.

ALSO READ: ARCTIC; EXPLORATION; GREENLAND; HENSON, MATTHEW.

PECOS BILL When pioneers settled the American Southwest, they encountered many hardships. The land was rough and everyday life was hard and often lonely. In order to keep themselves amused, cowboys began telling tales about an imaginary "super cowboy" named Pecos Bill. Although there was never a real Pecos

▲ *Lester Pearson, Canadian statesman.*

▲ *Robert Peary, United States polar explorer.*

PEKING

Peking's famous *Gate of Heavenly Peace* stands at the southern edge of the city. It overlooks a vast square where parades and firework displays are held on national holidays.

Bill, his fame grew as the tales about him were written down and published for everyone to read. Edward O'Reilly wrote some of the first Pecos Bill stories, which were published in *The Century Magazine* in the early 1900's.

According to stories, Pecos Bill fell out of his pioneer family's wagon when he was a baby. A pack of coyotes found him and raised him as one of them. Pecos Bill grew up believing he was a coyote—until he noticed that he had no tail! Some of the amazing things Pecos Bill was said to have done were riding a cyclone, lassoing a railroad train, and digging the Rio Grande to get water for his cattle.

No one knows what became of Pecos Bill. One story tells how he put fish hooks and barbed wire into his whiskey to make it stronger—and died from indigestion.

ALSO READ: BUNYAN, PAUL; LEGEND.

PEKING (or BEIJING) Peking is the capital and second largest city of China. It is also China's educational, cultural, financial, and transportation center. The city lies on a large plain between the Pei and the Hun rivers in northeastern China. About six million people live in Peking.

There has been a city on the site of Peking for more than twenty centuries. When the Mongols from central Asia conquered China, their emperor, Kublai Khan, made it his capital and called it Khanbalik. In the 1200's, Marco Polo, a trader from Venice, Italy, spent many years in the city.

Two series of great Chinese emperors, the Mings and the Manchus, built their palaces in the city and called it "Peking," meaning "northern capital." General Chiang Kai-shek, former leader of Nationalist China, moved his headquarters to the south and from 1928 to 1949 the city was renamed "Peiping," or "northern peace." When the Communist Chinese captured mainland China, they restored Peking as the capital.

Peking is made up of cities within cities, all formerly surrounded by huge mud-brick walls. The heart of old Peking was the Tatar or Inner City. Within the Inner City was the Imperial City, where the government had its offices and government officials lived. Inside the Imperial City was the famous "Forbidden City," where the emperor himself lived. Nearly a square mile (2.5 sq. km) in area, it contained the imperial palace and grounds encircled by high pink-washed walls and a deep canal, or moat. It was heavily guarded, and few people ever got inside the Forbidden City. There was once a walled city for foreigners in Peking.

Today, tourists can enter the Imperial and Forbidden cities and visit the beautiful temples and palaces. The Temple of Heaven and the summer palace of the Manchu emperors are in the south of the city. The Communist Chinese have done much to clean up the old city and are constructing new buildings. Peking's industries produce iron and steel, petrochemicals, electronic and communications equipment, and textiles.

In 1989, Tiananmen Square in Peking was the site of a terrible massacre when thousands of demonstrators were killed and injured by troops.

ALSO READ: CHINA.

▼ *Peking, the capital of China, has a mixture of old and new buildings. The ancient Forbidden City (in the foreground) was once occupied by the Chinese emperors.*

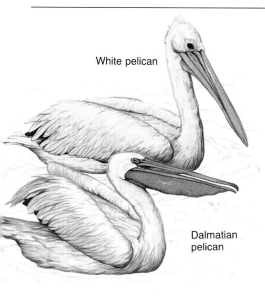

White pelican

Dalmatian pelican

▲ *The white pelican is one of the two kinds found in North America. The Dalmatian is a Eurasian species.*

PELICAN A pelican is a large, web-footed, fish-eating bird. Pelicans range from four to six feet (1.2 to 1.8 m) long and have very powerful wings, with wing spreads of up to ten feet (3 m). They have long beaks. The upper half of a pelican's beak is hooked at the end. The lower half consists of an elastic pouch of skin that is attached to the neck. The pelican uses the pouch as a scoop to catch fish, which it swallows soon after it catches them. Young pelicans feed on half-digested fish brought up from the stomach into the pouch of the parent.

There are ten different kinds of pelicans distributed throughout the warm and temperate parts of the world. North American pelicans include the white pelican (the largest type of all) and the brown pelican (now an endangered species).

White pelicans live in large colonies, usually on an island. Their nests are crude heaps of earth, gravel, and rubbish, in which they lay one to four white eggs. Brown pelicans nest in low trees. White pelicans catch fish by chasing them in the water. Brown pelicans dive upon fish to catch them.

ALSO READ: BIRD.

PENDULUM Cuckoo clocks and grandfather clocks have pendulums. A clock pendulum is very simple. It is nothing more than a weight that swings on the end of a long metal rod. The pendulum makes the clock keep accurate time.

Watch a pendulum very closely. Notice that it does not slow down or speed up. It swings back and forth at a constant speed. A pendulum will slow down eventually, if it is left to swing by itself. But clocks have a special device, called an *escapement*, that gives the pendulum a tiny push at regular intervals. This tiny push keeps the pendulum swinging steadily. The escapement is driven by a spring or by a falling weight.

The weight on the end of the pendulum's rod is called the *bob*. A heavy bob will keep a pendulum swinging for a very long time. But it is the length of the rod that determines how fast the pendulum swings back and forth. If the pendulum has a long rod, the bob swings back and forth slowly. If the rod is short, the pendulum swings back and forth quickly. This is why the short pendulum on a cuckoo clock moves faster than the long pendulum on a grandfather clock.

The Foucault Pendulum A French scientist, Jean Bernard Léon Foucault, invented a pendulum in 1851 that proved that the Earth turns. The Foucault pendulum is a very long wire with a heavy bob. It is usually hung from the ceiling so that it is free to swing to and fro in any direction. Sometimes the bottom of the bob is pointed, and it makes a mark in a circle of sand beneath the pendulum when it swings through its course. As long as nothing interfers with the swinging of the bob, the bob will continue to swing back and forth in the same direction through space. But the marks it makes in the sand will change, covering more and more of the circle. It looks as if the pendu-

▲ *An early pendulum clock. Because a pendulum always takes the same time to swing to and fro, it can be connected to a clockwork mechanism to make a reliable timepiece. The first working pendulum clock was made by Christiaan Huygens in Holland in 1657.*

The use of the pendulum to regulate clocks was first suggested by the great Italian scientist Galileo. While in Pisa cathedral during his first year at the university there, Galileo noticed that a lamp hanging from the ceiling was swinging to and fro with a very regular motion. He timed the swings by feeling the pulse on his wrist and discovered that as the distance of the swings grew less, the lamp slowed down. Each swing took exactly the same time whether the swing was big or small. Galileo was only 17 when he made this discovery.

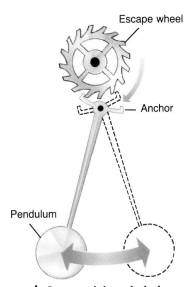

▲ *In a pendulum clock there is a toothed escape wheel driven by a spring or by a weight. The escape wheel is controlled by an anchor that rocks back and forth. The anchor is connected to the pendulum that swings at a constant rate. So the escape wheel turns at a constant rate too, and turns the hands through gears.*

▼ *The Emperor is one of two kinds of penguin that breed on the continent of Antarctica. Chinstrap, macaroni, and gentoo penguins all breed on sub-Antarctic islands. All penguins live in the Southern Hemisphere and come ashore to raise their young.*

Emperor penguin

lum has been swinging in a circle. Scientists know that, according to the laws of nature, the pendulum has kept on swinging in the same direction in space. It is the Earth that has turned around under the pendulum, changing the marks in the sand.

ALSO READ: CLOCKS AND WATCHES, EARTH.

PENGUIN Penguins are flightless swimming birds. They live in the Southern Hemisphere from the Antarctic regions to the Galápagos Islands, which are near the equator in the Pacific Ocean west of Ecuador. The 18 kinds of penguins range in height from 12 to 48 inches (30 to 120 cm).

Penguins look like small people in dress suits. They are white in the front, with black or blue-gray on the back and shoulders. In some species, the white feathers have patches of yellow or orange. The feathers of all species are tiny and thick.

Penguins' wings are rigid because they have no joints. The wings are useless for flight, but they make excellent flippers for swimming. When swimming, a penguin moves its wings together like oars—forward, then backward. Penguins stand erect on land because their short legs are placed so far back on their bodies. They walk slowly with a comically dignified waddle. However, penguins can move rapidly over ice and snow by sliding on their breasts and bellies.

Penguins feed on fish, crustaceans, and other sea animals, which they

Chinstrap penguin

Macaroni penguin   Gentoo penguin

▲ *A pair of King penguins. Penguins use their wings as paddles for swimming.*

catch while in the water. A thick layer of body fat keeps them warm and enables them to go for long periods of time without eating.

At breeding time, penguins gather on land in large colonies. The female usually lays only one or two eggs. The male and female of most species take turns incubating the eggs. In some species, the eggs are kept warm in a pouch above the penguin's feet. The birds go without food during the 18 days it takes the eggs to hatch. Newly hatched penguin chicks are covered with grayish, downy feathers. The male of some species feeds the baby for a short time on a liquid food he brings up from his own stomach. Both parents usually share the responsibility of feeding the chicks partly digested food.

The Antarctic emperor penguin, about four feet (120 cm) tall, is the largest species. The males incubate the eggs on their feet. The smallest penguin, only about 12 inches (30 cm) tall, is the blue penguin of southern Australia and New Zealand. The jackass (or blackfoot) penguin of southern South America and South Africa is named for its braying, similar to that of a jackass or donkey.

ALSO READ: BIRD, FLIGHTLESS BIRDS.

PENICILLIN see ANTIBIOTIC.

PENN, WILLIAM (1644–1718)
William Penn, an English Quaker, founded the city of Philadelphia and the colony (now the state) of Pennsylvania. Penn, born in London, England, was converted to Quakerism while he was studying at Oxford University. Little religious freedom existed in England at that time, and the Society of Friends (the Quakers) was treated unfairly. Penn was imprisoned for writing religious and political essays based on Quaker beliefs.

In 1681, King Charles II gave Penn a grant of territory in North America in payment for a debt owed to Penn's father. Penn sent colonists to settle there, and then he sailed for America in 1682. He established friendly relations with the Indians, whom he generally treated fairly. Penn planned and named the city of Philadelphia. During his nearly 30 years as governor of Pennsylvania, he based the colony's government on Quaker ideals: peace, religious freedom, and democratic government. Because of this, many Quakers followed Penn to the new colony.

Penn had to return to England on business in 1701. He became very ill there and was never able to go back to the colony he had founded.

ALSO READ: PENNSYLVANIA, SOCIETY OF FRIENDS.

PENNSYLVANIA Pennsylvania is called the "Keystone State" because it was in the center of the original 13 states. Six states were north and east of it, and six states were south of it.

Pennsylvania is one of the Middle Atlantic States. It is bordered on the north by Lake Erie and New York and on the east by the Delaware River, which separates the state from

New York and New Jersey. Ohio and West Virginia are to the west, and West Virginia, Maryland, and Delaware border Pennsylvania on the south.

The Land and Climate Pennsylvania is mostly highland. It has two small lowlands. One is a narrow strip of plain beside Lake Erie. The other is part of the Atlantic Coastal Plain, along the Delaware River. All the rest of the state is in a highland, the Appalachian mountain system. Northern and western Pennsylvania are in the part called the Allegheny Plateau. Parallel mountain ranges curved through the center of the state. They begin at the Maryland border and continue to the Delaware River. In the southeast is the rolling Piedmont. It lies also between Maryland and the Delaware River.

Two long rivers cut through the Appalachians in eastern Pennsylvania. One is the Susquehanna, and the other is the Delaware, which forms the state's eastern border.

Pennsylvania has a varied climate. The Allegheny Plateau is cold in winter. In summer, its ridges are pleasantly cool. The valleys between the ridges, however, are quite warm then. Summers in the Piedmont and on the strip of Atlantic Coastal Plain are long and hot, and the winters are mild. Mountains protect southeastern

▲ *The tranquil setting of an Amish farm in Lancaster County, Pennsylvania.*

William Penn wanted to call his colony Sylvania, meaning "forest land." But King Charles added the prefix Penn, in memory of William Penn's father.

▲ *Philadelphia, the largest city in Pennsylvania, is the fifth largest in the United States. With its metropolitan area (including Trenton and Wilmington) added, Philadelphia ranks as the nation's fourth most populous urban region.*

America's oil industry was born near Titusville in northwestern Pennsylvania. The first oil well was drilled there in August, 1859, by a blacksmith, "Uncle Billy" Smith. He was working for Edwin Drake, a retired railroad conductor.

Pennsylvania from cold northwest winds. Rain and summer warmth help farming.

History The most important Indians here were the Lenni-Lenape, who also lived in the valley of the Delaware River. These Indians are usually called Delawares.

Swedish people were the first Europeans to settle in Pennsylvania. They had a colony in Delaware. Some of them moved a short distance north on the Delaware River. In 1643, they built a fort on an island. On the Pennsylvania side of the river, they built a village named Upland. In 1655, the Dutch made the Swedish settlements part of New Netherland. Nine years later, the English took over New Netherland, including the Swedish settlements.

Pennsylvania is also called the "Quaker State." The Quaker William Penn sent colonists from England to found the colony of Pennsylvania (meaning "Penn forest land") in 1681. Penn himself came a year later. Penn changed the name of the town of Upland to Chester. He signed treaties of friendship with the Delaware Indians and purchased land from them. He founded the city of Philadelphia.

The colony of Pennsylvania attracted settlers from many countries. Welsh Quakers, German Mennonites, Moravians, Italian and French religious groups, and people from other colonies came. Most of the early colonists were Quakers from England, Wales, and Scotland. Germans who settled in Pennsylvania after the 1680's lived in their own groups on farms and spoke in a German dialect, which became known as "Pennsylvania Dutch."

The French built Fort Duquesne where Pittsburgh stands today. After the British won the French and Indian War of the 1700's, a British fort was built on the ruins of Fort Duquesne and was named Fort Pitt, after Britain's prime minister.

Pennsylvania played a big part in the American Revolution. The First Continental Congress met in Philadelphia in 1774. The Declaration of Independence was adopted in 1776 by the Second Continental Congress in Philadelphia's Independence Hall. The Constitution of the United States was drawn up at Philadelphia. Delaware was the first state to ratify (approve) the Constitution and Pennsylvania was the second.

Coal mining boomed in Pennsylvania, as did the making of iron and, later, steel. Where rivers weren't deep enough for boats, canals were dug. Railroads were built. Pennsylvania grew into a state of miners and factory workers, as well as farmers.

In the Civil War, Pennsylvania was the only Northern state to be the site of a major battle. Confederates under General Robert E. Lee invaded it in 1863, but they were turned back at the Battle of Gettysburg.

Pennsylvanians at Work After the Civil War, the coal, steel, and oil industries expanded greatly in Pennsylvania. The Pittsburgh area in the west became a factory center. In the east, industry grew in the towns of Scranton, Reading, Easton, Allentown, and Bethlehem. Ships were built along the coast.

Pennsylvania has a good location for manufacturing. Millions of customers live in or near the state. Transportation by water, rail, and road is available. Iron ore from Minnesota can reach Pennsylvania easily by way of the Great Lakes. Ships from Philadelphia can reach the Atlantic Ocean by way of the Delaware River and the Delaware Bay. Pittsburgh, a city with great iron and steel mills, is also an important river port. It is located where the Monongahela and Allegheny rivers join to make the Ohio River. Nearly all the country's anthracite (hard) coal is mined in Pennsylvania, which also has valuable deposits of

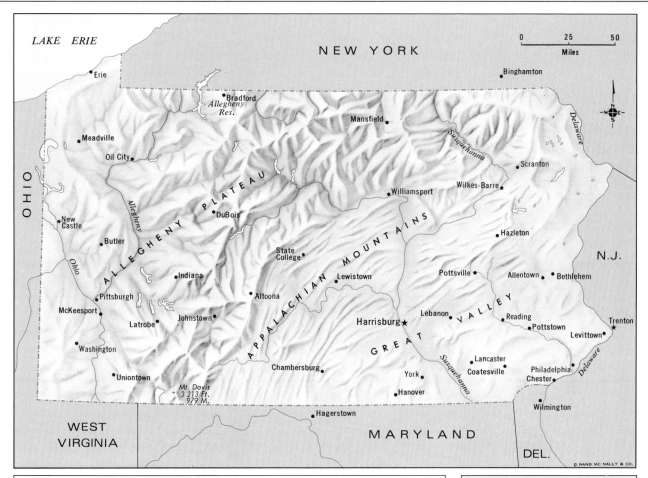

LAKE ERIE

NEW YORK

0 25 50
Miles

Erie

Binghamton

Bradford
Allegheny
Res.

Mansfield

Meadville

Susquehanna

Delaware

Oil City

Scranton

OHIO

ALLEGHENY PLATEAU

Wilkes-Barre

Williamsport

New
Castle

DuBois

Hazleton

Butler

State
College

N.J.

Allentown Bethlehem

Pottsville

Indiana

APPALACHIAN MOUNTAINS

Lewistown

Ohio

Altoona

Reading

VALLEY

Pittsburgh

Lebanon

Pottstown

Trenton

McKeesport

Harrisburg ★

Levittown

Latrobe Johnstown

GREAT

Lancaster

Washington

Susquehanna

Coatesville

Philadelphia

Chambersburg

York

Chester

Uniontown

Mt. Davis
+ 3,213 Ft.
979 M.

Hanover

Wilmington

Hagerstown

WEST
VIRGINIA

MARYLAND

DEL.

© RAND MC NALLY & CO.

STATE EMBLEMS

Mountain Laurel

Hemlock

Ruffed Grouse

PENNSYLVANIA

Capital
Harrisburg (51,500 people).

Area
45,333 square miles
(117,403 sq. km). Rank: 33rd

Population
11,853,000 people. Rank: 4th

Statehood
December 12, 1787

Principal rivers
Allegheny River
Susquehanna River
Monongahela River
Delaware River

Highest point
Mt. Davis; 3,213 feet (980 m)

Largest city
Philadelphia
(1,654,000 people)

Motto
"Virtue, Liberty and
Independence"

Song
None

Famous people
Stephen Foster, Benjamin West
David Wilmot, Lee A. Iococca,
Martha Graham.

▲ *Sunset over Pittsburgh, with its many bridges spanning the Allegheny, Monongahela, and Ohio Rivers.*

bituminous (soft) coal. Petroleum, natural gas, and other minerals are found in the state. Pennsylvania leads in the making of iron and steel.

Other important industries include textiles, paper, lumber, and food products. On the farms, many fruits and vegetables are grown to supply city markets. Farms also yield livestock and dairy products.

The Pocono Mountains and many other woodland areas of Pennsylvania provide places to ski, to go boating on lakes, or to enjoy camping, fishing, and hunting.

Historical areas also draw tourists to the state. They visit the restored Independence Hall at Philadelphia and go on to Revolutionary battlegrounds. Brandywine State Park near Delaware marks an old battlefield. British and German troops defeated the outnumbered Americans there in 1777. Washington's ragged little army camped at Valley Forge in Pennsylvania. The Valley Forge State Park has huts like those in which the soldiers lived. At the old ironworks in Hopewell Village National Historic Site, cannon were cast for General Washington.

ALSO READ: APPALACHIAN MOUNTAINS; CONSTITUTION, UNITED STATES; DECLARATION OF INDEPENDENCE; FRENCH AND INDIAN WAR; GETTYSBURG ADDRESS; INDEPENDENCE HALL; LIBERTY BELL; PENN, WILLIAM; PHILADELPHIA; SOCIETY OF FRIENDS.

PENS AND PENCILS Pens and pencils are instruments used for writing. Pens are used for writing with ink. Pencils may contain one of several writing substances—graphite and clay, slate, or wax.

Probably the first writing instruments were sharp pieces of rock or bone. The ancient Egyptians and Greeks made pens from the reeds of the calamus plant. In the 100's B.C., the Romans began using quills (large, strong tail feathers of birds, such as geese and swans) as pens. The word "pen" comes from the Latin word *penna*, meaning "feather." Quills were widely used from the A.D. 700's to the 1800's when metal pens were first made. These pens consisted of a metal pen point, or nib, attached to a wooden holder. As with the quill, the nib was dipped in ink for writing. Metal pens and holders are still used today, mostly for special kinds of lettering.

These metal pens were replaced for general use, however, by more efficient kinds of pens. In 1884, Lewis E. Waterman, an American inventor, patented an improved *fountain pen*. A fountain pen has an ink barrel in the holder and a metal point, permanently attached. The even flow of ink from the barrel to the point is controlled by an automatic "feeder," which releases ink to the tip as it is needed. Many fountain pens have disposable ink cartridges. *Ballpoint pens*, first sold in 1946, also carry their own ink supply. But the ink in a ballpoint pen is thicker and greasier than ordinary ink. Instead of a sharp point, a ballpoint pen has a tiny metal ball that turns, releasing ink evenly. Two other types of pens in use today are *felt-tip marker pens*, first sold in 1951, and *fiber-tip marker pens*, introduced in the early 1960's. These pens can be used to write on paper, glass, plastic, and metal.

The lead pencil, another important tool for writing, has no lead in it at all!

▼ *Inside a ballpoint pen is a thin tube of ink. At the tip of the tube is an opening with a tiny ball in it. Many ballpoint pens have push-button actions that push the ink tube forward for writing and retract it when the pen is not in use.*

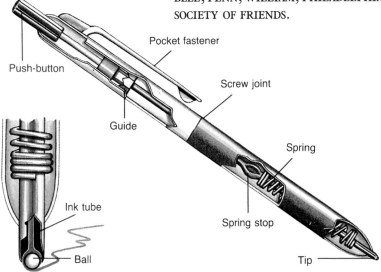

Push-button

Pocket fastener

Screw joint

Guide

Spring

Ink tube

Spring stop

Ball

Tip

Lead was once used in pencils, so the modern pencil became known by the same name. The "lead" pencils most often used today consist of a mixture of graphite (a soft, black mineral) and clay encased in a painted wood covering. Colored pencils are usually made of chalk, clay, or wax, mixed with coloring pigments. They may have wood casings, or they may have a strip of paper wound around them.

In modern graphite pencil factories, powdered graphite is mixed with water and clay to form the "leads." The more clay used, the harder the pencil lead will be. (Soft pencils make a dark, thick line. Hard pencils make a light, thin line.) The pencil leads are inserted into the grooves in little slabs of wood. Other grooved slabs are glued over them. Machines then divide the slabs into pencils. Afterwards, the pencils are polished and painted. Erasers are often attached on one end. The maker's name and a number indicating the pencil's softness are stamped on one side. The softest pencil is number 1 (mostly graphite), and the hardest is number 4 (mostly clay). The most widely used pencils are numbers 2 and 3.

ALSO READ: INK.

PERCENTAGE In mathematics you often have to work with parts of something. For example, you might want to know what part of all the voters voted for Mr. Pumpernickel. You can write this in fractions by saying that ⅗ (three-fifths) of the voters voted for Mr. Pumpernickel.

Percentage is a way of writing a fraction. Percentage fractions always have a denominator of 100. (20% = ²⁰⁄₁₀₀ or ⅕. 75% = ⁷⁵⁄₁₀₀ or ¾.) The % sign means "percent." It comes from the Latin phrase *per centum*, meaning "per hundred." If ⅗ of the people voted for Mr. Pumpernickel, this means that 60% (60 out of every 100) voted for him (60% = ⁶⁰⁄₁₀₀ or

⅗). If 100% of the people voted for him, that would mean everyone (¹⁰⁰⁄₁₀₀) voted for him.

Stores often use percentages when having a sale. Let's say a bicycle that usually costs $120 is on sale for 20% off. This means the sale price is 20% lower than the regular price. 20% = ²⁰⁄₁₀₀ or ⅕. One-fifth of $120 is $24, which means that the bicycle is on sale for $24 less, or $96.

Percentage is easily written in decimal numbers. To find the percentage, put the decimal point two places to the left in the percent number (20% = .20) and multiply. (20% of $120 = .20 × $120 = $24.) If 60% of 17,640 people voted for Mr. Pumpernickel and you want to know the exact number of people who voted for him, just multiply 17,640 × .60 to get 10,584 Pumpernickel voters.

■ LEARN BY DOING

A store announces a sale in which buyers can save 30%. If a camera usually costs $20, how much does it cost at the sale? (30% of $20 = .30 × $20 = $6. $20 minus $6 = $14.) If you want to change a percent to a decimal fraction, divide the percent by 100. Then move the decimal point two places left and drop the percent sign. For example, 50% = .50. Can you work out what 50% is as a common fraction? ■

ALSO READ: DECIMAL NUMBER, FRACTION, MATHEMATICS, NUMBER.

PERCUSSION INSTRUMENTS If you have ever beaten a drum, shaken a rattle, or hit a tambourine, then you have played a percussion instrument. Percussion instruments are those that produce sound by being struck or shaken. In a band or orchestra, percussion instruments play the rhythm. Many percussion instruments have no definite pitch and so cannot play melodies. You cannot play a tune on a bass drum, for exam-

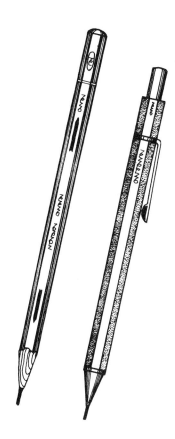

▲ *Two kinds of pencil: a regular wooden pencil (left) and a propelling pencil (right) that has replaceable leads.*

▲ *Timpani or kettledrums are percussion instruments. The tightly stretched drumskin vibrates when hit by the mallet. The frame and the air inside the frame vibrate, too. The bigger the skin is, the deeper the sound.*

▲ *When a great ruler of ancient times went on a journey, his band played for him. At the front of this band is a mounted drummer.*

ple. But pianos, xylophones, kettledrums, chimes, and sets of bells can sound various pitches and are able to play melodies.

The tone of a percussion instrument is made by striking metal (triangles, bells, chimes, gongs, cymbals), wood (rattles, wood blocks, castanets), or a stretched skin (drums, tambourines). The tone quality of each instrument depends on the material it is made of, as well as the way it is struck. In playing a drum, you can strike it with a wooden drumstick to produce a sharp, clear sound. Hitting it with a padded stick produces a duller, muffled sound. Hitting or rubbing the drum with a brushlike drumstick produces a swishy, crackling, or scratchy sound. Striking a drum with your hands produces a variety of different sounds.

Piano tone is produced by felt-covered mallets (hammers) striking against tight metal strings each time a key is pressed. Kettledrums (timpani) can produce a variety of tones when the player tightens or loosens the skin of the drumhead. Chimes, xylophones, and marimbas are played by striking metal or wooden tubes or bars of varying lengths. Each tube or bar is tuned to a particular pitch. A

◀ *A rock drummer. The drum kit includes different sized drums and cymbals.*

celesta is a keyboard instrument that produces bell-like tones caused by hammers striking metal plates when the keys are pressed. The snare drum has a rattling sound along with the beat of the striking drumsticks. The rattle is caused by metal snares (wires stretched across the bottom, inside of the drum) that vibrate against the lower drumhead.

Steel drums make good musical instruments. During World War II, U.S. Navy oil drums were made into musical instruments on Caribbean islands. Empty oil drums of varying sizes produce a range of notes. The bottom surface is used as the drumhead and is struck with sticks or with the hands, producing soft, ringing tones. The glockenspiel is a band instrument that looks like an upright xylophone. It is played by striking the metal bars. The glass harmonica consists of a set of glasses of various size that produce tones when the player draws a moistened finger around the rims.

The musicians in the percussion section of a symphony orchestra or band must be skilled players of almost all the instruments mentioned in this article. In jazz and rock bands, the drummer often plays complicated rhythmic solos.

■ **LEARN BY DOING**

You can make a set of steel drums by collecting empty metal cans of various sizes. Each can should produce a different tone. Try out various tone qualities by striking the bottom surfaces with objects, such as the wooden end of an unsharpened pencil, the eraser end of the pencil, a small screwdriver, or whatever you think may produce an interesting sound. Tilting the drums slightly when you play them will make the sounds sharper and clearer. ■

ALSO READ: BELL, MUSIC, MUSICAL INSTRUMENTS, ORCHESTRAS AND BANDS, PIANO, XYLOPHONE.

PERFUME Perfume is a substance that has a pleasant smell. Perfumes are used mainly in cosmetics. They may be in the form of a liquid that you put on your skin or clothes to make yourself smell pleasant. Or they may be mixed with a cream or soap. Face and body powders, lipsticks, and other cosmetics are often scented with perfume. Perfumes are also used to hide unpleasant odors in inks, paints, insecticides, and plastics. Cologne is made from perfume.

Perfume is made of two main kinds of ingredients. Natural perfume ingredients are those obtained from plants and animals. Synthetic, or artificial, perfume ingredients are made from chemicals. Synthetic ingredients give almost the same odors as natural ones do. Most perfumes made today are entirely synthetic or contain many synthetic ingredients.

The most important part of a perfume is made up of one or more *essential oils*. These provide the distinctive odor of a natural perfume. The essential oil evaporates easily and quickly at ordinary temperatures. This evaporation carries the perfume into the air, so that you can smell it. Essential oils come from various parts of plants. Rose scent comes from the essential oils pressed from rose petals. Violet and lavender scents come from both the flowers and the leaves of these plants. Bark and wood provide essential oils for cinnamon, rosewood, and cedar-scented perfumes. Fruits, such as oranges and lemons, and seeds, such as anise and nutmeg, also provide essential oils. *Aromatics* are synthetic products that give off strong odors. Another part of a perfume is a *fixative*. It holds the perfume ingredients together and makes the odor last longer. The best fixatives are obtained from the scent glands of certain animals. Musk comes from the musk deer of Asia. Castor comes from beavers, and civet from civet cats. Another fixative is made from ambergris, which comes from the stomachs of sperm whales. However, not everyone believes it is right to use animals (especially rare ones) for this purpose. Synthetic and plant substances can also be used as fixatives. *Solvents* are the materials in which the essential oils, the aromatics, and the fixatives are dissolved. The most widely used solvent is a particular kind of alcohol. It has no odor of its own, and it evaporates along with the essential oil.

A perfume may be a mixture of as few as 10 ingredients or as many as 200. Most perfumes are made up of about one-tenth essential oils, aromatics, and fixative, and nine-tenths solvent. Perfume may be mixed with punk (dried plant material) and pressed into cakes. This makes *incense*, which can be lighted and burned to give off a perfumed smoke.

Perfume-making is an ancient art. The Egyptians used fragrant woods and flower petals to make perfumes. They often embalmed their dead with substances containing strong perfumes. The Greeks and the Romans learned to make perfumes from the Egyptians. But after the fall of the Roman Empire, Europeans stopped making perfumes. It was not until the 1500's that perfumes again became popular in Europe. By that time, France had established itself as the center of the perfume industry. Today, France exports most of the world's expensive perfumes. But the United States is the largest producer of perfumes.

ALSO READ: COSMETICS.

▲ *Modern perfumes are a mixture of natural and artificial substances. The perfume industry is a huge international business.*

▼ *Some of the ingredients of perfumes come from plants, while others are taken from animals. The perfumer extracts the essential oils that contain the delicate fragrances.*

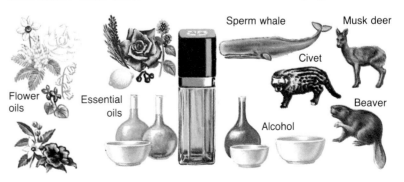

Flower oils
Essential oils
Sperm whale
Musk deer
Civet
Beaver
Alcohol

▲ *Eva Perón rose from poverty to fame as the first lady of Argentina.*

The nearest we can come to perpetual motion is an artificial satellite in orbit around the Earth. The initial push of the rocket that put it into orbit keeps it going for years. But eventually the satellite will fall to Earth because even in space there are a few atoms of matter to cause friction and slow it down.

PERISCOPE see LENS, SUBMARINE.

PERÓN, JUAN (1895–1974) AND EVA (1919–1952). Juan Domingo Perón was president of Argentina, first from 1946 to 1955, and again briefly from 1973 to 1974. He was born near Lobos, in Buenos Aires province, and became a soldier. In 1943, he helped overthrow the government of President Castillo. He sought the support of the country's workers, and on his election to the presidency in 1946 swore opposition to all who oppressed Argentina's poor.

Perón was greatly helped by his wife, Eva. They had married in 1945. Born Eva Ibarguren in 1919, she had worked her way from poverty to success as a film actress. Alongside President Perón, she helped bring in reforms such as votes for women and better health services. "Evita," as she was known, became immensely popular. Her death in 1952 shocked Argentina. Because of her rise from poverty to be joint leader of her country, Eva Perón is still admired by many Argentinians.

Perón's policies did not bring economic success, and he was opposed by the Catholic Church. In 1955 the army overthrew his regime, and for years Perón lived in exile in Spain. But many Argentinians remembered "Perónism," and in 1973 he was elected as president once more. His government was short-lived, for Perón died in 1974. His second wife, Isabel, succeeded him, but her government was ended by military overthrow in 1976.

ALSO READ: ARGENTINA.

▶ *This perpetual motion machine was the invention of Leonardo da Vinci. The bulbs on the arms were to be filled with mercury; as the mercury shifted, it was supposed to keep the wheel turning.*

PERPETUAL MOTION Something that is perpetual will last forever. A perpetual motion machine would be a machine that could run forever without using any outside energy. It would have to supply all of its own energy. There are no perpetual motion machines.

There is one very good reason why no machine can supply all of its own energy. That reason is the *law of conservation of energy*, one of the basic laws of physics. This law says that energy can never be created or destroyed. Energy can only be changed from one form to another. For instance, when an automobile engine burns gasoline, it changes the chemical energy of the gasoline into heat energy. The heat energy in turn is changed into the mechanical energy that moves the automobile. You can make one kind of energy out of another kind of energy, but you cannot end up with more energy than you started with. And this is just what a perpetual motion machine would have to do. It would have to make some energy out of no energy.

But what if we gave the machine a

little push, just to get it started? Would this kind of perpetual motion machine be possible? The answer is still no, because of friction.

Whenever one thing rubs against another, friction resists the rubbing. Friction changes mechanical energy into heat energy. Even just moving through the air produces friction. A machine will always produce some friction. The friction will drain some of the machine's mechanical energy by changing it to heat energy.

The heat energy could not be used to run a perpetual motion machine because of the *second law of thermodynamics* (the study of heat energy). This law says that heat energy always flows from a warm body to a cold body. There is no way for a machine to keep all of the heat energy it produces. Some of the heat energy is always going to escape. And if a machine loses any energy at all, it cannot be a perpetual motion machine. Pushing a perpetual motion machine to get it started gives it mechanical energy, but after a while all of this mechanical energy will be eaten up by friction, and the machine will stop.

The first design for a perpetual motion machine was drawn up in the 1200's. Seven weights were attached to seven arms that swung from the rim of a wheel. The idea was that as the wheel turned, the weights coming over the top would swing out and down. At the same time the weights on the side moving up would be tucked in close to the wheel. The force of the moving weights would turn the wheel.

There were two things wrong with this idea. One was that the wheel lost energy through friction. The other was that there were always more weights tucked in on the "up" side than moving on the "down" side. The extra force each moving weight had was canceled out by the fact that there were more "dead" weights on the other side. Despite these problems, many people, including the great artist and inventor Leonardo da Vinci (1452–1519) have tried to invent a perpetual motion machine based on this idea.

Modern science has led to many new ideas for perpetual motion machines using atomic energy, electrical energy, or the heat energy held by lakes and oceans. However, the law of conservation of energy (now the law of conservation of mass-energy) and the second law of thermodynamics are still believed to be true. So there will never be a perpetual motion machine.

ALSO READ: ENERGY, FRICTION, PHYSICS, RELATIVITY.

PERRAULT, CHARLES (1628–1703) Charles Perrault, a French poet, is best remembered for a collection of fairy tales. He was born in Paris. After studying in Orléans, he became a lawyer. Perrault later became secretary to the prime minister of King Louis XIV. In this position, he helped promote the arts and sciences in France.

Perrault published *Contes de ma mère l'oye* (Tales of Mother Goose) in 1697. "Sleeping Beauty," "Little Red Riding Hood," "Hop-o'-My-Thumb," "Bluebeard," "Puss-in-Boots," and "Cinderella" are among the tales in the collection. Perrault's tales were translated into English in 1729. In 1765, John Newbery, an English publisher, brought out a book of children's poems, called *Mother Goose's Melody*.

Perrault did not actually make up the stories in the first *Mother Goose* collection. They were already very old folktales passed down through the centuries from parent to child. But Perrault was the first to write them down in simple language for children to enjoy.

ALSO READ: CHILDREN'S LITERATURE, FAIRY TALE.

There have been many perpetual motion frauds. One of the most famous was carried out by John W. Keely in the United States in 1870. He said he had invented a "hydro-pneumatic-pulsating-vacuo-engine" that would go on working forever using "etheric" force. The machine was a complete fraud, but Keely collected a great deal of money in support of his invention. He also said that with one gallon of water he could propel a large steamship from New York to Liverpool.

▲ *A scene from* Puss-in-Boots, *by Charles Perrault.*

▲ *Oliver Hazard Perry in 1813 at the Battle of Lake Erie, which took place during the War of 1812.*

▼ *Perseus used his shield as a mirror. He gazed at the Medusa's reflection, avoiding her fatal stare.*

PERRY, OLIVER (1785–1819) AND MATTHEW (1794–1858)

The naval hero, Oliver Hazard Perry, was born in South Kingston, Rhode Island. His brother, Matthew Calbraith Perry was born in Newport, Rhode Island. He too served in the U.S. Navy.

Oliver became a midshipman in the Navy and served in the Mediterranean Sea during the war with the Barbary pirates. At the outbreak of the War of 1812, Oliver Perry was given command of the U.S. naval force on Lake Erie. In 1813, at Erie, Pennsylvania, he ordered ten ships to be built, equipped, and manned. He met and defeated the British fleet on Lake Erie with these warships. During the battle, Perry sent the words, "We have met the enemy and they are ours." After the victory, he became a hero.

Oliver Perry was later sent to the Mediterranean Sea, to fight the Barbary pirates. He caught yellow fever after completing a mission to Venezuela in 1819. He died in Trinidad. A monument in his honor stands in Newport, Rhode Island.

Matthew Perry followed in his brother's footsteps. He also joined the Navy and worked to change ships from sail to steam. He commanded the *Fulton*, one of the first steam-powered vessels and the first U.S. Navy steam warship.

In late 1852, Matthew Perry was sent on a mission by President Fillmore to negotiate a treaty with Japan for trade between the two countries. Until that time, Japan had refused to trade with the West. Perry anchored his fleet in Edo (now Tokyo) Bay when he arrived there on July 8, 1853. This display of armored sea power influenced the Japanese to agree to a treaty. The treaty was signed in 1854, opening trade between Japan and America.

ALSO READ: JAPAN, WAR OF 1812.

PERSEUS

According to Greek mythology, Perseus was a son of Zeus, the leader of the gods. His mother was a human woman named Danaë. When Perseus was a grown man, a king named Polydectes fell in love with Danaë and wanted to marry her. Knowing that Perseus was against the marriage, Polydectes sent him on a deadly errand. He ordered Perseus to kill the Medusa, a horrible female monster with snakes for her hair. Polydectes thought that Perseus would never come back alive, because any man who looked at the Medusa would be turned into stone. Perseus used a bright shield as a mirror with which to see the Medusa and cut off her head without looking straight at her. Perseus returned to Polydectes, holding the head of Medusa. In surprise, Polydectes looked at the head and was immediately turned into stone.

ALSO READ: GODS AND GODDESSES, LEGEND, MYTHOLOGY.

PERSIA

The Persian Empire once stretched from India in the east to Greece in the west, as far north as the Danube River, and southwest to Egypt on the African continent. Iran now occupies the area that once was the center of the empire.

Persian art and literature have lasted through the centuries. The religion called Zoroastrianism spread throughout the empire. A Persian teacher and prophet named Zoroaster (or Zarathustra) began the worship of Ahura Mazdah (or Ormazd), god of light, truth, and goodness.

Persia was settled by nomads (wandering people) who moved down from the Caucasus Mountains in central Asia. People who settled in the mountains were known as Medes, and those who went to the valleys became known as Persians. Cyrus the Great united the tribes in the 500's

B.C. and formed a nation. Cambyses II, son of Cyrus, conquered Egypt.

Darius I extended the empire to its greatest area. The Persians governed their provinces by law—the Law of the Medes and the Persians. Roads were built. Coins were used in trade. Susa, the old capital, was a great city. Darius built a magnificent new capital, Persepolis. Its impressive buildings were decorated with carvings.

The Greeks defeated Darius at the Battle of Marathon and later defeated his son, Xerxes. In the 300's B.C., Persia fell to Alexander the Great of Macedonia. The Arab conquest of Persia in the A.D. 600's introduced the Muslim faith, Islam, into Persia. The word *Persian* is still used today to describe things that came from that part of the world, such as Persian cats and Persian carpets.

ALSO READ: ALEXANDER THE GREAT, ANCIENT CIVILIZATIONS, IRAN, ISLAM.

PERSPECTIVE see DIMENSION, DRAWING, PAINTING.

PERSPIRATION see SKIN.

PERU Peru, the third largest South American country, was the center of the great ancient Inca Indian civilization. Later, it was the richest Spanish land in the Americas. Today, Peru is an interesting mixture of the Indian and Spanish past and the present.

The long coastline of western Peru extends along the Pacific Ocean. Ecuador and Colombia are Peru's northern neighbors. Brazil and Bolivia border Peru on the east, and Chile is south. (See the map with the article on SOUTH AMERICA.)

Peru is more than three times the size of California. It is divided lengthwise into three main regions. The costa, or coastal plain, has a dry climate. In the north, there are places where a whole year passes with no rainfall at all. Peru's capital, Lima, is located midway on the country's coast. It is a large city whose buildings reflect both Spanish colonial days and modern progress. Callao is the nearby seaport. The Sierra region is made up of the high plateaus and valleys of the Andes Mountains. The Andean region contains many valuable mineral resources. Peru has important copper and iron mines, and exports most of its metals.

An area known as the Montaña makes up the largest region. It consists of the steep eastern mountain slopes, foothills, and plains. Some of the densest forests in the world cover the Montaña, where primitive Indian tribes still live.

Indians make up nearly one-half of the Peruvian population. Most of them are poor and uneducated, and many speak only their tribal languages, although Spanish is the official language of the country. Many

▲ *This picture made of glazed bricks shows a Persian soldier of the imperial guard. The royal guards were known as the "Immortals," because their number was always kept at 10,000.*

PERU

Capital City: Lima (6,500,000 people).
Area: 496,225 square miles (1,285,216 sq. km).
Population: 22,250,000.
Government: Republic.
Natural Resources: Copper, iron ore, lead, oil, silver, zinc, gold, coal, phosphates, potash.
Export Products: Fishmeal, cotton, sugar, coffee, copper, iron ore, refined silver, lead, zinc.
Unit of Money: Sol.
Official Languages: Spanish, Quechua.

▲ *The city of Cuzco in Peru was once the Incas' capital. To the right is the site of the old main square where Inca ceremonies were held.*

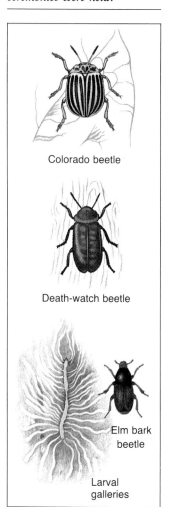

Colorado beetle

Death-watch beetle

Elm bark beetle

Larval galleries

Peruvians are of mixed Indian and Spanish descent. Others have a Spanish or European background.

Although the coastland is dry, farming is made possible by irrigation. Large farms raising cotton, rice, and sugarcane form green oases in the barren landscape. In the Andes Mountains, the Quechua and Aymara Indians farm small plots of potatoes and grains suited to high elevations. Thousands of Indians work in the rich sierra mines at higher altitudes than the lowland Indians and Europeans can stand in comfort. In the mountain regions, Indians tend flocks of sheep, llamas, and alpacas. The llama is also used as a pack animal to carry heavy loads.

Peru is a world leader in the fishing industry. Fish meal and fish oil are leading products. In the 1970's and 1980's, catches declined because of overfishing and unusual conditions affecting offshore ocean currents.

Spain ruled Peru for more than 250

◀ *Insect pests can damage our crops, our buildings, and the trees we enjoy around us. Shown here are the Colorado beetle, which attacks potato crops; the Death-watch beetle, which attacks woodwork in old buildings; and the Elm bark beetle, which damages trees.*

years, until independence was won in 1821. The country is now ruled by a president and legislature. In the mid-1980's, the government faced opposition from a left-wing guerrilla group named the "Shining Path."

ALSO READ: CONQUISTADOR; INCA; PIZARRO, FRANCISCO.

PEST CONTROL In 1980, the United States began fighting a war against an invader. The invader was a tiny insect, only 2–3 millimeters long. It was the Medfly, or Mediterranean fruit fly, which threatened Californian fruit farms.

In Europe these flies are not such a threat as they were in California. In America they are a pest. A pest is any animal that eats or spoils our food, or any plant that grows on land we need for crops. Most animal pests are insects or other tiny creatures, but larger animals such as rats may also be pests.

People control pests in various ways. They kill rats by trapping them or putting down poison. Insects are generally attacked with *pesticides*, chemicals that kill the insects. One of the best-known pesticides is DDT, a chemical that is very efficient in killing insects. But unfortunately DDT has harmful side-effects. It remains in the ground for a long time. It is absorbed by plants and by the animals that eat the plants. Animals at the top of the "food chain," such as hawks, may be badly affected by the poison. So too may humans. If we eat plants and animals sprayed with DDT, our bodies absorb the DDT. For these reasons, since 1972 the use of DDT has been banned in the United States.

Another way to control pests is *biologically*, by using the pests' natural predators. For example, at one time, ladybugs were imported from Australia into California and Florida. Ladybugs feed upon the cottony-cushion scale insect, a major pest of citrus fruit.

In the 1920's Australia had to import a moth to eat the prickly pear. This South American plant had been introduced as a garden ornament but became a pest when it spread over valuable grazing land.

ALSO READ: CATERPILLAR, INSECT, POLLUTION, RATS AND MICE.

PET Pet animals are fun, but they often are a lot of trouble to keep. You must feed most pets every day and take proper care of them so that they do not get sick. You must also housebreak some pets.

Talk to your parents about having a pet. When you are in school, or if you should get sick, your parents may have to take care of your pet for you. You must decide with your parents where the pet is to sleep or where its cage is to be.

When you decide what kind of pet you want, you should learn something about the animal. Find out what it will eat and what sort of special care, if any, it will need. Learn the animal's habits and behavior and how to train it to obey you. Exotic animals, such as monkeys or snakes, do not generally make good pets. It is cruel to keep wild animals (such as birds or squirrels) in captivity.

The most important thing about choosing a pet is to make sure it is healthy before you bring it home. Choose a pet that looks clean. It should also be lively and energetic. Do not buy an animal that has a runny nose, runny eyes, or sores.

Before you bring a pet home, you must have a place ready for it. For example, do not buy a goldfish without first preparing an aquarium to put it in as soon as you get home. If your pet needs a cage, the cage must be all ready when you bring the animal home. Have on hand the kind of food your pet eats. (Find out what foods

SOME COMMON PETS

◀ *A pet turtle needs a place to hibernate if you live where the winters are cold.*

Veiltail

▶ *Goldfish like these fancy varieties can be kept in a coldwater tank.*

Black-eyed Moor

Fantail

▼ *People enjoy listening to the song of the canary. Canaries are popular as cage birds.*

▲ *A pet rabbit needs a warm, dry hutch for shelter. It also likes an outside run.*

▼ *Cats are favorite pets, but they are independent and will come and go as they please.*

▲ *A miniature poodle. People have kept pet dogs since ancient times and have developed an astonishing variety of dog breeds.*

The average healthy cat eats more animal protein a day than the average person in the Third World.

▼ *A horse enjoys a visit from its young owner. When a horse is kept in a field, the owner must check that the fences are secure and that there are no poisonous plants the horse might eat.*

are bad for your pet so that you can avoid them.) You must know how much food your pet eats so that you do not overfeed it.

Many animals are nervous and frightened. You must give a new pet time to settle down and become used to its new home. Do not pick up your pet without first learning how to hold it properly. Some animals hate to be carried or handled very much. Never force your pet to let you carry it.

Some Common Pets CATS AND DOGS. These animals are the most popular pets in the world. They are also the friendliest and easiest to care for. But they are not always friendly to each other, so you may have trouble keeping both a cat *and* a dog as pets.

Most dogs need room to run and plenty of exercise. Dogs also need to be trained in obedience. Cats also enjoy going outdoors, but they can live contentedly as "house cats." You may be able to get a kitten or a puppy free by looking in the classified ads of a newspaper. People whose pets have litters are usually happy to give the babies to a good home as soon as they are old enough. If you want a pure-

bred animal, however, you will probably have to pay a lot of money for it. Do not tease or try to frighten a cat or dog. They will scratch or bite in self-defense. For further information, see the articles on CAT and DOG.

FISH. Fish make very colorful and, of course, quiet pets. Even if you live in a small apartment, you probably have room for a fish tank. Before you buy any fishes, you should have your aquarium ready. For instructions, see the article on AQUARIUM. Once the aquarium is prepared and you have the proper food, fish are very easy to care for. For further information on kinds of fish, see the article on TROPICAL FISH.

BIRDS. Certain birds have been bred as pets and are used to living in cages or in larger enclosures called aviaries. Canaries, which can be trained to sing, are very popular pets. Male canaries imitate the songs of other birds. Parakeets, parrots, and mynah birds also make interesting pets because they can be taught to talk. Pigeons are occasionally kept as pets. Some people make pets of chickens and ducks, birds that are not kept in cages. Most birds will thrive on a diet of seeds, fruits, nuts, and green vegetables. Your pet store can advise you on feeding the kind of bird you choose.

COMMON RODENT PETS. Hamsters, gerbils, and guinea pigs are the most popular rodent pets. For information on their care, see the article on GUINEA PIGS AND HAMSTERS.

Mice—from a pet store—also make good pets. Buy a mouse that has bright eyes and a smooth, shiny coat. You can keep a mouse in a small wire cage or in an aquarium tank. Buy as large a cage or tank as you can because mice need room to run around and play. Mice also need a little closed room in their cage where they can sleep. The cage should always be kept clean.

You can feed a mouse either once or twice a day. Mice will eat oats and seeds and bread soaked in milk. Mice also eat green vegetables. Give your mouse only what it will eat at one meal. Make sure you clean the food dish every day. Always keep fresh water for the mouse to drink.

RABBITS. Rabbits make fairly inexpensive pets. Buy a bright-eyed, plump rabbit from a pet store. Pick it up gently, and do not handle it very much until it gets used to you. *Never* pick up a rabbit by the ears.

A rabbit should live outside in a wire-mesh pen, or hutch. A rabbit likes privacy, so part of the pen should be closed off as its bedroom. Hay or straw make a nice bed. Change your rabbit's bedding at least twice a week, and clean the hutch at least once a week.

Rabbits eat greens, such as lettuce, spinach, clover, and beet greens, and grains, such as oats or bran. They also like turnips, carrots, and apples. They need a high nutrient diet, so they are usually fed a special food bought at a pet store. Keep fresh water and a piece of rock salt in your rabbit's hutch. It will also appreciate having some hay around for snacks. Rabbits need to chew on twigs to keep their teeth healthy. Wash your rabbit's dishes after each meal.

Some Unusual Pets Some people enjoy unusual pets, such as frogs, turtles, and lizards. Such animals have unusual water, temperature, and food requirements, and you should be aware of their special life cycle and habitats. See the article on TERRARIUM for information on keeping these animals.

Whatever pet you choose, you must make sure that it stays clean, healthy, and well fed. Animals can take care of themselves in their natural surroundings, but when they live with you, they need your help. If your pet has runny eyes or nose or seems sick or unusually tired, you should take it to a *veterinarian*, or animal doctor. Some animal diseases can be given to human beings, as well as being

harmful to your pet. Veterinarians can cure most animal diseases and give you advice on caring for your pet. With the proper care and attention, your pet can remain a playful friend and comforting companion for a long time.

ALSO READ: AQUARIUM, CAT, DOG, DOMESTICATED ANIMALS, GUINEA PIGS AND HAMSTERS, LIZARD, PARROTS AND PARAKEETS, RABBITS AND HARES, SNAKE, TERRARIUM, TROPICAL FISH.

PETER THE GREAT (1672–1725) Peter the Great was the name given to the czar (ruler) of Russia, Peter I. He was the first czar to make Russia into a great power in Europe.

Peter was crowned czar when he was 10 years old. He grew up to be tall and massively strong. He was fiercely independent. His great interest was in sailing and shipbuilding. When he was 17, Peter dismissed his sister Sophia, who had ruled during his childhood, and took control of the government. He traveled abroad to study, visiting England, Germany, and Holland.

Russia at that time was an inland country, with no seaports. Peter built a great fleet of ships and captured the Turkish port of Azov on the Black Sea. He then declared war on Sweden and seized several provinces along the Baltic Sea. In one of these provinces he built a new capital, St. Petersburg (now Leningrad).

Peter greatly admired the new inventions and modern governments of western Europe. Russia, in comparison, was a backward country. Peter began to reorganize the Russian government along Western lines. He made the Russian people adopt Western dress and habits. Anyone who continued to wear the traditional beard and long robes was heavily fined. Peter built new factories and encouraged trade with Western countries. The old Russian nobility, who rebelled against the changes, were put

▲ *Raccoons have been kept as pets when raised from babyhood. But wild animals were not meant to make tame pets and are best left to the wild.*

▲ *Peter the Great, ruler of Russia.*

Peter the Great had such a passion for ships and shipbuilding that he worked in shipyards in Holland and England while he was the czar of Russia.

▲ *These stone "tree trunks" are in the Petrified Forest National Park in eastern Arizona.*

▼ *The world's first oil well, in Titusville, Pennsylvania. This well struck oil on August 28, 1859.*

down with great cruelty. Before Peter died, he decreed that his wife, the empress Catherine, should succeed him. She was the first woman to rule Russia.

ALSO READ: CATHERINE THE GREAT, RUSSIAN HISTORY.

PETRIFIED FOREST The Petrified Forest in northern Arizona is the world's largest and brightest collection of petrified wood. About 200 million years ago, this area of the desert was a land of lakes and swamps. Trees grew in the highlands surrounding the swamps. When a tree died and fell, it was carried by streams into the swamps and became buried there. Water seeped through the mud into the dead tree. The minerals (mostly silica) in the mud and water seeped inside the tree cells and hardened, like plaster poured into a mold. Gradually, the wood fibers were replaced by silica and hardened into stone (petrified). Every little detail of the log was preserved. Other minerals, such as iron oxide, jasper, agate, and quartz, added color and sparkle to the petrified wood.

Some of the stone logs in the Petrified Forest are more than 100 feet (30 m) long and 6 feet (2 m) in diameter. One arched log forms a natural bridge, called the Agate Bridge. Petrified wood is harder than steel and heavier than ordinary wood. One log of petrified wood weighs more than three logs of freshly cut wood of the same size.

The Petrified Forest officially became the Petrified Forest National Park in 1962. Visitors from all over the world come to see the magnificent petrified trees, as well as many relics of prehistoric Indians.

ALSO READ: FOSSIL, GEOLOGY.

PETROLEUM Petroleum is a thick liquid mostly found beneath the Earth's surface. The word petroleum means "rock oil." Petroleum is usually called *oil*. It ranges in color from light brown to nearly black. Most scientists believe that petroleum is the decayed remains of tiny animals and plants that lived in shallow seas millions of years ago. Heat and pressure in the Earth's crust covered the decaying plant and animal remains with layers of rock. Squeezed together, the plant and animals remains turned to liquid petroleum. In this way, underground stores of petroleum were formed. Some of this petroleum was forced to the Earth's surface when the

Drake's Oil Well

▲ *The top of the drill pipe is suspended from the top of the tower of an oil derrick. The drill is lengthened by adding sections of pipe.*

▲ *A Texas oil field. Here, the oil lies underground, and extracting it is easy.*

rock above it was worn down by erosion and then cracked.

Finding Oil People have been obtaining oil from surface pools for thousands of years. But underground petroleum was not used until 1859, when the first oil well (a hole drilled from the Earth's surface to an underground pool) was made by Edwin L. Drake near Titusville, Pennsylvania. His discovery, plus the invention of the internal combustion engine (which burned oil) in the late 1800's, started an oil boom that was the beginning of the petroleum industry.

The world's largest known oil deposits lie in the Middle East, in the countries of Saudi Arabia, Iraq, Iran, and Kuwait. The Soviet Union also has very large oil reserves and is the world's leading oil producer today. Other major oil-producing nations include Mexico, the United States, Libya, Venezuela, China, Nigeria, the United Kingdom, Indonesia, Algeria, and Canada.

Oil companies hire geologists to find regions where oil will most likely be found. Oil geologists explore an area by using electronic instruments that reveal what is beneath the Earth's

surface. But drilling an oil well is the only way to find out for certain whether oil is located in the area. Since World War II, drilling below the ocean floor off the coast, called *offshore drilling*, has proved very productive. Offshore oil drilling in the United States is done off the coasts of California, Texas, Louisiana, and Alaska. There are other offshore oil fields in Europe, in the North Sea, and also in Australia.

Transporting Oil The transportation of petroleum is an important business, in the North Sea, and also in Australia. Oil is pumped from the wells through huge underground pipes, often over thousands of miles to *refineries*. There, the crude oil is "refined" or purified, and petroleum products are made. If the petroleum is not sent by pipeline, it is carried in ships called tankers or in railroad tank cars. The refineries deliver petroleum products the same way.

At an oil refinery, the various oils and other materials, called *fractions*, in crude (unrefined) oil are separated. In the process used, called *fractional distillation*, petroleum is heated in closed containers. As the temperature is raised, one fraction after another boils. The vapors (gases produced by boiling) of each fraction are piped out

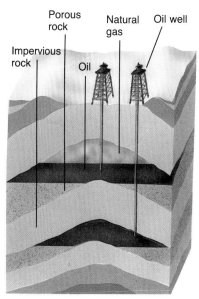

▲ *Oil and natural gas are "fossil fuels" that are formed in pockets between porous rocks (rocks that allow liquids to soak through) and impervious rocks (rocks that do not allow liquids to soak through).*

▼ *Venezuela has rich petroleum deposits in the inland sea of Lake Maracaibo, where the water is shallow enough to make drilling less difficult than in the rougher open seas.*

▲ *Part of an oil refinery. In a refinery, crude petroleum is broken down into useful forms such as gasoline and heating oil.*

During the 1991 Gulf War, the price of petroleum reached record highs until Kuwait was liberated.

of the container. When they are cooled, they become liquid again. The liquids formed are the lighter petroleum products, such as gasoline, kerosene, and heating oil. Other refining processes produce different petroleum products, or *petrochemicals*.

Petroleum is one of the most important materials in the modern world. Fuels, such as gasoline, kerosene, and diesel oil, provide the power for automobiles, boats, airplanes, and other vehicles. Fuel oil is burned for heat. Hundreds of other useful products are made from petroleum. Examples of these petroleum products include perfumes, insecticides, paint thinner, cosmetics, detergents, and explosives.

The Future of Petroleum New oil fields (areas covering petroleum pools) are continually being found and drilled. Yet in spite of these discoveries, petroleum is being used faster than it is being found. Some scientists predict that the world's petroleum supply will be used up by early next century. By then petroleum may be too valuable to be burned as gasoline in cars. Oil can also be extracted from shale, a kind of rock, and from tar sands, but getting the oil out of them is very expensive. Scientists are working on new methods of extractions from oil shale and tar sands, for these are probably the petroleum sources of the future.

ALSO READ: DISTILLATION, DRILLING RIG, FUEL, GASOLINE, GEOLOGY, KEROSENE, NATURAL GAS, PIPELINE.

PHARAOH   see EGYPT, ANCIENT.

PHILADELPHIA Philadelphia is the largest city in Pennsylvania and fifth largest in the United States. Almost five million people live in and around Philadelphia. This city of great historical importance is located

where the Schuylkill and Delaware rivers meet.

The name, Philadelphia, means "brotherly love" in Greek. It was chosen by the city's founder, William Penn, in 1682. Penn and his Society of Friends, called Quakers, planned the city as a place where people would have freedom in their worship and their daily lives.

The First and Second Continental Congresses were held in the city, and the Declaration of Independence was signed in Independence Hall in 1776. This historic site is now a national shrine, which also contains the famous Liberty Bell. Nearby is Congress Hall, where the first Congress met.

Philadelphia served as capital of the United States from 1790 to 1799. Although the seat of government was moved to Washington, Philadelphia

▼ *Philadelphia's Independence Hall was built between 1732 and 1741.*

continued to expand and prosper. The first bank in the new nation was established in the city. Several industries grew up, first in textiles and clothing, printing and publishing, and later in metals and machinery. Petroleum products and chemicals are important industries.

Philadelphia became a great seaport and now has nearly 300 piers and wharves. Its naval base is one of the largest in the country.

The reputation for religious freedom, associated with Philadelphia since William Penn, attracted many people persecuted in their homelands. The Quakers and refugees from many countries came to make a new life in the city. Many blacks from the southern United States settled here. Blacks form about one-third of the population in the central city of Philadelphia.

The University of Pennsylvania, founded in 1740, and Temple University are two of the many schools and colleges in Philadelphia and its suburbs. Fairmount Park, a wooded area of more than 3,500 acres (1,416 ha), extends for ten miles (16 km) and contains the Zoological Gardens, natural settings for summer concerts and plays, and many restored colonial buildings.

ALSO READ: DECLARATION OF INDEPENDENCE; FRANKLIN, BENJAMIN; LIBERTY BELL; PENN, WILLIAM; PENNSYLVANIA; SOCIETY OF FRIENDS.

PHILIP, KINGS OF FRANCE
Six kings of France were named Philip.

Philip I (1052–1108) was the son of King Henry I of France. Philip became king after the death of his father in 1060. The French kings at this time ruled only a small territory in the center of France. The rest of the land was controlled by powerful French nobles. In 1066, the strongest of these nobles, Duke William of Normandy, invaded England and became its king. He warred with Philip.

Philip II (1165–1223) was the son of King Louis VII of France. He succeeded his father in 1180, at the age of 15. When he came to the throne, a large region of France was controlled by King Henry II of England. But Henry's sons were ready to rebel against their father and to deceive one another. Philip used their quarrels to aid him in winning back most of the English lands in France, including Normandy. Because of this, he was called "Philip Augustus." (Augustus comes from a Latin word meaning "magnificent.") In 1214, Philip won a great victory over the armies of England, Flanders, and the Holy Roman Empire. After that, France was an important power.

Philip Augustus was the first of the French kings to bring most of France under his control. He took power away from the nobles and appointed his own magistrates (officials) to oversee each of the French provinces. Philip gave special privileges to the French merchants and encouraged the growth of the cities. He had Paris walled, and its streets were paved for the first time.

Philip III (1245–1285) was the son of the French king, Louis IX, or Saint Louis. Philip succeeded his father in 1270. Louis had been a powerful king, much loved by the French people. But Philip was weak and spiritless. He depended very much on the advice of others. His uncle, Charles of Anjou, encouraged him to fight an unnecessary war against Aragon, a kingdom in Spain. The French were defeated and Philip was killed in the final battle.

Philip IV (1268–1314) was known as "The Fair." He succeeded his father, Philip III, in 1285. The most important event in the reign of Philip IV was his quarrel with the leader of the Roman Catholic Church, Pope Boniface VIII. The Roman Catholic clergy in France has always considered the pope to be their only leader.

▲ *Philip I, king of France from 1060 to 1108.*

▲ *Philip IV (the Fair), king of France from 1285 to 1314.*

▲ *Philip VI, King of France from 1328 to 1350.*

▲ *Philip II, king of Spain from 1556 to 1598.*

▲ *Philip IV, king of Spain from 1621 to 1665.*

Philip II built the huge Escorial palace and church about 30 miles (48 km) from Madrid, Spain. It took 21 years to build and now contains one of the world's finest collections of paintings, books, and manuscripts. Philip II and most of his successors are buried there.

But Philip now claimed that the king should have the power to collect taxes from the clergy. The quarrel lasted until Boniface died in 1303. Two years later, a French bishop was elected pope. Philip encouraged the new pope to move from Rome to Avignon in France.

Philip V (1294–1322) was the second son of Philip IV. Philip became king after the death of his older brother, Louis X, in 1317. Some people in France claimed that Louis's baby daughter should have been the new ruler. They refused to support Philip. But he strengthened his control over the country by setting up militias (small citizen armies) in the cities.

Philip VI (1293–1350) was the grandson of Philip III. He was the first king of the Valois dynasty (ruling family). Philip succeeded his cousin, King Charles IV, as king of France in 1328. King Edward III of England, who was the grandson of the French king, Philip IV, claimed that he should have been crowned king of France. This quarrel led to the outbreak of the Hundred Years' War between France and England. Edward defeated Philip at the great Battle of Crécy in 1346.

ALSO READ: ENGLISH HISTORY; FEUDALISM; FRENCH HISTORY; HUNDRED YEARS' WAR; WILLIAM, KINGS OF ENGLAND.

PHILIP, KINGS OF SPAIN Five kings of Spain were named Philip.

Philip I (1478–1506) was called "The Handsome." He was the son of the Holy Roman Emperor, Maximillian I. In 1499, Philip married Joanna, the daughter of King Ferdinand V and Queen Isabella I of Spain. Ferdinand and Isabella were joint rulers of the two great Spanish kingdoms, Aragon and Castile. When Isabella died in 1504, Philip and Joanna became rulers of Castile. Philip died suddenly at the age of 28.

Philip II (1527–1598) was the son of King Charles I of Spain. Charles was also the Holy Roman Emperor. In 1556, Charles abdicated (gave up his throne) and broke up his enormous empire. Philip became king of Spain and ruler of the Spanish lands in the Netherlands, Italy, and the Americas. Philip was now the most powerful ruler in Europe. He spent much of his reign fighting rulers of other countries who were jealous of his power. Spain was already at war with France when Philip came to the throne. He defeated the French in two great battles. Philip had married Queen Mary I of England. But after Mary died, a quarrel broke out between Spain and England. Philip, as the most powerful Roman Catholic king, was the defender of the Catholic Church in Europe. The new English queen, Elizabeth I, who was a Protestant, sided with Philip's enemies. In 1588, Philip sent a mighty fleet of ships, called the Armada, to invade England. But the Spanish ships were put to flight and destroyed by the English navy and by terrible storms at sea.

When Philip died, Spain's great power was beginning to weaken. Philip's wars had cost vast amounts of money that the country could not afford. Many people lived in terror of the Inquisition, a court that questioned and tortured anyone suspected of being a heretic (one who opposes an official religious dogma) or a nonbeliever in the Roman Catholic Church. The Protestants in the Netherlands had rebelled against Spanish rule and were demanding their independence. Philip insisted on settling every matter of government himself. He was very hardworking, but his lands were too large to be governed properly by one person.

Philip III (1578–1621) succeeded his father, Philip II, in 1598. Unlike his father, Philip was not interested in the business of government. He let his favorite counselors govern Spain.

The Spanish people grew poorer, while the king spent money on festivals and amusements. The Greek painter, El Greco, was working in Spain during Philip's reign. The Spanish writer, Miguel de Cervantes, author of the novel, *Don Quixote*, also lived at this time.

Philip IV (1605–1665) succeeded his father, Philip III, in 1621. Like his father, Philip left the business of government to his favorites. His chief interests were hunting and the arts. The painter Diego Velázquez painted many pictures of Philip IV and his family. The country, meanwhile, grew poorer and weaker. Portugal broke away from Spain and chose its own king. Philip was forced to give the people of the Netherlands their independence.

Philip V (1683–1746) was the grandson of the powerful French king, Louis XIV. The Spanish king, Charles II, who had no children, chose Philip as his successor. But when Charles died in 1700, the rulers of England and the Holy Roman Empire refused to recognize Philip as king of Spain. They were afraid that he would join together the two great kingdoms of France and Spain. This fear provoked a war, the war of the Spanish Succession, in which France and Spain were defeated.

ALSO READ: ENGLISH HISTORY, FRENCH HISTORY, HOLY ROMAN EMPIRE, NETHERLANDS, PORTUGAL, SPANISH ARMADA, SPANISH HISTORY.

PHILIPPINES The more than 7,000 islands that make up the Philippines stretch out in the western Pacific Ocean about 100 miles (160 km) south of Taiwan and form the Republic of the Philippines in southern Asia. Borneo is to the southwest. (See the map with the article on ASIA.) The biggest islands are Luzon in the north and Mindanao in the south. Most of the people live on the eleven largest islands. Some of the islands are so small they are not even named. Manila, the chief port and largest city, is the capital.

The islands are the tips of mountains that are partly under the ocean. Earthquakes sometimes shake the islands, and volcanoes erupt. The climate is humid and warm all year in the lowlands, and cooler in the mountains. Typhoons (hurricanes) often strike during the rainy season.

Orchids and other flowers, plants, animals, and birds make the islands a natural wonderland. Deposits of chromite, nickel, and copper are among the largest in the world. Gold and silver are mined. The coastal waters are full of fish and mollusks, including the pearl oyster.

Most of the people live in small villages and make their living from farming. They raise crops of sugarcane, fruits, rice, coconuts, vegetables, and Manila hemp. Valuable timber grows in the mountains.

The people of the Philippines are called Filipinos. During prehistoric

▲ *Terraced fields flooded for rice growing in the Philippines.*

PHILIPPINES

Capital City: Manila (1,860,000 people).
Area: 115,831 square miles (300,000 sq. km).
Population: 65,505,000.
Government: Republic.
Natural Resources: Crude oil, nickel, cobalt, silver, gold, copper.
Export Products: Electronics, clothes, minerals and ores, farm products, coconut products.
Unit of Money: Peso.
Official Language: Pilipino.

▲ *Plato, Greek philosopher.*

▲ *Immanuel Kant, German philosopher.*

▲ *John Locke, English philosopher.*

times, Malayan peoples came to the islands at different times. They settled in all parts of the islands and developed many speech dialects and local customs. Spanish people arrived in the 1500's, and many Chinese came in later years. Most people speak Pilipino, the national language, which is based on a Malayan dialect called Tagalog. Many people also speak English and Spanish. The Philippines is the only Asian country with a large Christian population.

Ferdinand Magellan, a Portuguese navigator serving Spain, discovered the Philippines on March 14, 1521. Later, Spanish explorers named the islands after Philip II of Spain. In 1898, after the Spanish-American War, the islands were turned over to the United States. William Howard Taft became the first civil governor of the islands. The U.S. Congress passed a bill in 1934 that granted the Philippines independence by 1946. It provided for a temporary commonwealth supervised by the United States, but with an elected Philippine president and a constitution. In 1935, the Filipinos adopted a constitution and elected Manuel Quezon as their first president. In December 1941, Japan invaded and occupied the islands. U.S. forces returned in 1944 and defeated the Japanese in 1945. The Philippines gained full independence on July 4, 1946.

Ferdinand Marcos, who was elected president in 1965, restricted the activities of his opponents in the 1970's. In 1986, he was opposed in the presidential elections by Mrs. Corazon Aquino. Marcos won, but the elections were proved to be a fraud. Marcos fled the country and Mrs. Aquino became the new president. The new government faced economic problems and rebel opposition.

ALSO READ: ASIA; MACARTHUR, DOUGLAS; MAGELLAN, FERDINAND; SPANISH-AMERICAN WAR; TAFT, WILLIAM HOWARD; WORLD WAR II.

PHILOSOPHY The word "philosophy" comes from two Greek words meaning "love" and "wisdom." A philosopher, therefore, is one who loves wisdom enough to spend most of his or her time and energy in search of it. The word "philosophy" is often used to mean a set of basic values and attitudes toward nature, society, and life in general.

Philosophers Philosophy as a serious study probably began in ancient Greece between 600 and 430 B.C. The ancient Greek philosophers were not satisfied with the mythology of their time. They wanted to explain the nature and origin of the universe through reasoning and observation. The Greek philosophers dealt with many interesting ideas. Among the topics they investigated were politics, beauty, nature, logic, and moral values. The Greek philosophers are one of two important sources of philosophy in the Western world.

The other major source is the ancient Hebrew prophets. The writings of these prophets and the history of the Hebrew people are recorded in the Bible. In it are discussed many of the same questions that occupied the Greek philosophers. Together, the Greek (Hellenic) and Israelite (Hebraic) writers form the beginning of philosophy in the Western world. Most important Western philosophical ideas can be traced to one of these two sources.

As time passed and the world changed, so did philosophy. In the Middle Ages, philosophy was dominated by the Roman Catholic Church. During that time, philosophers, notably St. Thomas Aquinas, were concerned with the conflict between faith and reason. With the Renaissance, philosophy turned away from the supernatural to natural explanations of the external world. During the 1600's, philosophers became more daring in their thinking. They believed that people should question all established ideas. On this basis, they constructed many new views of the world and people's place in it.

The German philosopher, Immanuel Kant, believed that reality extends far beyond what a person's five senses tell him or her, but that a person's knowledge of reality cannot extend further than the senses. He also believed that the existence of God was proved by the existence of nature. (All the things in the natural world must have been created by someone—and people call the creator, God.) The English philosopher, John Locke, influenced political thought with his belief that all people have certain basic rights that their governments should protect.

In the Eastern nations of China and India, philosophy is as old as in the West. Two of the most important Chinese philosophers were Confucius and Lao-tse. Confucius taught that people should be kind to one another and respect their elders. Lao-tse encouraged people to follow the course of nature and live simply. Oriental philosophy is closely tied to religion. It contains many wise sayings and much advice on the best way to live. It is only in recent times that Western thinkers have discovered the great wisdom of Oriental philosophy.

Some Philosophical Questions For thousands of years, people have sought answers to several basic philosophical questions.

AESTHETICS. Think of something that seems beautiful to you. It might be something from nature, such as a flower or snow on a branch. Or it might be something artistic, such as a poem, a song, a painting, or a piece of sculpture. Now ask yourself, "What makes this seem beautiful to me?" Many philosophers have dealt with this question and others like it. Some find beauty in order and precision, others in the pleasure experienced through the senses. Still others find beauty in the ideas that the work of art contains. This area of study is known as aesthetics.

METAPHYSICS AND EPISTEMOLOGY. Sometimes we may feel that what we see is not all there is to the universe—and even that there is more to it than the most powerful telescopes and microscopes can reveal. Metaphysics attempts to understand the nature of ultimate reality—the reality of which we see only a small part—through reasoning. But we must understand how we look at reality and think about it, since we distort reality, or fail to see it entirely, in our looking and thinking. The study of the origin, nature, and methods of knowledge is epistemology.

ETHICS. This area of philosophy tries to determine what is right and wrong. It tries to answer the question, "How does a good and honorable person act?" There are many views on what the ethical person should do, but they all concern a person's responsibility—to oneself, to one's country, or to one's God. Some ethical standards have even been made into laws in an effort to make people behave honorably.

Everyone is a philosopher because an important part of growing up is developing a personal philosophy. Each person eventually has to decide who mankind is, why he or she is here, and what is right and wrong in life.

ALSO READ: ARISTOTLE, CONFUCIUS, JEWISH HISTORY, PLATO, RELIGION, SOCRATES.

▲ *René Descartes, French philosopher and scientist.*

Philosophers will often ponder over the oddest questions. It is said that two famous 13th century philosophers, St. Thomas Aquinas and Albert the Great, used to argue for hours about how many angels could sit on the point of a pin.

PHOENICIA Phoenicia was an ancient region in the Middle East. It extended for about 200 miles (320 km) along the eastern coast of the Mediterranean Sea. Most of Phoenicia is now the modern country of Lebanon. The Phoenicians were great seafarers and traders. They were known throughout the ancient world

▲ *A lion, carved in ivory, from Phoenicia. It was made in the 8th or 9th century* B.C., *when Phoenician art was highly prized.*

▼ *Office workers use photocopiers all the time, and it is very much taken for granted as an essential tool in the modern word-processing world.*

for the purple dye that they made from a type of mollusk. Their most important invention was an alphabet. This alphabet was copied by the Greeks, with whom the Phoenicians traded. It developed eventually into the alphabet we use today.

Phoenicia was made up of self-ruling city-states. Its two greatest cities were Sidon and Tyre. Phoenicians are called Sidonites in the Bible. Phoenicia was originally ruled by Egypt. But the Phoenicians rebelled, and by 900 B.C. they had won their independence. Phoenician traders sailed to ports all over the Mediterranean. They even ventured into the Atlantic Ocean, possibly sailing as far as England. Phoenicia founded several colonies, including Carthage in North Africa. In the 700's B.C., a series of foreign invasions of Phoenicia began. Phoenicia was conquered by the Assyrians and then the Persians. The Greek general, Alexander the Great, invaded Phoenicia in 332 B.C. He besieged Tyre for seven months before the city surrendered. In 64 B.C., Phoenicia was made a part of the Roman Empire.

ALSO READ: ALEXANDER THE GREAT, ALPHABET, CARTHAGE, LEBANON.

PHOENIX see ANIMALS OF MYTH AND LEGEND.

PHONICS see READING.

PHONOGRAPH see RECORDING.

PHOTOCOPIER A photocopier is a machine that can copy a picture, a page of a book, or a letter in seconds. Before photocopiers were invented, there was no way of making quick copies. People had to write out a page, trace a drawing by hand, or make a "carbon copy" of a letter using inked paper.

When you press the button on a photocopier, a bright light comes on inside. It lights up the page or drawing. A lens inside the machine projects an image of the page or picture onto a metal drum.

This drum is electrified so that its surface has an electric charge all over it. When the image is projected onto it, the light in the bright parts of the image destroys the electric charge. Only the dark parts of the drum are still electrified.

A black powder is dusted over the drum. It clings only to the parts of the surface that are electrified. When a sheet of paper is pressed against the drum, the powder comes off and an image of the page or picture forms on the paper. This process is called xerography.

Fax machines also produce copies of pages or pictures. They send signals to each other through a telephone line. One machine can copy a page or drawing "scanned" in the first machine.

PHOTOELECTRICITY When leaving a large supermarket, you may have passed through a door that opened for you automatically. You didn't have to push the door or touch it in any way. The door may have been opened by an "electric eye," a device operated by photoelectricity.

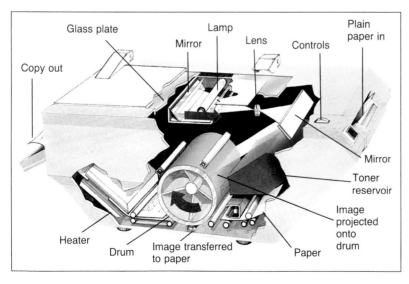

Glass plate — Lamp — Mirror — Lens — Controls — Plain paper in — Copy out — Mirror — Toner reservoir — Image projected onto drum — Heater — Drum — Image transferred to paper — Paper

How Photoelectricity Works Photoelectricity is a type of electric power produced by light. Light is a form of energy. Certain metals, such as cesium and potassium, give off electrons when struck by light. These metals are called "light-sensitive." Electric eyes, which are also called phototubes or photoelectric cells, contain light-sensitive metal plates. So, when light strikes an electric eye, electrons are produced. These electrons form a weak electric current, which can be amplified to work a switch.

In the case of the automatic door, an electric eye is attached to one side of the passageway. A thin beam of light shines across the passageway onto the electric eye. When a person cuts the beam, he or she interrupts the light rays. This sets off the switch that opens the door.

Photoelectricity is used to produce power for many other machines. Some burglar alarms, for example, use electric eyes. If a burglar passes through a door where light is shining on an electric eye, an alarm will go off. Street lights turn on automatically by means of electric eyes. Motion picture projectors use photoelectricity to produce sound.

ALSO READ: BATTERY, ELECTRICITY, ELECTRIC POWER, LIGHT.

PHOTOGRAPHY Have you ever thought about the many ways photography is used? Newspapers, magazines, and books are filled with photographs. Posters, shop window displays, and advertisements all make use of photographs. Tiny strips of microfilm record the printed pages of books, newspapers, and other materials. We use photocopying machines to make photographic copies of letters and other documents. X-ray photography is used in medicine and industry. Remote controlled cameras in spacecraft photograph distant planets.

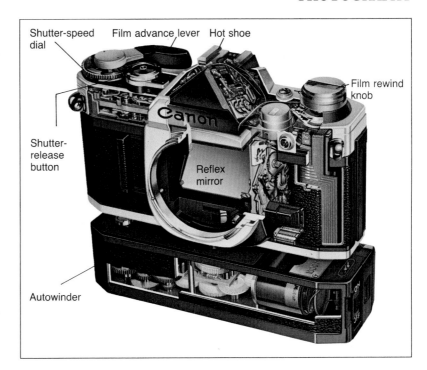

Shutter-speed dial   Film advance lever   Hot shoe

Film rewind knob

Shutter-release button

Reflex mirror

Autowinder

Taking Photographs There are all kinds of cameras, some very expensive. Yet a simple camera and film are all you need to take a photograph. Most cameras fall into two categories: reflex and non-reflex. A non-reflex camera has a direct-vision viewfinder, for viewing, framing, and perhaps even focusing the subject. A reflex camera allows you to view and focus on the subject through the lens using a mirror and prism system inside the camera. Many popular 35-mm single lens reflex (SLR) cameras come into this category. More advanced are large-format SLR and twin-lens reflex (TLR) cameras. For professional studio work, many photographers prefer a large bellows camera.

Small pocket cameras use cartridge film that is easy to insert and remove. Most 35-mm cameras use either cassette or roll film. Bellows cameras use sheet film. A recent development is the magnetic disk film camera. And there are also throwaway cameras, bought ready-loaded with film, which are thrown away after the film has been exposed and developed.

With a modern camera, all you have to do is aim the camera at your subject and press the button that

▲ *The working parts of a modern 35mm single lens reflex (SLR) camera.*

▲ *Holding the camera level should be fine for most shots. The lower picture shows how to hold the camera in an upright position, which you may need to do for some shots.*

▲ *This drum processing kit is a practical way to do your own color printing. The exposed print is placed into the drum, and each chemical solution is added as required. A motor rotates the drum to make sure the chemicals cover the surface of the print evenly.*

▼ *The photographer has included a horse and wagon in this picture to add extra interest and contrast to a tranquil sunset landscape.*

opens the shutter. Light enters the camera through the lens when the shutter snaps open, and this produces a chemical change on the film. This is *exposing* the film.

Each type of film has a particular sensitivity to light. This is the film speed. You can find a film's speed from the ASA numbers on the film and its carton. For example 50 ASA is slow (the film needs long exposure in poor light but is good for detail). 200 to 400 ASA is fast (good in most lights and can "freeze" a fast-moving subject).

Using the viewfinder on your camera, you can adjust your position to take the kind of picture you want. It is most important to hold the camera steady when taking a picture. Moving the camera will blur the image on the film. Always wind on the film after taking a picture. If you expose the same piece of film twice, you will get a double image—two photographs mixed together.

Aim your camera so that sunlight does not shine directly at the lens. Direct sunlight produces unwanted reflections and glare in the finished photographs. If you are taking photographs indoors, or where the light is not strong, you will need a flash attachment or some other bright light source.

■ **LEARN BY DOING**

Once you have some skill at taking good, sharp photographs, you can try some special effects with your camera. Try adjusting the light for an indoor photograph so that light hits your subject from an unusual angle— from one side, from above, from below. Take several pictures of the same subject, changing the direction of the light each time. The various light directions will produce many different moods, even though the subject is the same.

Even if your camera does not have an adjustable lens, different effects can be achieved by turning the camera. Try taking pictures of the same object, each time turning your camera so the view is wide, or long, or at an angle. Close-up shots make interesting photographs. Try some close-up views of a person, a leaf, a reflection, a crack in the sidewalk, a doorknob, the spokes of a bicycle wheel, or anything you think looks interesting.

Action shots make exciting photographs. By setting the shutter at a high speed, you can capture a moving subject without blurring the picture. You can get the feel of movement in a

▼ *This photograph shows how natural light from a window can give an interesting "softness" to the picture.*

▲ *A fantastic close-up of a bee. The insect "took its own picture" by crossing an infrared beam that fired the camera.*

negative is a transparent, "backwards" version of your original picture. The lighter areas show up dark on the negative, and the darker areas come out light.

After the negative image is fully developed, the film is placed in a tank containing a "stopper" solution, then in cool water to wash off the chemicals. The developing process must always be timed. If a film is left in a developer solution too long, the picture turns almost black. After being washed, the film is placed in a solution called hypo (short for hyposulfite). This is a mixture of chemicals that hardens the film and fixes the image to make it ready for printing after drying.

Printing Photographs In printing a photograph, you use the negative image to make a *positive image*. A positive shows the final picture just as you photographed it. The negative is pressed tightly against a sheet of special paper that is sensitive to light. When light is directed through the negative to the paper, a chemical change takes place on the paper. The paper is developed, fixed, and washed to make the photograph.

Small photographs can be enlarged by projecting the negative through an enlarger, which has a lens that makes

▲ *By using a long exposure and moving the camera, a photographer can "paint" a picture on film. Here, a surrealistic image has been created from traffic lights.*

photograph by using a slower shutter speed and following the movement of the subject by slowly turning your body to keep the subject in your viewfinder.

You can produce some interesting photographs by aiming your camera from an unusual angle. You might photograph a tree by lying down underneath it and pointing your camera right up into the branches. You can also "frame" your subject by shooting a picture through a window, door, archway, or grove of trees so that the window, archway, or trees surround the edges of your picture. ■

Developing Photographs Most people have the exposed films developed professionally. Some people enjoy developing their own film. Developing must be done in a totally dark room. If light should strike the film before it is developed, your photographs will be ruined. Darkrooms can be lit with a "safe light" (usually a special red light bulb) that will not damage the film.

Exposed film is first placed in a developer solution. The developer makes a chemical change on the film that brings out a negative image. The

▼ *In the early days of photography, the equipment was heavy, so the photographer carried it on a handcart. This large 19th-century plate camera stood on a tripod.*

▲ *This rare old photograph shows President Abraham Lincoln posing in a chair.*

Photosynthesis is possible because a leaf exposes a lot of moist cells to the air in order to take in carbon dioxide. But this also means that the leaf loses water by evaporation. In one summer's day, a tree may lose water weighing about five times as much as its own leaves. In temperate climates, as much water is lost from plants in this way as flows out to the sea from rivers.

the image bigger, just as a slide projector can enlarge small pictures by projecting them on a screen. The enlarger projects the magnified image onto light-sensitive paper. When the paper is developed, an enlarged print comes out.

An instant camera, such as a Polaroid, uses a special film that does not produce a regular negative. The undeveloped print is ejected from the camera just seconds after you snap the picture. It develops right in front of your eyes.

Color film for regular cameras comes in two types. Color-negative film produces a negative from which a print can be made. The other type produces transparencies, or slides, which are made on a piece of film, instead of being printed on paper. Transparencies must be held up to a light, or projected on a screen, in order to be seen.

History of Photography The earliest known photograph was made in 1826 by a French chemist, Joseph N. Niépce. He placed a light-sensitive metal plate in a camera, set the camera on a windowsill, and left the shutter open for eight hours. It took eight hours to get an image on the plate because the chemicals were very slow in reacting to light.

Since that first photograph, faster and more accurate films have been developed. Louis Daguerre invented a way of making positive images right on the metal plates used in the camera. These metal photographs (called daguerreotypes) were very popular. Tintypes were another kind of metal photograph that produced a negative image against a black background. The black background made the negative look like a positive image.

The first flexible film, made of celluloid plastic, was invented in 1887. In 1888, George Eastman made a simple camera that was light in weight and easy to use. These two inventions made photography a popular hobby

for everyone. People began taking "snapshot" pictures, of themselves, the places they visited, in fact, of practically everything. The invention of reliable color film in 1935 added even more to people's enjoyment of photography.

Careers in Photography Many people have jobs to do with photography. Professional photographers may take pictures of famous people, models, buildings, wildlife, or family weddings. Press photographers take pictures for newspapers and magazines.

In the TV and movie world, there are careers for cameramen, cinematographers, technicians, and editors. Also, photography is now widely used in many branches of science, including medicine. Many colleges offer courses in photography and film production.

ALSO READ: CAMERA, MICROFILM, MOTION PICTURE, PHOTOCOPIER, TELEVISION.

PHOTOSYNTHESIS Green plants make their own food. They take in water and carbon dioxide and produce sugar. This food-making process is called photosynthesis. For photosynthesis to take place, green plants must be exposed to light.

Carbon dioxide gas is a part of air. Air enters a plant through stomata (tiny holes) in the surfaces of its leaves. Water is taken into a plant through its roots. The water rises up the stem to the leaves, and there the water and carbon dioxide combine and form sugar. This combination is a *chemical reaction*. Chemical reactions cannot take place without energy. The energy in photosynthesis comes from light. This light energy is stored in *chlorophyll*—the green substance that gives most plants their color. Chlorophyll causes the reaction.

Photosynthesis takes place in many complicated steps. But the process

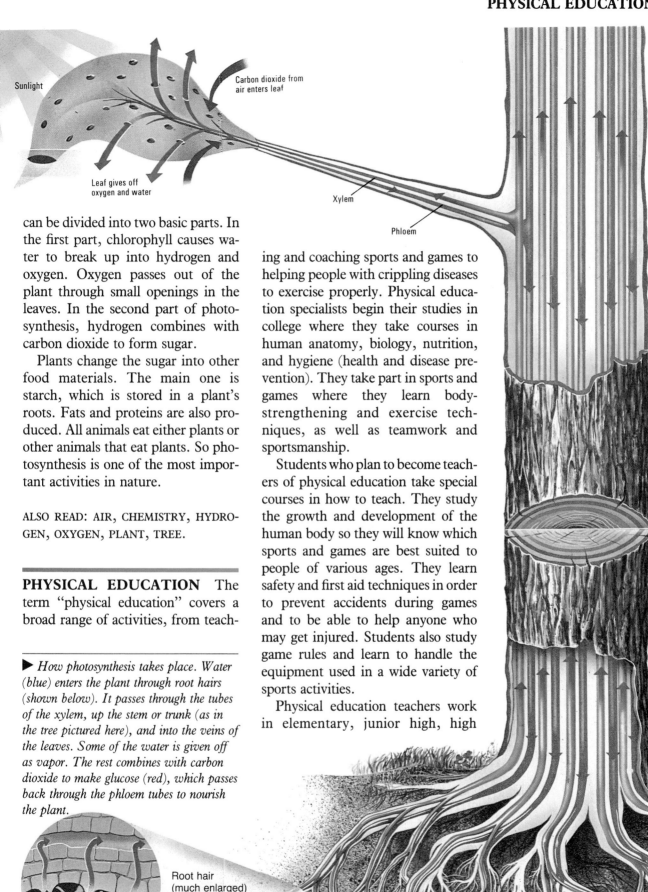

Sunlight

Carbon dioxide from
air enters leaf

Leaf gives off
oxygen and water

Xylem

Phloem

Root hair
(much enlarged)

can be divided into two basic parts. In the first part, chlorophyll causes water to break up into hydrogen and oxygen. Oxygen passes out of the plant through small openings in the leaves. In the second part of photosynthesis, hydrogen combines with carbon dioxide to form sugar.

Plants change the sugar into other food materials. The main one is starch, which is stored in a plant's roots. Fats and proteins are also produced. All animals eat either plants or other animals that eat plants. So photosynthesis is one of the most important activities in nature.

ALSO READ: AIR, CHEMISTRY, HYDROGEN, OXYGEN, PLANT, TREE.

PHYSICAL EDUCATION The term "physical education" covers a broad range of activities, from teach-

▶ *How photosynthesis takes place. Water (blue) enters the plant through root hairs (shown below). It passes through the tubes of the xylem, up the stem or trunk (as in the tree pictured here), and into the veins of the leaves. Some of the water is given off as vapor. The rest combines with carbon dioxide to make glucose (red), which passes back through the phloem tubes to nourish the plant.*

ing and coaching sports and games to helping people with crippling diseases to exercise properly. Physical education specialists begin their studies in college where they take courses in human anatomy, biology, nutrition, and hygiene (health and disease prevention). They take part in sports and games where they learn body-strengthening and exercise techniques, as well as teamwork and sportsmanship.

Students who plan to become teachers of physical education take special courses in how to teach. They study the growth and development of the human body so they will know which sports and games are best suited to people of various ages. They learn safety and first aid techniques in order to prevent accidents during games and to be able to help anyone who may get injured. Students also study game rules and learn to handle the equipment used in a wide variety of sports activities.

Physical education teachers work in elementary, junior high, high

▲ A young student completes a somersault over a vaulting horse under the supervision of a physical education teacher. Gymnastic exercises like this play an important role in physical education.

▲ The Dutch physicist, Christiaan Huygens, explains his wave theory of light to King Louis XIV of France in 1678. Huygens's theory changed optical science.

schools, and colleges. They are employed in camps, playgrounds, and community recreation centers. Physical education specialists are employed by the military and by police departments. Since exercising has been proven to reduce stress in people, large corporations often have exercise and recreational facilities in their buildings. Physical education specialists frequently direct exercise programs for company employees.

Everyone in the field of physical education must work closely with other people. For this reason, most physical education specialists receive training in psychology and in group dynamics (how people in a group or team get along together). A physical education teacher may find a child who is afraid to play certain sports. The teacher must find out why the child is afraid and try to help him or her. A physical therapist helping patients improve their physical conditions can also help them overcome depression and unhappiness. If you should decide on a career in physical education, you will be helping other people to live healthier lives.

ALSO READ: ANATOMY, BIOLOGY, EXERCISE, GYMNASTICS, HEALTH, NUTRITION, PSYCHOLOGY, SPORTS.

▶ Albert Einstein (1879–1955), the greatest physicist of the 20th century.

PHYSICS Have you ever wondered how a television set works? How is it possible to receive a picture out of thin air? What happens when you turn on a flashlight? How does the electricity in the battery turn into a beam of light? What makes an airplane fly? Why is it that a piece of wood floats, but a piece of iron sinks? To find answers, you must go to the science of physics. Physicists study and experiment with *matter* and *energy* in order to find out how things work.

Matter Sand, plastic, glass, steam, wood, metal, milk, and cloth are all substances that you know. There are many other substances in the world, and all of them together are called matter. Matter has two characteristics, or *properties*. All matter has the property of *mass* (it offers resistance to any force that tries to move it) and the property of *volume* (it takes up space). A tiny grain of sand or a microscopic atom both have mass—even though the mass is very small. You cannot put two atoms or grains of sand in exactly the same place at the same time. They both have volume (take up space), and so they cannot both use the same space at the same time.

Energy Physicists study matter to find out how it is built and how it reacts to energy. The ability to work, or move in some way, is called energy. Eight basic forms of energy are heat, electricity, light, sound, mechanical (potential or kinetic), nuclear, chemical, and magnetic.

Heat energy is used to operate steam engines, to cook food, to warm houses, and to do many other things. *Electric energy* is used for producing light and for running all kinds of machines. A photographer uses *light energy* for taking pictures. When you speak, you use *sound energy* to make others hear you. When you pedal a bicycle, you use *mechanical energy* to make the wheels move. *Nuclear energy* is used to explode atom bombs, produce electric power for cities, and drive ships. *Chemical energy* holds together the molecules of chemical compounds. *Magnetic energy* lifts certain metals against the force of gravity.

Physics is the study of nature, and the first scientists to study physics were known as "natural philosophers." Mostly, they guessed how things happened. For instance, the Greeks guessed that matter was made of atoms. In this case, they were right, but guesswork was often wildly wrong. Today, physicists work by theory and experiment; they work out an idea, or theory, often using advanced mathematics, and then they test the correctness of the theory by carrying out experiments. The need to carry out precise experiments made it necessary to have accurate systems of weights and measures, as well as accurate instruments to do the weighing and measuring.

Today, when you study physics, you learn how matter and energy work together. Through a knowledge of physics, people have been able to produce all kinds of machines—from simple can openers to very complicated computers and rocket systems. Astrophysicists study outer space and the movements of planets, stars, and galaxies. Nuclear physicists study the tiny, but extremely powerful, atom and its parts. If you decide to study physics, you may one day discover something about the universe and how it works that people have never known before.

For further information on:
Elements of Physics, *see* ATOM, COLOR, CRYOGENICS, ELECTRICITY, ENERGY, FIRE, FLUID, FRICTION, GAS, GEAR, GRAVITY AND GRAVITATION, HEAT AND COLD, LIGHT, LIQUID, MACHINE, MAGNET, MATTER, MEASUREMENT, MOTION, NUCLEAR ENERGY, ORBIT, PERPETUAL MOTION, PHOTOELECTRICITY, RADIATION, RADIOACTIVITY, RELATIVITY, SOLID, SOUND, SPACE, SPECTRUM, VACUUM, WAVE, WEIGHT, X-RAY.
Physicists, *see* ARCHIMEDES; BACON, ROGER; BOHR, NIELS; COPERNICUS, NICOLAUS; CURIE FAMILY; EINSTEIN, ALBERT; FARADAY, MICHAEL; FERMI, ENRICO; GALILEO GALILEI; GALVANI, LUIGI; NEWTON, SIR ISAAC; PLANCK, MAX.

▲ *Isaac Newton (1642–1727) was the first systematically to set out the laws of the universe. His most important work was done before he was 30 years old.*

MAJOR FIELDS OF STUDY IN PHYSICS

Mechanics
Forces and motion, and how they affect matter. Includes *fluid mechanics*, the study of liquids and gases, and *solid mechanics*, the study of solids. Solid mechanics can be divided into *statics*, the study of bodies at rest, and *dynamics*, the study of bodies in motion. A similar division can be made for fluid mechanics.

Optics
Light: what it is, how it behaves, and how it can be used.

Thermodynamics
Heat: how it can be used, and how it changes to and from other forms of energy.

Acoustics
Sound: how it is produced, transmitted, and received. Includes *ultrasonics*, the study of sound waves that are too high-pitched to be heard by human beings.

Electricity and Magnetism
Electrical charges and magnetic forces and effects. These are closely related because an electric current produces a magnetic field, and a magnetic field can produce an electric current. Includes *electronics*, the study of electrons and how they move.

Atomic, Molecular, and Nuclear Physics
Atomic physics is the study of atoms as a whole. Molecular physics is the study of atoms in groups, *molecules*. Nuclear physics is the study of *nuclei*, the hard, inner core of atoms, including the nature of subatomic particles and other tiny bits of matter.

Solid-State Physics
The physical properties of solids, especially crystals.

Cryogenics
Extremely low temperatures and their effects, including *superconductivity*.

▲ *Computers help physicists store data, and work out complicated experiments. The latest types use microchips to transmit and store information.*

Products of Physics, *see* COMPUTER, DIESEL ENGINE, ELECTRIC POWER, ELECTRONICS, ENGINE, GEIGER COUNTER, GYROSCOPE, JET PROPULSION, LASERS AND MASERS, MOTOR, PENDULUM, PUMP, RADAR, RADIO, ROCKET, SCALE, TELEVISION, TEMPERATURE SCALE.

PHYSIOLOGY   see HUMAN BODY.

PIANO   The piano is probably the best known of all Western musical instruments. Pianos are used in chamber and symphony orchestras. Singers, instrumental musicians, and dancers often use piano accompaniment. There are pianos in many homes and most schools.

The largest pianos are the concert grands (about nine feet , or 3 m, in length) and the baby grands (about five feet, or 1.5 m, in length). Both have wing-shaped bodies and are used mostly by serious and professional musicians. Console or spinet pianos are most often found in homes and schools. Their bodies are compact, and they fit easily in small spaces or against a wall. Upright pianos are similar to consoles, but they are taller.

The piano is a combination percussion and stringed instrument, operated by a *keyboard*. The keyboard consists of 88 white and black keys. Ask someone to play some notes on a piano while you look inside. Each key

The piano has changed very little since the 1860's. People have experimented with different shapes, two keyboards, pedal boards, and electronic reproduction, but none of these have caught on for the concert platform.

▲ *This piano was given by its maker, Thomas Broadwood, to the German composer Ludwig van Beethoven in 1818.*

controls a felt-covered *hammer* inside the piano. When you press a key, a hammer moves up and strikes a set of two or three wire strings. Each set of strings is tuned to a particular pitch, so that each piano key sounds a different note. The lowest-pitched keys are on the left side of the keyboard, the high-pitched keys are on the right.

As you press a key, the hammer rises and at the same time the *damper* moves away from the strings. The damper is a small, felt-covered piece of wood that rests on a set of strings to keep them from vibrating and producing a tone. The damper stays on the strings until a key is pressed. Then it moves off the strings so that the hammer can hit the strings and make a tone. When you release a key, the damper falls back onto the strings and silences the tone. If you press a key and hold it down, the hammer will hit the strings and then move back a short way allowing them to vibrate.

Underneath the piano keyboard near the floor are a set of foot pedals. The damper pedal on the right raises all the dampers inside the piano. This lets all the strings vibrate freely and allows tones to "overlap"—keep on sounding while other tones are being played. The soft pedal on the left shifts all the hammers to one side so that they strike only one string in each set. This produces a softer tone. Some pianos have a third pedal between the other two called the *sostenuto* or sustaining pedal. This pedal releases dampers on only those keys that are pressed down and then released by the pianist.

The piano was first invented about 1709 by an Italian harpsichord maker named Bartolommeo Cristofori. He wanted to combine in one instrument the delicate sound of the *harpsichord* and the power of the *clavichord*. These two keyboard instruments were popular in the 1600's and 1700's. Harpsichord tones are pro-

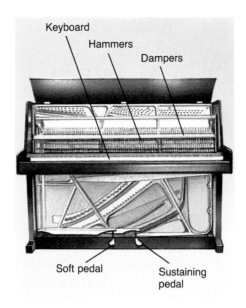

Keyboard
Hammers
Dampers
Soft pedal
Sustaining pedal

duced by quills that pluck the strings. Clavichord tones are made by leather pieces that rub the strings. Cristofori's first piano had leather-covered hammers that hit the strings. The loudness or softness of the tone depended on how hard the player hit the keys. The word "piano" is an abbreviation of the Italian word *pianoforte*, meaning "soft-loud." The instrument was given this name to describe its variety of sounds.

In the 1760's, Johann Christian Bach (a son of Johann Sebastian Bach) performed a series of concerts on the piano. This gave many people a chance to hear the new instrument, and by the beginning of the 1800's, the piano had become very popular. Through the years, improvements were made in the tone quality and pitch of the piano.

ALSO READ: BACH FAMILY, MUSIC, MUSICAL INSTRUMENTS, MUSICIAN, PERCUSSION INSTRUMENTS, STRINGED INSTRUMENTS.

PICASSO, PABLO (1881–1973) As a young lad in Spain, Pablo Picasso could draw amazingly well. A portrait he did of his father looks like the work of a grown artist, but Picasso was in his early teens when he

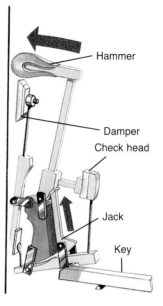

Hammer
Damper
Check head
Jack
Key

▲ *An upright piano (left) and the mechanism that works the hammers as the piano keys are played. The hammer head strikes the string, causing it to vibrate and make a sound. At the same time, the damper moves away from the string, so that it is free to vibrate. A check keeps the hammer near the string in case the same note is to be repeated. When the key is released, the jack moves down and the hammer falls away from the string. The damper then moves back, to stop the string's sounding.*

▲ *The artist Pablo Picasso, with a piece of his sculpture.*

▲ Acrobat with a Ball, *by Pablo Picasso.*

▲ Paulo as Pierrot with Mask, *also by Picasso, who enjoyed painting children.*

It is said that Picasso could draw before he could talk. At the age of 14 he spent one day on an art school test that most people needed a month to take. By 16 he had passed all the tests that Spain's art schools could offer.

drew it. He was not quite 20 when he left Spain for Paris. Almost at once, he was a success as an artist—selling pictures and even having an exhibition of his work. Soon he was in the middle of the exciting modern art movement in Paris. For well over a half century, he was to be a great leader in the visual arts.

Picasso's talents were varied. He not only painted pictures and murals, but he also did sculpture and even designed stage costumes and scenery. Unlike most painters, he did not develop one particular style of painting. He would paint one way for a few years, then change his style so much that the new work would look like that of a different person!

Soon after arriving in Paris from Spain he went through his "blue period" (1901–1904). He painted sad figures and mournful faces in gloomy shades of blue and gray. Perhaps he was lonely for Spain. Then he went into his "circus period," when he did the painting shown here—*Acrobat with a Ball.* Picasso loved the circus and the make-believe that goes with it. Once a week he would go to the part of Paris where the circus people lived, to paint clowns, acrobats, and bareback riders. In the painting, he has caught the graceful acrobat in the delicate act of balancing on a big ball. Contrast this with the powerful wall of muscle and strength in the back and silhouette of the other figure.

Next, Picasso went into his "rose period"—a pink, happy time, as shown in his canvases from those years. You can read in the article on MODERN ART about the next period— the development of cubism, a very important era in modern art history. He continued to change his styles.

One of his favorite subjects for many years was his son, Paulo. He first sketched him on the day he was born, and he continued to sketch and paint pictures of the boy all the time he was growing up. In the painting shown here, *Paulo as Pierrot with*

Mask, he is dressed in the floppy costume of a famous French pantomime figure.

One of Picasso's best-known paintings is *Guernica*, done in 1937 during the Spanish Civil War. Nazi airplanes had bombed the Spanish town of Guernica. Picasso was outraged by news of the death and destruction and put these feelings into a painting 26 feet (8 m) long. It is painted in black, white, and gray, and shows people dying, and suffering through the raid.

Picasso became famous and wealthy. His pictures sold for large amounts of money in his lifetime. Some of his little drawings attained fame—such as his *Dove of Peace*, a sketch of a neighbor's pigeon that has become known the world over as a peace symbol. In his long, productive life he experimented with many new ways of painting, searching for new forms of visual expression.

ALSO READ: MODERN ART.

▼ *Picasso painted this portrait of his mother when he was only 14 years old.*

PICCARD, AUGUSTE AND JACQUES see DEEP-SEA LIFE, OCEAN.

PICTURE WRITING see HIEROGLYPHICS, WRITTEN LANGUAGE.

PIERCE, FRANKLIN (1804–1869)

Franklin Pierce, the fourteenth President of the United States, served during a time when the country was expanding westward and increasing its population with thousands of immigrants. It was also a period when bitter feelings were developing between the North and South that would lead to the Civil War.

Pierce was born in Hillsboro, New Hampshire. His father, General Benjamin Pierce, had been an officer during the American Revolution and governor of New Hampshire. Franklin attended Bowdoin College in Maine and graduated third in his class in 1824. A college friend, the writer Nathaniel Hawthorne, once spoke of Pierce's "fascination of manner" that lay "deep in the kindness of his nature."

After studying law, Pierce served in the United States House of Representatives and in the Senate. At the start of the Mexican War, he enlisted as a private, but soon became a brigadier general. In 1852, he was elected President by a large majority over his former military commander, General Winfield Scott.

During Pierce's administration, the United States, through the Gadsden Purchase in 1853, bought a tract of land from Mexico. The purchase, which added land to the southern borders of Arizona and New Mexico, completed the continental expansion of the United States. Pierce influenced the Senate to ratify a trade treaty with Japan in 1854, which had been arranged by Commodore Matthew C. Perry of the U.S. Navy.

Pierce tried to settle differences between the North and the South and included people from both sections in his Cabinet. When Pierce signed the Kansas-Nebraska Act, a law passed by Congress in 1854, many of his former admirers turned against him. The act created new territories, Kansas and Nebraska, out of Indian lands in the West. It stated that settlers in each territory would decide for themselves whether to allow slavery. This law made it possible for slavery to spread and thus helped create conflict between people who wanted slavery and those who did not. The Northern Democrats refused to nominate Pierce for a second term. Pierce opposed slavery himself, but he feared the unity of the nation was at stake.

Four years after Pierce returned to New Hampshire, the Civil War be-

Just two months before Franklin Pierce's inauguration as president, his 11-year-old son was killed in a railroad accident. The president's wife, Jane, secluded herself upstairs in the White House for nearly half the President's term of office. Jane Pierce became known as "the shadow of the White House."

FRANKLIN PIERCE
FOURTEENTH PRESIDENT   MARCH 4, 1853–MARCH 3, 1857

Born: November 23, 1804, Hillsborough (now Hillsboro), New Hampshire
Parents: General Benjamin Pierce and Anna Kendrick Pierce
Education: Bowdoin College
Religion: Episcopalian
Occupation: Lawyer
Political Party: Democratic
State Represented: New Hampshire
Married: 1834 to Jane Appleton (1806–1863)
Children: 3 sons (one died in childhood)
Died: October 8, 1869, Concord, New Hampshire
Buried: Concord, New Hampshire

Every part of the pig can be eaten or used for something. It has been said that the only useless part of the pig is its squeal.

The highest number of piglets born in one litter is 34. The heaviest hog ever recorded weighed 2,552 pounds (11,570 kg). It was raised in Henderson County, Tennessee.

▼ *A domestic sow with her litter of piglets (one of which is much fatter than the rest). The smallest and weakest piglet in a litter is known as the "runt."*

gan—a war to which he was bitterly opposed. He believed it was a tragedy that could have been prevented.

ALSO READ: KANSAS; MEXICAN WAR; NEBRASKA; PERRY, OLIVER AND MATTHEW.

PIG The pig is probably descended from the wild boars that roamed over Europe, Asia, and Africa more than 5,000 years ago. Wild boars still roam over parts of Europe and Asia. A wild boar has two small tusks growing out of its lower jaw. The tusks can be very dangerous weapons. Pigs raised on farms usually get used to the presence of human beings, but wild boars are mean animals with vicious tempers. Pigs are considered to be one of the most intelligent of all hoofed animals.

Pigs are often called hogs or swine. A male pig is usually called a boar and a female pig, a sow. Pigs are cloven-hoofed animals with heavy, round bodies and short legs. Their skins are thick and partly covered with rough bristles. The pig has a long, flexible snout containing its nostrils and mouth, which has 44 teeth.

Pigs have been kept as domesticated animals since prehistoric times. Pigs are omnivorous, which means that they will eat anything that is vegetable or animal. When people

▲ *Domestic pigs are descended from the wild boar, a woodland animal with a bristly coat and sharp curving tusks.*

discovered that pigs were easily raised, they began to breed them in large numbers. Pork, ham, bacon, and spareribs all come from the meat of pigs. A pig's meat can be smoked or salted and can then be kept for a long time without spoiling. Lard, the fat of the pig, is used in cooking. Pig intestines are used as the casing for sausages. The pig's hide, when tanned, becomes the leather known as pigskin, used to make such items as gloves and luggage. The stiff bristles from the pig's hide are made into paint brushes.

A sow gives birth from eight to 20 baby pigs at one time—two or three times a year. Pigs reproduce more rapidly and mature earlier than many other common meat-producing animals. Baby pigs are called piglets. A piglet weighs about two and one half pounds (1 kg) at birth but gains weight quickly. When it is only one year old, a piglet can weigh 250 pounds (110 kg). The largest breeds may weigh as much as 600 pounds (270 kg) when they are full-grown.

Many different breeds of pigs have been developed in various parts of the world to meet local climate and pasture conditions. Eight separate breeds are widely raised in the United States. In modern farming practice, pigs are fed on a carefully balanced diet containing proteins, carbohydrates, and minerals.

Like other animals, pigs are subject to a number of diseases—some of which are also dangerous to human beings who may eat meat from infected animals. In the United States, the U.S. Department of Agriculture supervises and regulates the raising and processing of pigs throughout the country.

ALSO READ: FOOD PROCESSING, MAMMAL, MEAT.

PIGEON Almost anywhere in the temperate or tropical parts of the world, you can find pigeons. You can see them in city streets and parks, in the country, and in the woods. Pigeons are medium-sized, stout birds. They have short, rounded beaks, topped by a fleshy part, called a cere, through which the nostrils open. Pigeons are very strong fliers. They walk strutting, with their toes pointed slightly inward. People who walk with their toes pointed inward are said to be "pigeon-toed." Most birds tip their heads back after each sip when drinking. Pigeons, however,

---

▼ *The mourning dove is a pigeon that is adapted to life in hot deserts. It needs little water and can withstand high temperatures.*

put their beaks in the water and pump the liquid down their throats, keeping their heads lowered. Some pigeons are called doves, but all belong to the same family of birds, the *Columbidae*.

A female pigeon lays two white eggs in a crudely built nest. Both parents take turns sitting on the eggs. The newly hatched pigeons cannot eat solid food. The parents feed them pigeon's "milk." This is a liquid formed in the crop (a pouch in the throat) of the adult pigeon, and squeezed through the mouth into the throats of the pigeon chicks. Half-grown pigeons are called squabs. Some people raise pigeons for the squab meat.

There are more than 300 kinds of domestic and wild pigeons. The kind you see in parks and city streets is the common pigeon. The fantail pigeon can raise and spread its fanlike tail feathers. Most pigeons have 12 tail feathers, but the fantail has as many as 30. The tumbler pigeon turns somersaults as it flies. The homing pigeon can find its way back to its home from great distances. Homing pigeons have been used as message carriers, especially during wartime, and also as racing birds. Homing pigeons are taken sometimes several hundred miles from their home and then released. The pigeon that arrives home in the shortest time wins the race. The most common American wild pigeon is the mourning dove. It receives its name from the mournful sound it makes. The largest pigeon is the goura, or crowned pigeon, of New Guinea, which is three feet (90 cm) long.

The passenger pigeon used to be very plentiful in the United States. Once there were millions of them, but now they are extinct. Hunters killed so many of them through the years that now there are no passenger pigeons left. The last passenger pigeon died in the Cincinnati Zoo in 1914. Only 100 years before, John Audu-

▲ *City-dwellers the world over know the urban pigeon. This bird is descended from the rock dove. It lives wild in towns and cities, feeding on whatever it can find, as well as on food provided by passers-by.*

Pigeons were the main source of fresh meat for the people of the Middle Ages.

bon reported a flock of passenger pigeons so large that it took many hours for the flock to fly over him.

ALSO READ: AUDUBON, JOHN JAMES; BIRD; BIRDS OF THE PAST.

PIKE, ZEBULON (1779–1813)

Zebulon Pike was an American soldier and explorer. He was born in Lamberton (now part of Trenton), New Jersey, and entered the U.S. Army at the age of 15. In 1805, he was commissioned to lead a party to explore the upper regions of the Louisiana Purchase. He led the party into Minnesota searching for the source of the Mississippi River. He mistakenly believed he had found it, but snow and ice covered the source. Pike bought land from the Sioux Indians to set up a fort near the point where the Minnesota River flows into the Mississippi River.

In 1806 and 1807, Pike led another expedition to explore Colorado and New Mexico. In central Colorado, he sighted a mountain that was later named Pike's Peak, but he did not succeed in climbing it. He followed the Arkansas River and Red River to their headwaters. On that expedition, he was arrested by Spanish soldiers in the city of Santa Fe and put in jail. After his release, he wrote an account of his travels.

Pike was a brigadier general during the War of 1812 against the British. On April 27, 1813, he was killed while leading a successful assault on York (now Toronto), Canada.

ALSO READ: COLORADO, LOUISIANA PURCHASE, MISSISSIPPI RIVER, WAR OF 1812.

PILGRIM SETTLERS

The Pilgrim settlers were the group of English men and women who founded the first permanent European settlement in New England in 1620. Their

▲ *These pilgrim settlers, stepping ashore in America, are wearing the clothing that identified them as Puritans.*

▲ *This painting shows the settlers praying on board ship. The voyage across the Atlantic was treacherous and few had crossed before them.*

settlement was Plymouth Colony (now Plymouth, Massachusetts). The Pilgrims sailed to America in the ship *Mayflower*.

Among the 102 settlers who sailed on the *Mayflower* were 35 members of a religious group called the English Separatist Church. The Separatists had broken away from the official Church of England, which they considered sinful and corrupt. They were persecuted in England, and in 1608 and 1609 they had fled to the city of Leiden in Holland. But most of the Separatists longed to find a place where they could farm the land and practice their religion in peace. William Brewster, one of the founders of the Separatist Church, obtained permission from the Virginia Company to start a settlement in America.

In July 1620, the Separatists sailed to Plymouth, England. They were joined there by other settlers. All the Pilgrims were crowded onto the *Mayflower*, and Brewster was made leader of the expedition. The voyage was stormy. Many people became ill, and some died. A son was born to Stephen and Elizabeth Hopkins and was named Oceanus. Strong winds forced the *Mayflower* to sail too far north. In November, the Pilgrims landed on Cape Cod. This area was not yet under the rule of any European country. The Pilgrims drew up the Mayflower Compact, under which they agreed to obey the laws made by their leaders.

After exploring a few miles of the coast of Massachusetts, the Pilgrims founded the settlement of Plymouth. A Separatist leader, John Carver, was elected governor. Carver guided the Pilgrims through their terrible first winter, when half the people died. In March 1621, Carver arranged a peace treaty with the Indian chief, Massasoit, who ruled the whole area of eastern Massachusetts. Carver died the following month. William Bradford succeeded him as governor.

The Indians taught the settlers how to grow crops, such as corn and squash. The autumn harvest was so plentiful that Governor Bradford invited Massasoit to a great feast—the first Thanksgiving celebration. Bradford was reelected governor almost every year until his death in 1657. Under his leadership, the colony grew larger and new settlements were founded. Bradford arranged for the people to hold town meetings. Each settlement sent representatives to a general council at Plymouth, which made laws for the colony. Bradford was assisted by Edward Winslow, who also served as governor for three years. Winslow had married Susanna White, the widowed mother of Peregrine White, the first child born in Plymouth Colony.

Plymouth's small citizen army was trained by a professional soldier, Captain Miles Standish. He defended the colony several times against attacks by unfriendly Indians. A popular legend tells how Standish wanted to marry a young woman in Plymouth named Priscilla Mullens. Standish asked his friend John Alden to propose marriage for him. But Priscilla decided to marry Alden instead. John Alden served as an assistant governor of Plymouth.

The settlers were known for many years as the Forefathers. But William Bradford, in his book *History of Plimoth Plantation*, had called them "pilgrimes." After this book was published in 1856, the settlers were named the Pilgrim Fathers.

ALSO READ: MASSASOIT, MAYFLOWER, MAYFLOWER COMPACT, THANKSGIVING.

▲ *Pilgrims on their way to church. Some are carrying guns for protection against possible attack by Indians. At first, the Indians were friendly to the settlers, but later they became hostile.*

PIN In primitive times, a long thorn or sharp fishbone was probably used as a pin to fasten clothing. Pins made of bronze were used in ancient Rome. The development of the wire-making process led to the making of modern pins from brass, iron, and steel.

There are two main types of pins— straight, or common, pins and safety pins. Straight pins are used mostly in sewing. Safety pins, whose pointed ends slip into a protecting cap, are used mainly for pinning together clothing.

PINE see CONIFER.

PIONEER LIFE A territory yet to be explored is sometimes called a *frontier*. More than 200 years ago, pioneers moved into the unknown wilderness of North America where few people lived. As time passed,

The Pilgrims came mostly from East Anglia in eastern England. There is still a great deal in common between the speech of New Englanders and that of the people of East Anglia. There are many American English words that are no longer used in Britain, but many of these words would have been quite familiar to Shakespeare.

more and more people moved westward across the continent. The area once known as the frontier became settled. The settlers who moved there had to build their own houses, grow their own food, and attend to other needs themselves.

Frontier Houses   Most houses were built of logs, though some were made of clapboard—overlapping wooden boards—and others were made of stone. In some parts of the West, where there were few trees, families built houses of sod. Sometimes a group of families built log houses near a spring, and then built a log wall, or stockade, around the whole settlement as protection against Indian attacks.

Water had to be carried from lakes, rivers, or springs to the houses. In some areas, however, families dug wells near their homes. There was no plumbing in the early cabins.

Tables and benches were made of logs cut lengthwise. Legs were fastened to the curved side of a split log, and the flat side became the tabletop or the bench seat. Beds were often straw-filled mattresses on the cabin floor. Some settlers made wooden bed frames to which they tied ropes in crisscross fashion. The mattress rested on the rope network. Dishes and spoons were often made of wood, although some families brought pewter, silver, or china dishes with them when they moved West.

Family Life   The pioneer families had to make their own clothes. They hunted game for food and planted corn and other vegetables in their gardens. The Indians showed the first settlers what wild plants could be eaten or planted as crops.

Children had to help in housekeeping, gardening, taking care of chickens and cows, and other jobs. But they also found some time to play tag, Blindman's Bluff, or other games. They also played with homemade dolls, some carved from wood, some made of rags. They climbed trees, ran races, went swimming, and fished the streams.

The settlers had to travel to the nearest town to get certain supplies, such as salt, sugar, and spices. These were needed to preserve or pickle meat and other foods. The people took furs, homemade whiskey, corn, or fruit to be traded for whatever they needed. The loads were carried on pack horses, and the journey often took several days.

Families usually went to bed as soon as it was dark, and they got up at sunrise. If they stayed up after dark, they used homemade candles to light the rooms. Later, after towns began to grow, they used kerosene lamps.

Few schools or churches existed in the first settlements. In many pioneer families, the father read from the Bible before meals or at bedtime. Traveling preachers on horseback, called circuit riders, sometimes visited frontier families and held prayer meetings and Bible-readings in their homes. If there was no schoolhouse, children might be taught to read by their parents or by a neighbor.

▼ *A house goes up quickly with the help of many hands. Less fortunate pioneer families lived out in the open for many months before their homes were built.*

Hardships of Frontier Life Life on the frontier was lonely, and settlers occasionally visited neighbors who lived several miles away. Sometimes the hard-working farmers could enjoy being with other people at barn dances or picnics. Also, they all helped each other to build barns or other farm buildings. They joined with neighbors to help each other harvest crops, dig a well, or butcher hogs. If someone was sick or hurt, families used medicines or ointments made from the leaves and roots of plants and herbs they found, because few towns had a doctor.

Frontier life was very rough in both summer and winter. During summer dry spells, cows and other farm animals sometimes died from thirst and heat. Great armies of grasshoppers ate whole fields of wheat or other grain. The temperature often went down below freezing in the winter. The heat in many houses came only from the fireplace, and families often slept near the fire to keep warm. The cold weather, howling blizzards, and heavy snowstorms killed numerous cows and sheep.

The story of one pioneer family in Kansas tells of the terrible hardships. This family brought with them everything they owned—a bed, a few chairs, a table, four horses, two oxen, some vegetable seeds, and a plow. During their first winter, their oxen and one horse froze to death. The following summer their vegetable garden was ruined for lack of rain. The man of the family said, "In God we trusted. In Kansas we busted."

Despite the hardships, the pioneers kept pushing westward. Villages and towns were settled all along the wagon trails. Gold was discovered in California in 1848, and thousands of people rushed across the country to the gold fields. A coast-to-coast railroad was completed 21 years later, and the wild frontier was gradually tamed.

There are still many frontiers to settle. Vast, wild areas in the interior

of Australia are being explored and settled by "pioneers" from all over the world. Australia has fewer people than any other continent, except Antarctica, and the Australian government has encouraged people to settle there. Similar "pioneers" are also settling in previously uninhabited areas of Canada and in the Siberian region of the Soviet Union.

ALSO READ: AMERICAN HISTORY, CATTLE DRIVE, COWBOY, GOLD RUSH, OREGON TRAIL, RAILROAD, WESTWARD MOVEMENT.

PIPELINE The oil fields where petroleum and natural gas are to be found are often in distant deserts or under the sea bed. The oil and gas has to be brought to refineries for processing. Transportation of oil and gas is often done along a pipeline. Water and other liquids can be sent along pipelines.

Pipelines are large pipes that may be more than 3 feet (1 m) wide. They are made of steel and may be coated and lined with materials such as glass fiber and plastics to prevent corrosion. The pipes are often buried underground where they cross land. Pumps force the liquid or gas along the pipeline.

Some pipelines are very long. The Trans-Canada pipeline, which carries natural gas, is nearly 6,000 miles (9,656 km) long. Another long pipeline is the Trans-Mediterranean pipe-

▲ *A pioneer family photographed in front of their sod house in 1882 in South Dakota. By this date, pioneer settlers had more conveniences, such as glass windows, than those who had come earlier. Nevertheless, frontier life was still very tough.*

▲ *The famous Pioneer Woman Monument near Ponca City, Oklahoma, symbolizes the courage and determination of the women who helped settle the West.*

▲ *The Alaskan pipeline snakes its way through scenic conifer forests below Mount Wrangell, which rises 14,163 feet (4,317 m).*

▲ *Corsairs were pirates who terrorized travelers on the Mediterranean Sea in the 1500's. Their most famous leader was Barbarossa ("Redbeard"), a Turkish captain whose real name was Khayr ad-Din. Barbarossa turned the port of Algiers into a nest of fierce pirates.*

line, which carries gas from the Sahara Desert across the Mediterranean Sea to northern Italy. It is 1,500 miles (2,413 km) long. Under the sea, the pipe is covered in concrete to keep it from moving in the sea currents. In some places the pipeline spans undersea gulleys on steel supports.

Pipelines also carry materials such as coal, salt, chalk, and wood chips. These materials are forced through the pipe by moving water or air. Pipelines are also being built to carry bulky materials like grain in capsules, rather like small underground freight wagons.

ALSO READ: PETROLEUM.

PIRATES AND PRIVATEERS A pirate is a robber on the high seas. Pirates recognize no government and obey no laws. In the olden days, a pirate captain divided the shares of treasure—money and other valuables—among the crew. *Privateers* were commissioned by their country's government to raid and capture the commercial ships of unfriendly or enemy countries. When privateers captured a prize, they shared the booty with the government they served.

As long as ships have carried goods across the ocean, there have been pirates. The Phoenicians, early navigators in the Mediterranean Sea,

raided cargo ships. Vikings from Norway seized ships and raided villages along the coast of northern Europe. Arabs, called the Barbary pirates or corsairs, attacked and captured foreign ships along the Barbary Coast (North African coast on the Mediterranean Sea).

In the 1600's and 1700's, working conditions on merchant ships were poor. The food was bad, living quarters were crowded, and voyages were long. Sometimes sailors on merchant ships would rebel, or mutiny, against their captain and take over the ship. If this happened, the sailors could not go back to their home country or they would be thrown in jail. So they became pirates. Just before they attacked a ship, they raised the pirate flag, the "Jolly Roger," with its white skull and crossbones on a black background.

The most active period for pirates was between the 1500's and the 1700's. Spanish ships then traded between Spain and South and Central America. They were loaded with gold, jewels, and other booty from the lands the Spaniards had conquered. These treasure fleets attracted many pirates and privateers to the Caribbean Sea. The pirates who attacked Spanish ships off the mainland of South America (the Spanish Main) were known as *buccaneers*. They received this name from the *boucan*, or grill, they used for smoking and curing meat. They were also called *freebooters*.

One of the most famous buccaneers to attack these Spanish galleons was Henry Morgan. The British encouraged him to attack the Spanish. Morgan had a base at Port Royal, Jamaica. Port Royal was then called the "most wicked city in the world." Warehouses there bulged with the gold and silver bars, silks, and jewels the pirates had taken. Morgan not only captured ships, he also raided coastal towns in Venezuela and Panama. In a daring attack on Portobello, Panama, in 1668, Morgan and his 400 fighting buccaneers stormed and captured two well-defended forts. Then they seized the town itself. They held off a Spanish army force while Morgan obtained a ransom of 250,000 silver coins, silks, and 300 slaves.

English seamen and explorers such as Sir Francis Drake were also privateers. They raided Spanish ships with the full knowledge and blessing of the English queen, Elizabeth I. Captain William Kidd was a Scottish privateer. He wanted to be captain of a British man-of-war, but took charge of a privateer (the ship of privateers) instead. His ship roamed the Atlantic and Indian oceans, capturing merchant ships and searching for pirates that preyed on British shipping. But Kidd did not turn over a fair share of the booty to the government. He was brought to trial in England, found guilty, and hanged.

One of the most feared pirates to operate in the Atlantic Ocean and Caribbean Sea was Blackbeard. His real name was Edward Teach. He was given the name Blackbeard because he had a long, black beard, which he wore in braids to make himself look fierce. Blackbeard attacked many defenseless merchant ships that sailed along the Carolina and Virginia coasts between 1716 and 1718. The Southern planters grew furious as they lost their valuable cargoes. Finally a ship sent by the planters cornered Blackbeard off the coast of North Carolina. Blackbeard met his death fighting furiously with both sword and pistol.

Jean Laffite was a pirate who became an American patriot. He commanded a fleet of ships that put out from hidden coves of the Mississippi River delta. They raided both Spanish and neutral ships in the Gulf of Mexico. Laffite offered his services to the United States during the War of 1812. He and his crew fought on the U.S. side against England. He also helped General Andrew Jackson win the important Battle of New Orleans.

Later, he went back to pirating. In 1821, the United States sent troops to destroy his pirate colony. Laffite saw that he would be overpowered, so he had his crew abandon and set fire to the pirate town. Then Laffite quietly sailed away. Historians do not know what finally became of him.

Sea piracy is now mostly a thing of the past. Careful patrolling by modern navies and improved communications between ships have made it almost impossible. However, pirates still make raids particularly in the South China seas, preying on unarmed refugee boats and cargo ships. A new form of piracy—airplane hijacking—has also increased.

ALSO READ: BARBARY COAST; DRAKE, SIR FRANCIS; NAVY; SHIPS AND SHIPPING; SPANISH MAIN; VIKINGS.

PISTOL   see GUNS AND RIFLES.

PIZARRO, FRANCISCO (about 1478–1541) After Christopher Columbus first came to America, Spanish *conquistadors*, or conquerors, sought gold and other wealth in South America. One of the most famous conquistadors was Francisco Pizarro.

Pizarro was born in Trujillo, Spain. He came from a poor family and never learned to read and write. He became a soldier and adventurer with no training for governing a colony. After sailing to the New World in 1510, Pizarro joined Vasco Núñez de Balboa's colony in what is now Panama. When Balboa crossed the Isthmus of Panama and saw the Pacific Ocean in 1513, Pizarro was with him.

In 1532, a Spanish expedition led by Pizarro set out from Panama and sailed to Peru, where the Inca Indians had built a rich empire. The expedition landed on the coast of Peru at the time that two Inca rulers were quarreling over the throne. Pizarro and his soldiers captured and imprisoned

▲ *The English pirate Edward Teach, known as Blackbeard. His pirate ships preyed on merchant ships off the Carolina and Virginia coasts in the early 1700's.*

Blackbeard, one of the fiercest pirates, fought with lighted matches framing his face. He scared friends by firing pistols under the table and lighting pots of sulfur. In his last fight he suffered 25 wounds before he was shot dead. His head was put on a pole and shown to the Virginian settlers whom he had terrorized.

▲ *The Spanish conqueror Francisco Pizarro. With only a few men, Pizarro managed to gain control of the Inca Empire.*

▲ *Max Planck, German scientist who totally changed physics. His quantum theory enabled scientists to answer important questions about the nature of energy.*

Atahualpa, the Inca leader who had taken the throne. Pizarro received a huge treasure to free Atahualpa. But the Spaniards killed Atahualpa and many of his followers. Pizarro then seized the city of Cuzco (or Cusco), the great Inca capital.

After conquering the Inca Empire, Pizarro founded the city of Lima and called it the "City of Kings." He built a grand palace in Lima, now the capital of Peru. The Incas fought for years against their conquerors. In 1541, Pizarro was killed by the followers of his former partner, Diego de Almagro.

ALSO READ: BALBOA, VASCO NÚÑEZ DE; CONQUISTADOR; INCA; PERU.

PLAGUE   see CONTAGIOUS DISEASES.

PLANCK, MAX (1858–1947)   The German physicist Max Karl Ernst Ludwig Planck is famous because he was the first person to put forward the "quantum theory."

He was born in Kiel, Germany, and became professor of physics at Berlin University. He became interested in the way that objects behave when they are heated. If you have seen a piece of metal heated, you will know that it can become red-hot. Heated more, it would have become white-hot or even blue-hot. These different colors of light occur because the light being given off by the hot metal is of different wavelengths. The longer the wavelength, the less energy the light has; for example, red light has less energy than blue light and also a longer wavelength.

Planck wondered why a hot object did not give off light of all colors. The only way that he could explain what really happens was to say that energy comes in small "packages," or *quanta*. (The singular *quantum* is a Latin word meaning "how much".) The quantum is the smallest amount of energy that can exist: you cannot have half a quantum of energy.

Max Planck was awarded the Nobel Prize for physics in 1918.

ALSO READ: QUANTUM THEORY.

PLANET   see SOLAR SYSTEM.

PLANETARIUM   A planetarium is a building inside which a special projector projects (shows) a picture of the sky onto a rounded ceiling. This projector works in much the same way a movie projector or a slide projector works but looks and is more complicated. A planetarium projector (which by itself is usually just called a planetarium) is over 12 feet (4 m) high. It is shaped like a dumbell, with a large metal globe (ball) at each end and an open framework that looks like a cage between them. Each globe contains 16 different slide projectors, and the middle framework contains several more slide projectors. The projectors in the globes show the stars, and the projectors in the framework show the planets.

Inside a planetarium, you sit in a round room with a high, domed ceiling. In the middle of the room is the planetarium projector and an *astronomer* (a scientist who studies the stars and planets). When the lights in the room are turned off and the projector is turned on, it seems as if you are outdoors on a clear night. The ceiling is covered with stars, so that you seem to be gazing at the heavens.

In a planetarium you can be shown about three times as many stars as you could see on the clearest night outdoors. The planetarium will show you some stars that are usually too dim to be seen. Also, it will show you stars that you could see only if you were on the other side of the Earth. One globe of the planetarium projector shows the northern sky (that part of the sky seen from north of the equator), and the other globe shows the southern sky. The projector turns to show how the sky looks from different places. In a planetarium, you can see how the sky would look from any place on the Earth, and even from places in outer space.

The planetarium can also speed up the movements of the stars and planets. In a few minutes, it can show all the movements of one night or one year. It can show you what the sky looked like on any day in history.

Many planetariums are controlled by a computer, but while the show is running the astronomer explains what is happening in the "sky" and points out things you should notice. Planetariums often have special shows about imaginary trips through space.

The first planetarium was built by the Zeiss company in Germany in 1924, and the first planetarium in the United States opened in 1930. This was the Adler Planetarium in Chicago. Other large U.S. planetariums include the Fels Planetarium in Philadelphia, the Hayden Planetarium in New York, the Griffith Planetarium in Los Angeles, the Buhl Planetarium in Pittsburgh, the Morrison Planetarium in San Francisco, and the Morehead Planetarium in Chapel Hill, North Carolina.

ALSO READ: ASTRONOMY, CONSTELLATION, DAY AND NIGHT, ECLIPSE, OBSERVATORY.

PLANKTON see MARINE LIFE.

PLANT It is not hard to tell most plants from most animals. You can easily tell an oak tree from an ostrich or a rose from a rabbit. But exactly what makes plants different from animals? First of all, most plants contain a green substance called chlorophyll. Chlorophyll enables them to make their own food. Animals do not contain chlorophyll. Plants can take in

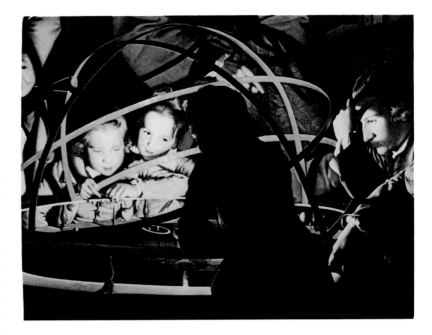

only dissolved or liquid substances. Animals can eat both solids and liquids. Plant cells are surrounded by hard cell walls made of cellulose. Animal cells contain no cellulose, nor do they have cell walls. Most plants cannot move around under their own power, but most animals can.

Some plants have animal characteristics and vice versa. A few tiny, one-celled, plantlike animals contain chlorophyll, while plants such as mushrooms do not. The plants called slime molds can move from place to place under their own power during one part of their lives, and so can many minute water-living plants.

Where Plants Are Found Plants live in nearly all parts of the world. Plants called lichens can grow in the extremely cold regions of the Arctic and Antarctic, and cacti grow in extremely hot, tropical deserts. Mushrooms can grow in dark caves, while algae can grow in the waters of seas, lakes, ponds, rivers, and streams. Plants are found at all levels of the land, from sea-level marshes to the peaks of high mountains. In the tropics, many kinds of plants grow in great numbers because the hot, humid climate is good for plant growth. Plants live in many different environ-

▲ The Orrery *by Joseph Wright. Such working models of planets in orbit around the Solar System can still be seen in many of our planetariums.*

Most trees or plants receive only about 10 percent of their nutrition from the soil. The other 90 percent comes from the atmosphere.

Bamboos only flower after long intervals. Some flower every 32 years, while others flower only every 60 years.

PLANT

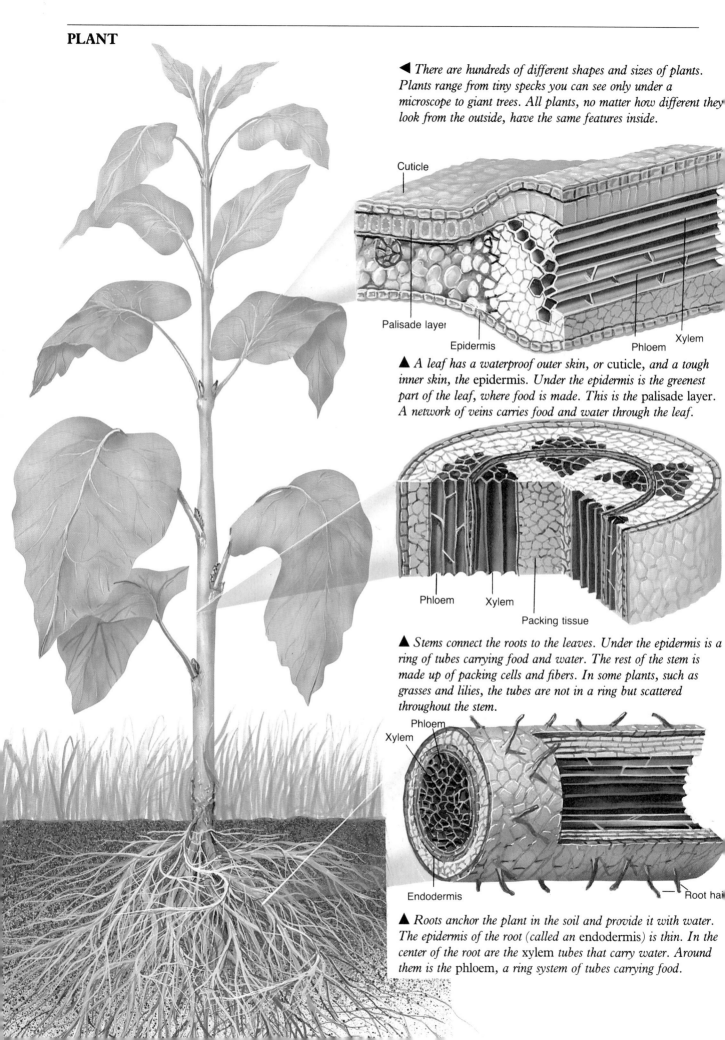

◀ *There are hundreds of different shapes and sizes of plants. Plants range from tiny specks you can see only under a microscope to giant trees. All plants, no matter how different they look from the outside, have the same features inside.*

Cuticle

Palisade layer

Epidermis

Phloem

Xylem

▲ *A leaf has a waterproof outer skin, or* cuticle, *and a tough inner skin, the* epidermis. *Under the epidermis is the greenest part of the leaf, where food is made. This is the* palisade layer. *A network of veins carries food and water through the leaf.*

Phloem   Xylem

Packing tissue

▲ *Stems connect the roots to the leaves. Under the epidermis is a ring of tubes carrying food and water. The rest of the stem is made up of packing cells and fibers. In some plants, such as grasses and lilies, the tubes are not in a ring but scattered throughout the stem.*

Phloem

Xylem

Endodermis

Root hai

▲ *Roots anchor the plant in the soil and provide it with water. The epidermis of the root (called an* endodermis) *is thin. In the center of the root are the* xylem *tubes that carry water. Around them is the* phloem, *a ring system of tubes carrying food.*

ments. They have been able to adapt very well to almost all possible living conditions (climate, soil condition, and so on) found on Earth.

Kinds of Plants *Botanists*, the scientists who study plants, have listed about 360,000 different kinds of plants. All plants together make up the *plant kingdom*, which is divided into four groups. The first group includes the simplest plants—*bacteria, algae, fungi*, and *lichens*—which have no stems, leaves, or roots. The second group, the *mosses* and *liverworts*, have parts resembling leaves, stems, and roots but lack food- and water-carrying tubes. The third group, the *ferns, club mosses*, and *horsetails*, have true leaves, stems, and roots, but lack seeds. The fourth group includes *seed plants*—cone-bearing trees (pines, firs, and so on) and flowering plants (grasses, roses, and so on).

Plant Structure CELL. Every plant consists of one or more tiny cells. Large plants contain many millions of cells. Each cell is surrounded by a *cell membrane*, which all living things have. Outside this delicate membrane is a *cell wall*, which is found only in plants. Cell walls are made of *cellulose*, a hard, nonliving material. The cell wall protects the plant cell and helps it keep its shape. Cell walls give strength to plant tissues. The strength of cotton, for example, comes from the cellulose contained in the cell walls.

ROOTS. All plants must take in water. Algae take in water directly through the cell walls and cell membranes all over the plant surface. Mosses have no true roots but grow a network of long cells. These cells act much like roots because they take in water. The fern group and the seed plants have real roots that are used to take in substances from the soil.

Root systems are of two main shapes. One consists of a single large root that grows straight downward

with many tiny, thin roots growing out from it. Carrots and trees have this kind of root, which is called a *taproot*. The other root shape looks like a large number of strings, all growing downward and outward from the base of the stem. These are called *fibrous roots*.

One of the main jobs of the root is to take in water and minerals from the soil. If you look very carefully at the thin ends of a root, you will see a fuzzy growth. This fuzz is made up of tiny *root hairs*. Each root hair is actually a single cell of the outer layer of the root. Growing roots have thousands of root hairs. Water and dissolved materials from soil pass through the walls and membranes of the root hairs. After water has entered a root hair, it is transferred from cell to cell toward the center of the root. From there, the water passes upward into the stem through long *xylem* tubes of cells, then outward to the branches and leaves. Another tube system, the *phloem*, carries food to the plant.

Another job of the root is to anchor a plant in the soil. The roots of large trees not only grow downward but also may grow more than a hundred feet outward from the tree. The roots must hold the tree upright against the force of strong winds.

Roots also store food. Sweet potatoes, radishes, carrots, and beets are roots in which plant food has been stored.

▲ *The hazel tree has hanging catkins that consist of male flowers only. The female flowers are the small, red-tufted buds.*

The fastest-growing plant is the bamboo. Some of these plants have been measured to grow 36 inches (91 cm) in a single day. Can you work out what speed this is in inches per hour?

◄ *Lichens are strange plants. Each consists of a mixture of a fungus and an alga. You find lichens growing on tree trunks, old walls, and rocks. They are very hardy, but do not like polluted air, so they are not often found in the center of a big city.*

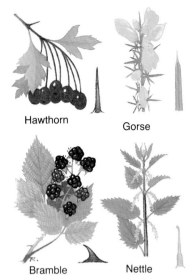

Hawthorn   Gorse

Bramble   Nettle

▲ *Some plants protect themselves from being eaten by animals by having prickles or thorns, either on their leaves or on their stems. Thorns are in fact modified twigs. The sting of a nettle comes from the hairs on the leaves; each hair is hollow and pumps out poison if disturbed.*

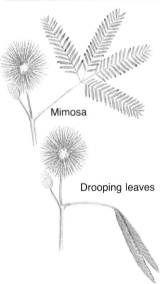

Mimosa

Drooping leaves

▲ *Plants are sensitive to touch, sound, gravity, and light. The Mimosa pudica plant, for instance, has leaves that droop if you touch them. A gentle touch may cause just one leaf to droop, but a large disturbance can affect the whole plant—showing that a "message" has been transmitted through the plant.*

STEMS. The stem supports the leaves and flowers of a plant. Leaves may be attached directly to the stem, or they may be attached by short stalks. Some stems branch many times, and the leaves are attached to the smaller branches. Leaves of trees are attached to smaller branches called twigs.

The stem helps turn the leaves of a plant toward the light, without which the plant cannot make food. If you look at the leaves of a plant that has been sitting near a window, you will see the leaves are turned toward the sunlight. If you turn the plant around so that the leaves face away from the light, in two days the leaves will have turned back toward the light again. The movement of a plant in response to an outside force is called *tropism.*

Most plant stems store some food, usually only temporarily. However, some stems are the main storage area of the plant. The thick horizontal stems of the iris are storage stems. The main job of a stem is to conduct water and dissolved materials from the roots to the leaves, flowers, and fruit of the plant. Liquid food materials made in the leaves also move downward through the stem from the leaves to the roots. The liquid food material in the leaf stalk is called sap.

■ LEARN BY DOING

Cut an inch (2.5 cm) off the bottom of a fresh celery stalk that has leaves. Put the end of the stalk into a glass of water containing a drop or two of ink or food coloring. In about an hour, you will see that the stalk and leaves have become streaked with the color of the water. If you cut across the stem, you will see colored dots. These dots mark the cell tubes that transport water and sap through the leaf stalk. ■

Most stems grow above the surface of the ground, but some grow underground. The white potato is an underground stem that stores food.

Some stems, such as tree trunks, have a tough outer covering of dead cells that make up the outer bark. Deeper, just inside the inner bark, is the *cambium* layer that causes the tree to grow in diameter. The cambium causes wood cells to form that carry water and minerals to the leaves. The cambium also makes tube cells for carrying food down the stem.

Celery and sunflowers are examples of herbaceous plants. They are not woody, although their stems may be quite tough. The cambium and conducting tubes, together with many tough fibers, form a ring in the stem.

LEAVES. Leaves are the food factories of a plant. Using water and carbon dioxide, the leaves make sugar. The leaves get energy for sugar-making from sunlight. The green-colored substance of plants, called *chlorophyll*, causes the sugar-making process to take place. The chlorophyll absorbs the sun's light energy that is needed for the process to take place. This sugar-making process is called *photosynthesis.* The sugar itself is used by the plant as food, or it may be converted to starches or oils for storage. The sugar is also used as the starting point for making cellulose and other materials, many of which are formed by combining the sugar with minerals obtained from the soil.

There are many kinds, shapes, and sizes of leaves. Tiny leaves, only one cell thick, are found on some kinds of mosses. Leaves of coconut palm trees may be 20 feet (6 m) long. The round, flat leaves of certain water lilies are more than 10 feet (3 m) across and can support small animals on the surface of the water. Leaves have many shapes. Some are round, others are long and thin. The needles of cone-bearing trees are leaves. Some leaves have smooth edges. Others are serrated (look like saw teeth). The broad, flat part of a leaf is called the *blade.* The stalk that holds the leaf to the stem is the *petiole.*

Leaves usually grow on a stem in

certain patterns. Leaves may be opposite each other on the stem. They may grow in a circle around the stem. Leaves are arranged so that they do not shade each other all the time and can get as much light as possible.

Within a leaf are tubes to conduct food and water. These tubes are called *veins*. The veins are spread out in a network that leads to the petiole. Scattered all over the underside of a leaf are tiny openings called *stomata*. Carbon dioxide, which is needed in photosynthesis, enters through the stomata. The oxygen that is produced during photosynthesis is expelled through the stomata.

Plant Reproduction One-celled plants reproduce by simple cell division. One cell divides into two cells, forming two new plants. Other plants, such as mushrooms and mosses, reproduce by forming tiny cells called *spores*. Each spore acts much like a seed. If it has good growing conditions, such as moisture and the proper temperature, it develops into a new plant.

The plants of the fern group grow from spores in two steps. First, the fern produces spores that grow into small plants that do not look like ferns. These plants produce male and female sex cells that unite and grow into a proper fern plant. This new plant then produces more spores.

Seed plants reproduce by means of male and female sex cells, in the process called *pollination*. In flowering plants, male sex organs, called *anthers*, produce *pollen*, which contains male sex cells. The pollen falls onto the female sex organ, called the *pistil*, which contains egg cells within *ovules*. Male cells from the pollen unite with egg cells to grow into *seeds*. Each seed contains a baby plant, called an *embryo*, and a supply of food, all enclosed in a tough coat. The seeds ripen and leave the plant. They may simply fall to the ground, or they may be carried long distances by wind,

water, or on the coats of animals. When a seed falls in good soil that has the proper moisture and temperature, the embryo starts to grow and bursts out of the seed coat. It is then a *seedling*. Some seedlings grow and scatter their own seeds in a few weeks, but trees take many years to grow up. Each plant has its own complete life cycle.

For further information on:
Kinds of Plants and Where They Grow, *see* ALGAE, BACTERIA, CACTUS, CITRUS FRUIT, CLUB MOSS, CONIFER, CORN, EVERGREEN TREE, FERN, FLOWER FAMILIES, FOSSIL , FUNGUS, GARDEN FLOWER, GRAIN, GRASS, HORSETAIL, HOUSE PLANT, INSECT-EATING PLANT, LICHEN, MOSSES AND LIVERWORTS, MUSHROOM, ORCHID, PALM, PARASITIC PLANT, PETRIFIED FOREST, PLANT DISTRIBUTION, PLANT KINGDOM, PLANTS OF THE PAST, POISONOUS PLANT, RICE, ROSE, SHRUB, TREE, VEGETABLES, WHEAT, YEAST.
Plant Products, *see* ALCOHOLIC BEVERAGE, CANDY, CHOCOLATE, COAL, COFFEE, COTTON, DYE, FLOUR MAKING, FOOD, FURNITURE, LUMBER AND LUMBERING, NATURAL RESOURCES, NUT, PAINT, PAPER, PERFUME, PETROLEUM, PLANT PRODUCTS, PLASTIC, RUBBER, SUGAR, TEA, TEXTILE, TOBACCO, WINES AND WINE MAKING.
Plant Structures and How They Work, *see* BULB, CELL, FERMENTATION, FLOWER, FRUIT, GROWTH, LEAF, PHOTOSYNTHESIS, REGENERATION, REPRODUCTION, RESPIRATION, SEEDS AND FRUIT, WOOD.
Raising Plants, *see* AGRICULTURE, BOTANICAL GARDEN, CONSERVATION, DROUGHT, EROSION, FERTILIZER, FORESTRY, GARDENING, GREENHOUSE, IRRIGATION, PLANT BREEDING, PLANT DISEASES, SOIL, TERRARIUM, TRUCK FARMING, WATER.
Sciences and Scientists Interested in Plants, *see* BIOLOGY; BOTANY; BURBANK, LUTHER; CARVER, GEORGE WASHINGTON; CHEMISTRY; ECOLOGY; LINNAEUS, CAROLUS; NATURE STUDY.

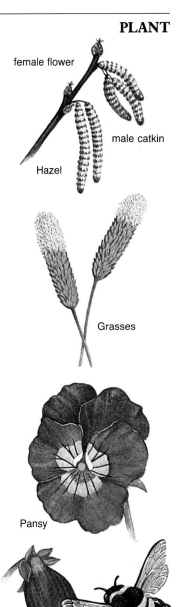

female flower

male catkin

Hazel

Grasses

Pansy

Foxglove

▲ *For grasses and catkins to reproduce, the wind blows pollen from male to female flowers. Other plants are aided by insects and birds. As a bee seeks nectar in a flower, it brushes against the pollen and carries it away to the next flower it visits. Some flowers, like the pansy, have "guide lines" to make sure the insect finds the pollen. Others, like the foxglove, are shaped so that the insect has to push its way inside and in this way gets coated with yellow pollen.*

▲ *Birch tree catkins releasing pollen into the wind. The catkins appear before the leaves, thus increasing the chances of pollination.*

▼ *Grafting a twig from one apple tree onto another. If the twigs are cut carefully as shown, then bound tightly together, they will grow together. In this way it is possible to grow two kinds of apple on one tree.*

PLANT BREEDING Oranges without seeds, giant roses, and stringbeans without strings are plant products that were created by the science of plant breeding. This branch of science breeds new plants or changes the characteristics of plants.

Plant breeding began thousands of years ago when primitive people noticed that certain plants gave better fruit than others of the same kind. People planted the seeds from this fruit and found that they grew into plants that bore the better fruit.

Modern plant breeding is based on the laws of heredity discovered by Gregor Mendel. These laws enable plant breeders to predict what kinds of plants their breeding experiments will probably produce.

One of the most useful modern methods of plant breeding is *cross-pollination*. Pollen from one plant is placed on the pistil of another. The plants that result from cross-pollinations are called crosses, or *hybrids*. By choosing the proper parent plants and planning the cross-pollination according to the laws of heredity, plant breeders can produce hybrids that are either completely new or are stronger, larger, or better in some way. An example of a new plant resulting from cross-pollination is *ugli fruit* (a cross between tangerine and grapefruit).

Although breeders can often predict what might happen when they cross-pollinate plants under experimental conditions, growing plants from seed does not necessarily produce more plants just like the parents. With trees and shrubs it can also take a very long time for a seed to grow into a mature plant. Breeders who need lots of identical plants often take *cuttings*. These are small twigs or shoots that will take root in the soil and quickly grow into new plants just like the original ones.

Another method, much used by fruit growers, is *grafting*. A live twig or bud from one kind of tree is attached to the live stump of another tree. The twig or bud is called a scion, and the tree it is attached to is the stock. The stock provides roots for the scion. The trunk and branches that eventually grow from the scion have the characteristics of the scion. For example, an apple grower may find a tree with bigger or tastier apples than on other trees. He or she cuts twigs with sturdy buds from the tree, and grafts the twigs to stocks of other apple trees. The apples that grow from the scions will be the same as those that grew on the tree from which the scion was cut. All the Baldwin apple trees in the world come from a grafted scion.

ALSO READ: AGRICULTURE; BURBANK, LUTHER; GENETICS; MENDEL, GREGOR; PLANT.

PLANT DISEASES Plants, as well as animals, suffer from disease. Scientists have not yet found a plant that is completely immune to disease. Plant diseases are caused by several kinds of parasites and by poor soil conditions. Plant diseases damage many millions of dollars worth of crops each year.

The most serious plant parasites

▲ *A potato plant with leaf roll virus. This disease makes the leaves so brittle that they rattle if the plant is shaken.*

are *fungi*. Next come *viruses*, and then *bacteria*. Fungi and bacteria are themselves plants. One-celled animals and microscopically small worms are other parasites that cause plant diseases.

Hundreds of different types of fungi live on plants. The harmful fungi are *rusts*, *smuts*, and *mildews*. Viruses live within the cells of the plants they attack. Bacteria usually occupy the spaces between the cells of a plant's tissues. These parasites cause a wide range of tumors, warts, and leaf spots. They may also cause the plants to wilt and various parts to rot away. They can stunt a plant's growth, causing it to be dwarfed.

High temperature, high humidity, and lack of sunlight favor the development of plant diseases. The parasites are carried from plant to plant by wind, rain, birds, insects, and people. Packing a few unhealthy fruits, vegetables, or grains along with healthy ones is another way of spreading plant diseases. Shipping diseased crops over long distances may spread a plant disease throughout a whole country.

Plant diseases caused by parasites can be fought by spraying crops with chemicals that kill the parasites. Another way is to breed plants that resist parasite infection. A third way is to prevent plants from being shipped or taken out of an area in which a plant disease is raging. This is usually done by inspecting or stopping crop shipments at the borders of states or countries.

Plants suffer disease due to poor conditions in their environment. The soil may have too much acid or too much alkali. It may contain too much or too little of the chemicals that plants need for healthy growth. Poor soil harms plants just as poor diets harm human beings. Plants often die from struggling to grow in poor soil. Severe air and water pollution kills plants or weakens them so much that they are easily infected by diseases.

ALSO READ: AIR POLLUTION, BACTERIA, DISEASE, ECOLOGY, FUNGUS, PARASITIC PLANT, PLANT, SOIL, VIRUS, WATER POLLUTION.

PLANT DISTRIBUTION Different kinds of plants grow in different places. Willows grow along the banks of streams. Cattails grow in swamps and marshes. Sunflowers grow in fairly dry areas with lots of sunshine. Cacti grow in extremely hot and dry desert areas. Every plant is adapted for life in a certain kind of environment, and if it is not adapted for a particular place it cannot live there. This is what plant distribution is all about. Maple trees, for example, need a certain amount of water in order to survive. A desert has hardly any water, so a maple tree will die if planted in a desert environment. Similarly, palm trees and cacti cannot grow in the cold climate of Alaska. The giant redwood trees of northern California cannot grow in Florida because there is not enough rain.

Plant Environment All plants are dependent upon a particular environment, which includes the climate, moisture, and soil type of the area, as

The biggest cactus is the saguaro of Arizona and Mexico. It has branches that grow to a height of 52 feet (16 m), about nine times the height of a man. Large saguaro cacti may weigh as much as two elephants. Three-fourths of this weight is in the water they store in their great stems.

▲ *Palms are plants that flourish only in tropical regions. These trees provide many useful products.*

PLANT DISTRIBUTION

□	Polar tundra and alpine tundra
■	Needleleaf forest (cool coniferous)
■	Sclerophyll forest and maquis (chaparral) (Mediterranean woodland)
■	Deciduous temperature forest
■	Evergreen tropical forest
■	Steppe and grassland
■	Desert and semi-desert
■	Savanna
■	Tropical deciduous seasonal forest
■	Evergreen temperate forest

▲ *This map shows the main vegetation zones of the world. Climate, soil, altitude, and the effect of people and animals are factors that determine plant distribution.*

well as other plants and animals that live there.

CLIMATE. The temperature in an area affects how fast a plant can take in food. Low temperatures slow down a plant's ability to take in food. In very cold northern areas, the ground is frozen during many months of the year. A plant needs water, but it cannot take in ice through its roots, nor can it dissolve the nutrients in frozen soil. Trees in cold environments have adapted by storing food in their trunks. The sap of evergreen trees and maples is an example of this food storage.

The amount of rainfall is another factor that determines plant distribution. Only part of a rainfall reaches a plant's roots. The rest runs off into streams or evaporates. Sometimes the water goes down too far into the soil so that plants with shallow roots cannot reach it. In rain forests, where there is a great deal of water and heat, plants grow very rapidly and reach very large sizes. Desert areas are hot and have very little rainfall. Plants living there must protect themselves from water evaporation and get as much moisture from the soil as possi-

ble. Cactus plants are shaped so that any rain falling on them immediately runs down to the ground to be absorbed by the roots. Cactus plants also have needlelike leaves. Raindrops do not cling to them and evaporate, as on larger-leafed plants. The rain quickly falls off the needles to the ground, where the roots absorb it.

Sunlight is necessary for photosynthesis (food making) to take place. All green plants need sunlight. But green plants that live in areas of little sunlight have developed adaptations to make food manufacturing faster and more efficient. Ferns, for example, grow on the floors of dense forests where very little light filters through the taller trees and shrubs. Ferns have developed broad leaves (called fronds) that fan out over a large area to capture as much available sunlight as possible.

Humidity is the amount of moisture in the air. High humidity keeps moisture in the soil from evaporating. Desert areas have little humidity, and evaporation takes place very quickly. Rain forests have the highest humidity. The soil stays moist all the time, and plants grow to very large sizes.

Wind causes a high rate of evaporation. Plants living in windy environments have to be able to absorb water quickly. They must also cut down the rate of evaporation from their leaves. Many mountain-living plants do this by means of a hairy covering on their leaves. Strong winds can uproot plants. In seacoast areas that have heavy winds, plants are short, or dwarfed. Their roots are spread out over a wide area in order to get water quickly and at the same time hold to the ground against the force of the wind.

SOIL.   Plants obtain water and nutrients from the soil. Sandy soil does not hold water for very long. Plants such as dune grass are adapted to sandy conditions. They have root systems that spread out in all directions to get water quickly as it filters through the sand. Clay soils hold water for long periods of time.

Soils vary in the amount and kinds of nutrients they contain. Plants that need a certain kind of nutrient, such as phosphorus, will grow best in soil that contains a great deal of it.

OTHER PLANTS AND ANIMALS.   A plant's survival depends on the other forms of life around it. In a garden environment, for example, weeds can use up the soil nutrients and water that were meant for flowers or vegetable crops. Plant parasites attack other plants and feed off them, either killing the plants or making them unable to produce seeds. The chestnut blight and Dutch elm parasites have destroyed whole families of trees in the United States.

Grazing animals feed on grasses. The droppings from these animals provide manure fertilizer that enriches the soil and helps the grasses and other plants to keep growing. Squirrels store food by burying thousands of nuts, such as acorns. The squirrel never eats all the acorns it buries, and so the buried acorns grow into oak trees.

People cultivate many crops, cut down many trees, and dig up the land to build highways and buildings. In all these activities, people change the distribution of plants. People also weaken and kill many plants with air and water pollution, as well as poor farming methods that reduce the nutrients in the soil. Much soil erosion (washing away of soil) and other loss of soil is caused by strip mining and improper farming practices. However, people are experimenting with plant breeding in order to create better kinds of vegetables, flowers, and trees. They are studying ecology to find out how plants and other forms of life are affected by changes in the environment. They are practicing conservation methods in order to save plants from ruin or extinction. People have built greenhouses so plants from

Plants can be found almost everywhere on earth. Divers found seaweed growing at a depth of 880 feet (270 m) off the Bahamas. At that depth there is almost total darkness.

MAIN PLANT ENVIRONMENTS OF THE WORLD

Tundra
Short, cool summers with very long days of continuous light. Soil frozen most of the year, but thaws down about two feet (61cm) in summer.
Main plants: grasses, dwarf shrubs, lichens, and mosses.

Coniferous Forest
Short, cool summers, but warmer than in tundra region. Long, cold winters with much snow. Soil completely thawed in summer.
Main plants: cone-bearing evergreen trees (spruces, firs, birches, and pines) and deciduous larches.

Deciduous Forest
Winters and summers about equal in length. Mild to fair temperatures. Soil rarely frozen. Medium rainfall. Great variety of plants.
Main plants: deciduous trees (those that lose leaves in autumn) and shrubs, with a carpet of small flowering plants.

Grassland
Evenly mild temperatures with seasonal variations and medium rainfall. Wide-open, flat, or rolling landscape.
Main plants: grasses with deciduous trees along edges of water bodies.

Desert
High temperatures, low rainfall, fast evaporation. Little plant cover. Soil dry and usually sandy.
Main plants: succulent species such as cacti, drought-resisting shrubs such as sagebrush and yucca trees, with a few short-blooming desert flowers after rainfall.

Tropical Rain Forest
High temperatures, high humidity, much rainfall. Heavy, very tall plant cover. Soil always moist.
Main plants: flowering evergreen trees, including palms, climbing vines, and aerial plants perched on the branches of the trees.

Aquatic Regions
Wide range of temperatures in bodies of fresh and salt water. Great variety of water plants.
Main plants: algae, duckweeds, sedges, and water lilies in ponds, lakes, and rivers; brown and red algae (seaweed) and eelgrass in oceans, mainly around the coasts.

▲ *Rivers and streams affect vegetation. Where slow-flowing rivers meet the sea, they deposit loads of silt and mud. This soil is colonized by grass and eventually by trees.*

▼ *Many plants have adapted to life in hot deserts. Cacti store all available water inside their fleshy stems, which are protected by thick, leathery skins. Other plants like the mesquite have long roots that seek out moisture deep underground.*

warmer regions can be grown in colder areas of the world. All of these things affect plant distribution.

FIRE. Uncontrolled fire is probably the worst enemy of plants. Fire burns, and plants cannot run away from the flames as animals can. A very big forest fire can totally destroy all the plants in an area. Those plants may never be seen again. The giant sequoias, and redwood trees grow only in a small area on the West Coast of the United States. It takes thousands of years for one sequoia to gain its full growth. One fire could destroy all the sequoia trees forever. Forest rangers and fire wardens constantly watch for the smallest signs of fire—both in forest and grassland areas. On the other hand, not all fire is bad. Foresters often use controlled fire to burn off forest undergrowth that has become too heavy and thick.

Barriers Plant distribution is also affected by natural formations, such as oceans, high mountains, wide deserts, and so on. These barriers keep the seeds of plants in one area from spreading to another area. So although conditions may be alike in the two areas, the plants they support may be different. Seeds that grow on an island in the middle of the ocean would have a hard time reaching the mainland. More than three-fourths of the plants growing in Hawaii, for example, do not grow in other parts of the world.

Temperature can also be a barrier. Plants that grow at the base of a tall, snowcapped mountain cannot survive the cold temperatures at the top. Seeds that may get blown to the top will not grow there. Very tall mountains have what is called a *timberline*. The timberline marks the greatest height at which trees are able to grow without freezing.

In some cases, people have overcome these natural plant barriers. The potato, for example, used to be found only in the Andes Mountains of Peru. In the 1500's, Spanish explorers brought potato plants back to Europe. Today, the potato grows in almost every cool climate.

ALSO READ: AIR POLLUTION, CACTUS, CLIMATE, CONSERVATION, DESERT, ECOLOGY, EROSION, FERN, FOREST FIRE, HUMIDITY, JUNGLE, PARASITIC PLANT, PHOTOSYNTHESIS, PLANT, PRAIRIE, RAIN AND SNOW, SOIL, TREE, TUNDRA, WATER POLLUTION.

PLANT KINGDOM All of the plants on Earth are members of the plant kingdom. In order to keep track of them all, botanists divide the plant kingdom into groups. The plants in each group are all alike in some way. Each large group is called a *division*. The members of a division are alike only in a few very general ways. A division includes thousands of kinds of plants that may look very different from each other. For instance, pond scum and mushrooms are members of the same division. A division is divided into smaller groups called *classes*. The classes are divided into *orders*, and the orders are divided into *families*. Families may still include a large number of members. The daisy family, for example, has 20,000 members. The group next smaller than a family is a *genus*, and the members of a genus are called *species*.

Mesquite
Century plant
Prickly pear
Saguaro
Ocotillo
Evening primrose
Barrel cactus
Creosote plant
Night-blooming cereus

Some Plant Divisions THALLO-PHYTES are simple flowerless plants without roots, stems, or leaves. They may have only one cell or millions of cells. Thallophytes include *algae, fungi, bacteria,* and *lichens.*

Algae contain chlorophyll, which means that they are green plants, although the green color may be hidden by other pigments. Algae vary from single-celled, microscopically small species to many-celled seaweeds up to 200 feet (60 m) long.

Fungi do not contain chlorophyll. This means that fungi do not make their own food and so do not need sunlight in order to grow. They get their food either by living on other plants as parasites or by living on the decaying remains of dead plants and animals. Mushrooms and molds are fungi, and bacteria are sometimes classed as fungi. Lichens are algae and fungi combined.

BRYOPHYTES are *mosses* and moss-like plants. Mosses are small, green, flowerless plants. Like all bryophytes, mosses have no real roots—just fine hairs that absorb water from the soil. Many *liverworts* are flat, branching bryophytes resembling green sea-weeds, although they live on land. Other liverworts are like mosses, and are among the simplest of all land plants.

PTERIDOPHYTES are complex plants that have true roots, stems, and leaves, but no flowers or seeds. *Ferns* are the main type of pteridophyte. Other pteridophytes include *club mosses* and *horsetails.*

SPERMATOPHYTES are the true seed plants. They also have roots, stems, and leaves. They include all flowering plants. Most plants we know today are seed plants. Seed plants replaced most of the other types of plants that existed in the past. This means that seed plants have been the most successful in adapting to climate and soil conditions that exist on Earth today.

There are two kinds of sperma-tophytes—*gymnosperms* and *angio-sperms.* The gymnosperms, or "naked seed" plants, include the coniferous (cone-bearing) trees and shrubs. They have conelike parts, such as the pine cones. Within the cones, the seeds of the plant lie exposed and unprotected. Pines, firs, spruces, hemlocks, and junipers are all gym-nosperms. The largest plants on Earth, the redwood trees, are also gymnosperms. The leaves of many gymnosperms are in the form of nee-dles, which remain on the plant all year round. This is why the trees are called "evergreens."

Angiosperms, or "covered seed" plants, include such different plants as grasses, maple trees, roses, and orchids. The seeds of these plants are protected with a fruit. There are over 200,000 species of angiosperms—more than half the number of all known plants.

The angiosperms are divided into two classes—*monocotyledons* and *dicot-yledons.* The seeds of monocotyledons contain a single seed leaf, or *cotyledon.* Grasses, including grains such as wheat, buckwheat, and rye, are monocotyledons. So are bananas, on-ions, coconut palms, and orchids.

The seeds of dicotyledons have two seed-leaves. There are nearly five times as many dicotyledons as mono-cotyledons, which means that dicoty-ledons are the best of all plants at adapting to different environments. The daisy family contains some of the most highly developed flowers, such as the goldenrod, aster, thistle, chry-santhemum, and dahlia. Some other dicotyledons are carnations, peonies, roses, blackberries, cherries, clover, chickweed, potatoes, tomatoes, to-bacco, melons, and poison ivy.

ALSO READ: ALGAE, BOTANY, EVER-GREEN TREE, FERN, FLOWER, FRUIT, FUNGUS, GRAIN, GRASS, LEAF, MOSSES AND LIVERWORTS, MUSHROOM, OR-CHID, PHOTOSYNTHESIS, PLANT, PLANT DISTRIBUTION, PLANTS OF THE PAST, ROSE, SEEDS AND FRUIT, TREE.

RECORD TREES

Tallest are the California coast redwoods, which grow over 300 feet (91 m) high.

Thickest trunk is that of a Montezuma cypress in Mexico, with a diameter of 40 foot (12 m).

Oldest are the bristlecone pines of Nevada, Califor-nia, and Arizona, nearly 5,000 years old.

Earliest surviving species is the maidenhair tree or ginkgo of China; it first ap-peared about 160 million years ago.

The living thing that grows to a greater length than any other is a plant—the giant kelp. It can grow to a length of 600 feet (183 m) or more, about twice the length of a football field.

GYMNOSPERMS

Gymnosperms are spermatophytes (seed-producing plants). They are woody plants, with naked seeds usually carried in cones. Included in the gymnosperms are ginkgoes, cycads, and evergreen conifer trees such as pine (*shown*), spruce, fir, cypress, cedar, hemlock, and redwood.

ANGIOSPERMS

Dicotyledons are plants with seeds containing two seed leaves. (A cotyledon is the primary leaf of the plant embryo: the *di* in the name simply means *two*.) Most trees and flowers are dicotyledons, or dicots for short. A familiar example is the violet (*shown*).

Monocotyledons, or monocots, are plants with seeds that contain only one seed leaf, or cotyledon (*Mono* means *one*.) Examples of monocots are grasses (*shown*), including wheat, coconut palms, and orchids. These plants are less adaptable than the much more widespread and numerous dicotyledons.

Pteridophytes are plants with true stems, roots, and leaves, but without flowers or seeds. They have what are called vascular tissues, containing tiny tubes through which water and food can pass. These tissues also help the plants to grow tall. This plant group includes club mosses (*shown*), horsetails, and ferns.

PTERIDOPHYTA

Bryophytes were the first plants to adapt to life on dry land. These primitive plants are green, but have neither flowers nor true roots. Most do have distinct stems and leaves. They are the simplest plants to produce embryos—tiny, part-developed plants that grow inside the parent plant. The bryophytes include mosses (*shown*) and liverworts.

BRYOPHYTA

SPERMATOPHYTA or SEED PLANTS

Thallophytes are simple plants without true leaves, stems, or roots. They reproduce by scattering tiny spores; although bacteria and some single-celled algae also multiply simply by splitting into two halves. Thallophytes include algae, bacteria, and fungi such as mushrooms (*shown*).

THALLOPHYTA

▲ *Corn is a useful plant. Apart from providing food, its stalks can also be used to thatch the roofs of houses. These Peruvians in distinctive shawls and hats are walking past a corn field in their village.*

▼ *Reeds are bound together to make these simple boats used on Lake Titicaca in the Andes Mountains of South America.*

PLANT PRODUCTS A very large number of products that are useful to human beings are produced from plants—more than from any other source.

Food is the most important product that comes from plants. There are cereals such as wheat, rye, barley, and corn. There are dozens of fruits—apples, pears, peaches, cherries, grapes, and so on. Berries and nuts, such as raspberries, blackberries, strawberries, peanuts, walnuts, and cashews, all come from plants. Vegetables, such as potatoes, tomatoes, peas, beans, celery, broccoli, lettuce, and onions, are all eaten by people. Spices, such as pepper, cinnamon, cloves, mustard, and ginger, are also plant products. Sugar comes from sugarcane, a member of the grass family, and from sugar beets, which are similar to regular garden beets. Coffee, tea, and hot chocolate are three popular beverages that are made from plants. The soybean is one of the main ingredients in such different products as margarine and plastics. Grasses and other plants are also of immense importance as food for our cattle and other livestock.

The most widely used building material is wood. Wood comes from trees, which are plants. Houses of wood have been built in every part of the world.

▲ *Quinine is a plant product that used to be used in the treatment of the disease malaria. The drug is extracted from the bark of cinchona trees.*

Stone, brick, earth, or baked mud houses usually have roofs, inside walls, stairs, window sashes, and other parts made of wood. In tropical countries, walls and roofs of houses may be made of coconut or banana leaves. Roofs of houses are also made of thatch—straw or twigs woven together. Wood logs are used to make jetties, wharves, docks, and telephone poles. Wood is still a favorite material from which to make boats. Much furniture is made of wood. Tables, chairs, desks, beds, bureaus, and cabinets may be made entirely or partly of wood. However, the commercial chopping down of millions of trees, particularly in tropical rainforests, is causing growing concern because of the change it is causing to our environment.

Tobacco is the leaf of a plant that is smoked in pipes, cigars, and cigarettes. Plant leaves are also the source of indigo and other dyes used for coloring cloth. The bark of many trees produces tannin, a substance used in tanning leather to make it soft as well as long-wearing.

Plants provide fibers that are made into cloth. Cotton and flax fibers are spun into thread, and the thread is

woven into cloth. Clothing, curtains, furniture coverings, and hundreds of other products are made from cloth. The raw material for the artificial fiber rayon is cellulose, which comes from plants. Rope is made from hemp fibers. Fibers of the jute plant are woven into burlap sacks and made into twine.

Paper is made from wood or linen (which comes from flax). Paper is used for writing, printing, or wrapping. It is made into bags, boxes, dishes, and many other products.

Certain trees secrete gums and resins, which harden in the air into sticky or stiff masses. Gums and resins have many uses. Gum arabic, which comes from acacia trees, is used in inks, glues, candies, and medicines. Rubber is made from a gum called latex that comes from the rubber tree. Pine trees give off a mixture of gum and resin that is made into turpentine, which is used in paints. Pine resin is used in the making of soap, sealing wax, varnish, lacquer, and paint. Chicle (the sap of a tropical evergreen tree, the sapodilla) is the main ingredient of chewing gum.

Except for nuclear fuel, all fuels are plant products. Wood is still burned as fuel in many parts of the world. Coal, lignite, and peat are fossilized plants that are burned as fuel. Oil comes from petroleum, which is partly the decayed and fossilized remains of blue-green algae.

Many plants are used as medicines or the sources of medicines. Quinine, once used to combat malaria, comes from the bark of the cinchona tree. Digitalis, for heart disease, comes from the foxglove plant. Ephedrine, for hay fever, comes from evergreen trees.

ALSO READ: ALCOHOLIC BEVERAGE, BUILDING MATERIAL, CANDY, CHOCOLATE, COAL, COFFEE, COTTON, DYE, FLOUR MAKING, FOOD, FURNITURE, LUMBER AND LUMBERING, NATURAL RESOURCES, NUT, PAINT, PAPER, PERFUME, PETROLEUM, PLANT, PLASTIC, RUBBER, SUGAR, TEA, TEXTILE.

PLANTS OF THE PAST Scientists believe that plants were the first living things. The oldest known fossils are remains of single-celled plants much like the single-celled blue-green algae plants of today. The rocks in which these fossils were found are thought to be nearly three billion years old.

For the first one and a half billion years in which there was life on Earth, many scientists believe that all living things lived in the ocean. The first plants were various kinds of bacteria and *algae*. Some single-celled algae became many-celled. These primitive plants resembled the seaweeds that live today in the ocean. Even primitive algae contained *chlorophyll*, the green substance that enables plants to make their own food using sunlight. The first algae must have lived near the surface of the water in order to get the needed sunlight. For many millions of years, they were the only living things on Earth.

After a time, plants like algae, but without chlorophyll, appeared. To get food, they had to live on other algae that were either alive or dead and decaying. These new plants were the first *fungi*. But because there are very few fossil fungi, botanists don't really know how they arose.

▲ *The Masai tribespeople of Kenya in Africa are nomads who wander from place to place. When they find a good place to make a village, they build huts from reeds and grasses.*

▲ *Fibers from the cotton plant are used to provide people with clothing and other useful materials. The cotton thread is woven into cloth on a loom.*

PLANTS OF THE PAST

The oldest plant fossil was found in Colorado in 1953. It is thought to be about 65 million years old.

The Land Plants About 420 million years ago, many scientists think that plants began to live on land. Among the first was a plant called *Cooksonia*; it was a leafless stalk just a few inches tall. The upper end branched, and on the branches were small pods. These held *spores*, the cells from which new *Cooksonia* plants grew. Another kind of early land plant was the *lichen*. A lichen is really two plants living together—an alga and a fungus.

The earliest land plants lived in mud at the shoreline of the ocean because there was no soil farther inland. The land was bare rock covered by rock dust that had been building up for millions of years. Some of this windblown dust piled up around the plants along the shore. When they died, their decaying remains mixed with the rock dust. This formed the first soil. Spores grew in the soil, and the plants that grew from them formed more soil when they died. It took about 100 million years from the time of the first land plants for most of the land to become covered with soil and plants.

As soil spread over the land, plants were able to grow bigger and bigger. There were tree-ferns 100 feet (30 m) tall and horsetails 60 feet (18 m) tall.

THE COAL FORESTS. About 340 million years ago, many scientists believe that the climate all over the Earth was tropical. It remained warm for about 60 million years. The land was often flooded by the ocean, which formed vast, swampy areas. In this warm, moist climate, plants grew abundantly. Besides tree-ferns and horsetails, there were *calamites*. These were related to the horsetails but grew to be 100 feet (30 m) tall and had whorls of flat or needlelike leaves. There were *scale trees*, whose trunks had scalelike scars where leaves had dropped off. *Seal trees* had seal-like scars where leaves had dropped off. About this time, *Cordaites* appeared. These were the first *conifers*, or cone-bearing trees—the ancestors of modern conifers.

All these plants grew quickly to gigantic sizes, died, and fell into the swamps. Layer upon layer of dead plants piled up and sank deep into the mud. The covering of mud kept them

▶ *The plants of the past included giant ferns and club mosses, like these shown growing in a prehistoric "coal forest." When these plants died and decayed, their remains formed coal seams underground. Scientists have found hardened fossil remains of the plants in these coal seams, and some of these fossils are shown in this illustration. From such fossils, scientists have been able to picture what these strange forests of the past were like.*

▼ *A small, low-growing seed fern overhangs a pool of water in the coal forest. Behind it, growing higher up the bank, is the small horsetail named* Sphenophyllum.

▶ *Medullosa was a common seed fern in the coal forests. Its thick, woody stems reached 5 inches (12 cm) in diameter, and its roots penetrated deep into the ground.*

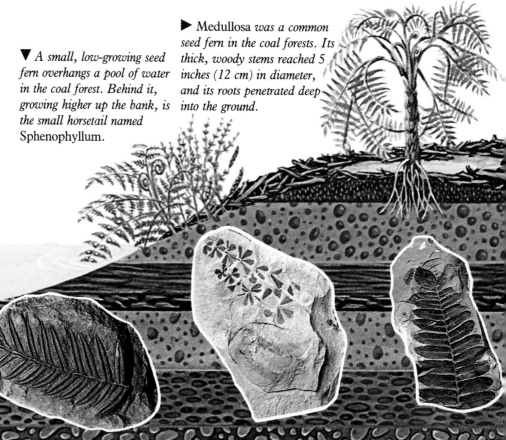

from decaying. The pressure of their own weight, together with pressure and heat from movement of the Earth's crust, slowly changed the deeply buried trees into coal.

SEED FERNS AND CONIFERS. Ferns reproduce by means of spores, but some early kinds of ferns bore seeds instead of spores. These seed ferns were the ancestors of the conifers. Seeds grew within the cones of conifers. Plants that bore seeds that were protected in fruits probably also developed from the original seed ferns.

CYCADS AND GINKGOES. About 250 million years ago, when the Earth was in one of its warm periods, many scientists believe that there appeared a kind of tree looking somewhat like a palm with a very thick, rough trunk. This was the *cycad*. Cycad trees spread widely over the Earth, and

▶ Lepidodendron *was the largest of all the club mosses, growing to a height of about 100 feet (30 m). Some specimens may have reached 130 feet (40 m). Its leaves grew directly out of the stems and branches. On older plants the leaves on the main stem fell off, leaving a pattern of diamond-shaped scars. There were four horizontal branching roots.*

◀ Psaronius *was a tree fern. A crown of leaves sprouted from the top of its stem. The stem appeared large, but most of it consisted of a thick covering of fibrous roots.*

◀ *The giant horsetail* Calamites *grew to a height of about 60 feet (18 m). It grew from a large underground rhizome.*

▲ *Today, many familiar articles are made of plastic. Yet the first plastic to be made completely from chemicals was not invented until 1907.*

then almost died out. Today, about 100 kinds of cycads grow in tropical areas, including Mexico and South America. From the conifers there came *Ginkgo* trees. These, too, spread widely, and then almost died out. Today, the maidenhair trees of Asia are the last of the ginkgoes.

Cereals, Fruits, and Grasses By about 65 million years ago, most of the kinds of plants living today had appeared. There were grasses, including wheat and rye. Flowering herbs as well as fruit and nut trees were growing. One 63-million-year-old rock contains the fossilized leaves of such well-known plants as pepper, alder, and walnut.

ALSO READ: ALGAE, BACTERIA, COAL, EARTH HISTORY, EVERGEEN TREE, EVOLUTION, FERN, FLOWER, FOSSIL, FUNGUS, GRASS, HORSETAIL, LICHEN, MARINE LIFE, OCEAN, PETRIFIED FOREST, PHOTOSYNTHESIS, PLANT, PLANT DISTRIBUTION, PLANT KINGDOM, SEEDS AND FRUIT, SOIL.

PLASTIC Plastic materials have become so numerous that you cannot go through a single day without touching something made of plastic. Toothbrushes, ballpoint pens, unbreakable dishes, cabinets and knobs for machines and appliances, light switches—all these things and many more are made of plastic.

It seems hard to believe that before 1869, there was no such thing as plastic. The first plastic, *celluloid*, was invented in 1869 by John Wesley Hyatt. A $10,000 prize had been offered to anyone who invented a material that could replace ivory for making billiard balls. In his experiments, Hyatt dissolved nitrocellulose and camphor in alcohol. This produced a solid, white material that could be pressed into blocks. The celluloid blocks could then be cut and ground into billiard balls. Mr. Hyatt won the

prize and patented his invention. For more than 40 years afterward, Hyatt's celluloid was the only kind of plastic.

Manufacturers began making it into combs and brushes, buttons, piano keys, handles, and stiff collars and cuffs for men's shirts. Celluloid also became the main material for making plates for false teeth. The celluloid plastic was lighter and had less taste than the hard rubber that had previously been used to hold false teeth. George Eastman, a manufacturer of photographic equipment, invented a way to make celluloid film. Photographers until then had been taking pictures on chemically treated glass plates. Celluloid film aided Thomas Edison in his invention of the movie camera that needed a continuous roll of film.

The main problem with celluloid was that it caught fire easily. In 1909, Leo Hendrik Baekeland, a Belgian chemist living in New Jersey, invented a new kind of plastic called *Bakelite*. Bakelite is hard to burn and impossible to melt. Telephone sets were among the first products made from Bakelite.

Since the early 1900's, many different plastics have been developed, each having a special characteristic or advantage that makes it good for various purposes. Some stand heat better, some withstand shock better, some can be used in liquid form, others can be spun into thread for making fabrics. Plastics are flexible. They can be made hard or soft. Colors can be mixed right into the plastic material, so plastic objects do not have to be painted. Plastics are easily shaped and molded, and they can be used together with other materials, such as metal, wood, and rubber.

The two main types of plastic are *thermoplastic* and *thermosetting*. The thermoplastic types become soft and lose their shape in intense heat, and harden again when cooled. Thermoplastics include acrylics, celluloids, nylon, and vinyls. The thermosetting

SOME PLASTICS

Name and Type of Plastic	Qualities	Some Products Manufactured from It
ACRYLIC (Thermoplastic)	Very strong. Withstands weathering and cold. Holds color well and is an excellent insulator. Has no odor or taste and is nonpoisonous.	Windows, eyeglass lenses and frames, signs, paints, storefronts, floor waxes, auto parts.
CELLULOSICS (Thermoplastic)	Four types—*Acetate, Butyrate, Ethyl Cellulose, Nitrate.* Strong, not easily scratched. Colorful, tasteless, nonpoisonous. Butyrate has slight odor but can be used outdoors. Nitrate is flammable.	*Acetate*—lampshades, toys, twine, vacuum-cleaner parts. *Butyrate*—underground pipe, tool handles. *Ethyl Cellulose*—camera cases, refrigerator and appliance parts. *Nitrate*—frames, table tennis balls, explosives.
EPOXY (Thermosetting)	Strong, hardens quickly. Not affected by heat, moisture, and chemicals. Resists weather well. Good adhesive qualities.	Paints, casting compounds, protective coatings, glues, adhesives, tools.
NYLON (Thermoplastic)	Strong, will not break if dropped. Can be sterilized by boiling. Good electrical insulator. Odorless, tasteless, nonpoisonous.	Fabrics, gears for machines, twine, spikes for athletic shoes, hinges, rollers, dishes, wire, insulation.
PHENOLIC (Thermosetting)	Takes rough use and is hard to scratch. Good heat resistance and electrical insulation. Resists moisture well.	Handles for kitchenware, household appliances, electric tools, telephones, light plugs, switches.
POLYESTERS (Thermosetting)	Can be made into very large products, as strong as product requires. Not easily scratched or scarred. Not affected by weather or water. Withstands shock and impact well.	Boats, car bodies, furniture, roofing, bathtubs, airconditioner cabinets, fishing tackle, roof tiles, fabrics.
POLYETHYLENE (Thermoplastic)	Can be used as liquid and in non-rigid forms. Seals out water but allows flow of oxygen. Can be sealed with heat. Comes in all colors as well as clear.	Plastic bags and food wrappings, squeeze bottles, athletic equipment, mixing bowls, bristles for brushes, ice trays, chair covers.
POLYSTYRENE (Thermoplastic)	Comes in all colors as well as clear. Resists very low temperatures. Seals out water. Good insulator. Surface wears well.	Wall tiles, toys, costume jewelry, shelves, freezer storage containers, dresser sets, refrigerator doors.
SILICONE (Thermosetting)	High elasticity. Can resist extreme heat and cold. Resists weather well. Good electrical qualities.	Elastomer in electrical insulation, seals for jet engines and aircraft windows, waterproof cloth and paper, oven gaskets, greases.
UREA (Thermosetting)	Good insulator. Not affected by chemicals. Not easily broken or scratched.	Buttons, buckles, tops for tubes and jars, clock cases, light reflectors, picnic equipment.
VINYL (Thermoplastic)	Can be made rigid or flexible—sheets, tubes, liquids, etc. Resists tearing and water. Sealed with heat. Usually no odor or taste. Nonpoisonous.	Raincoats, phonograph records, garden hoses, table mats, door mats, curtains, boots, auto upholstery.

types do not lose shape in heat but will keep their shape until destroyed. The thermosetting group includes phenolics, ureas, and polyesters. The chemical process that makes plastic is called *polymerization*. The molecules of the plastic-making materials (oxygen, hydrogen, chlorine, nitrogen, and sulfur) form long chains called *polymers*. Different polymers determine the various kinds of plastics.

Plastics are shaped in a number of different ways. *Molding* is done by putting the plastic materials in molds under heat and pressure. The material is forced into all parts of the mold. The plastic takes the shape of the mold and then hardens. When the

mold is opened, the plastic object is ready for use. Plastic toys are often made by molding.

Casting is similar to molding, except that when the melted plastic is poured into the molds, no heat and pressure are needed. The plastic is simply allowed to cool, and then the mold is removed.

Extruding means "squeezing out." You extrude toothpaste from a tube, and the paste has the shape of the tube's opening. Plastics softened by heat are extruded through a metal plate containing a hole of a particular shape. Plastic bars, tubes, and sheets are extruded. Extruded plastic can be fabricated—in other words shaped or

When the new nylon plastic stockings first went on sale in May, 1940, customers lined up outside stores in New York, Los Angeles, and many other cities. Four million pairs were sold in four days. During the next year more than 64 million pairs were manufactured.

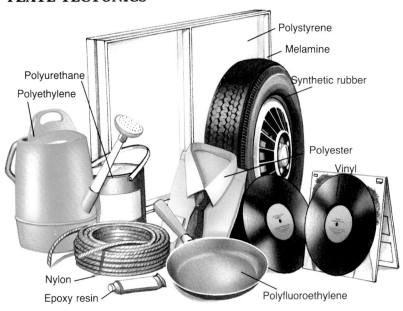

- Polyurethane
- Polyethylene
- Polystyrene
- Melamine
- Synthetic rubber
- Polyester
- Vinyl
- Nylon
- Epoxy resin
- Polyfluoroethylene

▲ *Plastics have innumerable uses because there are many different kinds. They can be soft or hard, rigid or flexible, clear or colored. Some plastic articles are shown here; look around your home and you will probably find even more.*

▲ *A bust (sculptured head) of the Greek philosopher Plato.*

carved by sawing, shaving, or drilling.

Calendering is putting a thin coat of heat-softened plastic on cloth. The coated cloth is put under pressure by running it through heated metal rollers. This presses the plastic into the fibers of the cloth. Products such as tablecloths, tents, and rainwear are made by calendering.

In *laminating*, a kind of "sandwich" is made by placing layers of plastic powder between layers of another material, such as wood or glass. The sandwich is put under heat and pressure. The plastic powder seals the layers of wood together, forming a strong sheet. Plywood and safety glass are made by lamination.

Although plastic is tough and flexible, it must still be treated with care. Certain hard plastics may break if dropped on a hard surface. Plastics cannot withstand rubbing with steel wool, sandpaper, or gritty cleansers. Their surfaces will become dull, scratched, and rough. Clean plastics with soap and damp cloths. Do not keep plastics, especially plastic toys, near heat or flames. Some plastics will burn rapidly, while others will melt.

If broken, most plastics can be readily repaired using adhesive.

ALSO READ: CHEMISTRY, DIES AND MOLDS, MANUFACTURING, SYNTHETIC.

PLATE TECTONICS Plate tectonics is the theory that the Earth's crust consists of several giant, movable plates of solid rock that "float" on the liquid, molten (melted) rock, or Earth's mantle, beneath. The movement of these plates is believed to cause the continental drift (slow movement of the land masses—continents—over the Earth's surface), earthquakes, and the formation of volcanoes and mountains.

Convection currents from the Earth's interior force molten rock to rise to the surface, spread over the ocean floor, and cool. At the same time, the molten rock spreads apart the heavy land masses. The plates push and slide against each other, bending, wrinkling, and causing geological changes. The theory of plate tectonics was first put forward by geologists in the 1960's.

ALSO READ: EARTH, GEOLOGY.

PLATO (about 427–347 B.C.) Most great thinkers in the Western world have been influenced by the ideas of the Greek philosopher, Plato. Plato thought deeply about all the major subjects that concern mankind. The questions he asked and the answers he suggested are still very meaningful to us today.

Plato was born in Athens, Greece. His real name was Aristocles. He was an excellent athlete as a youth and was given the nickname "Plato," which means "broad-shouldered." He became a student of the Greek philosopher, Socrates, and was deeply influenced by his ideas. The execution of Socrates in 399 B.C. by the Athenian government was a bitter blow to Plato. He left Athens and spent several years traveling.

Plato returned to Athens in 387 B.C. and set up a school called the Academy. People traveled from distant countries to hear Plato's lectures on philosophy. One of his greatest pupils was the Greek philosopher, Aristotle.

Plato wrote down his ideas in the form of *dialogues*, or discussions between people. In most of these dialogues, Socrates is portrayed as the teacher. The dialogues explain Plato's ideas on subjects such as politics, law, science, education, art, and the nature of knowledge. One of the best-known dialogues is *The Republic*, in which Plato describes his idea of an ideal, or perfect, government. He compares this government to an ideal person, who must be carefully educated to achieve qualities such as justice and wisdom.

ALSO READ: ARISTOTLE; GREECE, ANCIENT; PHILOSOPHY; SOCRATES.

PLATYPUS The duck-billed platypus is a *monotreme*, an egg-laying mammal. Like most monotremes, it lives in Australia and Tasmania. The platypus has a leathery bill that looks like a duck's bill, and a tail that looks like a beaver's tail with fur on it. When fully grown, a platypus is 16 to 24 inches (40 to 60 cm) long and weights up to four pounds (1.8 kg). The body is covered with a mixture of short, thick fur and long, shiny hairs. The legs are short and stubby and each webbed foot has five clawed toes. The male platypus has a poison spur on the ankle of each hind leg. The young platypus has small teeth, but adults have hornlike plates in their mouths for crushing and grinding food.

The platypus eats small fish and other animals it digs up from muddy stream bottoms, using its bill like a small shovel. It usually dives for food in the early morning and early evening. Normally it stays underwater for about a minute.

Platypuses live in burrows in the banks of streams and lakes. There are two kinds of burrows. One is the nest

▲ *The curious platypus has fur like other mammals, but it has webbed feet and a ducklike beak. It also lays eggs.*

where the female platypus lays her eggs and takes care of her babies. The other burrow is where the male lives, and where the female lives when she is not having babies.

The female platypus lays from one to three soft, leathery eggs, each less than an inch (2.5 cm) long. When the baby platypus hatches, it is blind and without fur. The mother platypus "sweats" milk into the fur of her belly, and the babies lick it. The young platypus lives in the burrow for four months, until it is almost full-grown.

The platypus has few natural enemies and may live to be 15 or more years old. However, in recent times, people killed many platypuses for their skins, and the species almost died out. Now there are strict laws against hunting them.

ALSO READ: ANIMAL, AUSTRALIA, AUSTRALIAN MAMMALS, MAMMAL.

PLUMBING The systems of tubs, basins, pipes, and drains that brings water into our homes and carries it away is called plumbing. A plumbing system consists of two parts—the piping and the fixtures. Piping is usually hidden beneath floors and walls. It carries the water to and from the fixtures. Fixtures are the parts of a plumbing system you can see. They include sinks, bathtubs, drinking fountains, and toilets. They may be made of porcelain, glass, copper, steel, or plastic. The word "plumbing" comes from the Latin word

The eyes, ears, and nostrils of the platypus shut completely when the animal dives under water. Although the animal is blind and deaf in the water, its soft rubbery bill is so sensitive the platypus has no difficulty in finding small creatures to eat.

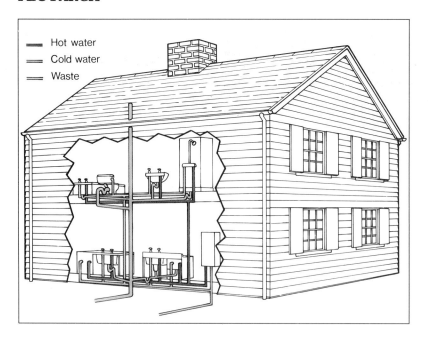

Hot water
Cold water
Waste

▲ *A simple diagram showing how home plumbing brings us fresh water and gets rid of waste. Most homes have plumbing.*

▲ *This painting of Plutarch, the Greek writer, was made sometime during the 1400's.*

plumbum, which means "lead."

The first known plumbing system, which was in Egypt, used lead pipe. Romans later used clay tiles and stone, as well as lead. Thomas Jefferson designed one of the first indoor plumbing systems in the United States in the late 1700's. But most Americans had no indoor plumbing until later.

Today, most people have some form of indoor plumbing. Most houses and buildings are connected to a public water supply, but homes in rural areas often get water from a well. Pipes carry clean water into the house and to the kitchen, the bathroom, and the laundry. Some of the water goes into a tank to be heated. Supplying clean water is the simpler part of plumbing. Getting rid of dirty water and wastes is more difficult. Plumbing must be designed to keep waste out of clean water supplies. Sewer gas and sewage are poisonous. Faulty plumbing that lets wastes enter the water people drink can cause diseases to start and spread.

Water traps keep sewer gas from entering homes. They are the U-shaped pipes under each sink. Water collects in the curve of the pipe and blocks the sewer gas from escaping through the sink drain. Vent pipes carry the gas to the roof, where it escapes into the air. Waste water is carried through a drain pipe into a sewer to be carried away from the house. In rural areas, water drains into a septic tank and cesspool (well for sewage) outside the house. Kitchen waste contains grease. Too much grease can combine with soapy water to block the sewers. Some kitchen sinks have grease traps that collect the cooking grease and let the water run through. These traps must be cleaned occasionally.

ALSO READ: WATER POLLUTION, WATER SUPPLY.

PLUTARCH (about A.D. 46–120) Plutarch was a Greek writer and teacher. His greatest works are a series of biographies (stories of people's lives) and essays. Plutarch was born in the city of Chaeronea, Greece. He was educated in Athens and became a teacher and writer. After returning to Chaeronea, he also worked as a government official and was made a priest. Plutarch's *Moralia* is a collection of about 78 thoughtful essays on many different subjects.

His best-known work is *Parallel Lives,* which contains 50 biographies of outstanding Greek and Roman soldiers, legislators, orators, and statesmen. Most of the biographies are written in pairs—one Greek and one Roman. The lives and accomplishments of the two persons are compared. A typical pair are the Greek-Macedonian conqueror, Alexander the Great, and the Roman emperor, Julius Caesar. *Parallel Lives* was translated into English in the 1500's. The English dramatist, William Shakespeare, based several of his plays on stories from Plutarch's biographies. *Parallel Lives* tells us a great deal about the history of ancient Greece and Rome in an entertaining way.

ALSO READ: GREEK LITERATURE.

PLUTONIUM see NUCLEAR ENERGY, RADIOACTIVITY.

POCAHONTAS (about 1595–1617)
Pocahontas was an Indian princess, the daughter of Powhatan. Powhatan was the chief of the Chickahominy Indians who lived along the coast of Virginia when the English settlers first arrived there. His real name was Wahunsonacock; the colonists named him "Powhatan" after his favorite village. Pocahontas's real name was Matoaka. Pocahontas was her nickname. It meant "playful one."

Powhatan ruled a confederacy of Algonkian-speaking Indians. The Indians fought to stop the settlers from taking their land. According to legend, Pocahontas saved the life of Captain John Smith (about 1580–1631). Smith was the leader of the English colony at Jamestown. He was on an exploring expedition when he was captured by the Indians. Pocahontas stopped her father's warriors from clubbing him to death. Later, in 1613, Pocahontas was kidnapped by the settlers and held as a hostage to prevent Powhatan from attacking the colony. She was converted to Christianity and baptized with the name Rebecca. In 1614, she married John Rolfe, a colonial leader. This brought

▼ *In 1613, Pocahontas was captured by the English settlers, taken to Jamestown, and baptized Rebecca.*

peace between the colonists and the Indians until 1618, when Powhatan died.

Pocahontas went with her husband to England in 1616. She met the king and queen and bore one son, Thomas, there. On her way back to Virginia in 1617, Pocahontas fell ill and died of smallpox.

ALSO READ: AMERICAN COLONIES; INDIANS, AMERICAN; JAMESTOWN; POWHATAN.

POE, EDGAR ALLAN (1809–1849) Edgar Allan Poe was one of America's greatest writers. He wrote poems, essays, short stories, and criticism. Poe was born in Boston. His parents were both actors. His father left the family when Poe was only a year old, and his mother died when he was three years old. John Allan, a Virginia merchant, and his wife raised Poe as a foster child. At college, Poe received little money to live on and turned to gambling. He quarreled with his foster father and was forced to leave college because of his debts. Poe starting writing and published his first work, *Tamerlane and Other Poems*, in 1827.

Poe wrote some of the first detective stories. He also wrote mystery and horror stories. "The Fall of the House of Usher," "The Tell-Tale Heart," "The Gold Bug," and "The Pit and the Pendulum" are among his most famous short stories. Poe's work and his ideas about writing and mankind influenced many other writers, including T. S. Eliot, James Joyce, and André Gide.

Poe married his cousin. They had no children. After his wife's death, Poe became extremely sad and sometimes drank heavily to relieve his grief. Found unconscious on a street in Baltimore, Maryland, Poe died in a hospital.

ALSO READ: LITERATURE.

▲ *Edgar Allan Poe, American writer.*

Edgar Allan Poe created the first ever private detective hero in his novels "The Purloined Letter," "The Murders in the Rue Morgue," and "The Mystery of Marie Roget."

▲ *The most famous woman poet of ancient times was Sappho, a writer of ancient Greece. She lived between 610 and 580 B.C. on the island of Lesbos in the Aegean Sea. She was so famous that her picture was put on coins and vases.*

▲ *John Keats, one of the greatest British poets of the Romantic period in the early 1800's.*

POETRY Poetry is the oldest form of literature. It probably began when primitive people started to chant or sing in time to the beating of a drum. Before people developed a system of writing, they found that the best way to remember a story was to sing it or put it in a certain rhythmical pattern. In this way, poetry was born. Poems were sung or recited for thousands of years before they were ever written down, and reading a poem aloud is still often the best way to appreciate it fully.

Poetry is a form of literature that uses words in more rhythmical patterns than in other kinds of writing or speech. Poetry is like music in that it creates beautiful sounds—but poetry creates them with words. Poetry expresses emotions and ideas in vivid language that excites your imagination and makes you "see" the poem's subject more clearly or in a different way.

Much poetry is written in *rhyme*. Rhyme means that the words at the end of a poem's lines sound alike. A simple rhyme is:

The world is so full of a number of *things*,
I'm sure we should all be as happy as *kings*.

"Things" and "kings" rhyme. Rhyme is not necessary in poetry, however. The use of rhyme simply depends on what the poet prefers. Many poets use rhyme in some poems but not in others.

Rhythm in poetry is the pattern of sound variations—loud, soft, long, short—that the poet uses to create a sense of movement. In speaking, louder and longer sounds are naturally stressed more than other sounds. When you read a poem aloud, you can feel the kind of movement the poet intended. If the poem is happy, you may feel as if you're running or skipping as you read. If the poem is sad, it may seem to move very slowly. Read these lines aloud, and feel the movement:

'Twas the night before Christmas, and all through the house,
Not a creature was stirring, not even a mouse.

This is called *metrical verse*, meaning "measured." ("Verse" is another word for poetry.) Meter has a regular, precise, rhythmical pattern. Meter is based on the *foot*, a group of one stressed sound and one or two unstressed sounds. (The sounds in each kind of foot are arranged in a certain order.) Every line of metrical verse contains a specific number of feet. When a poem is written in meter, words are arranged so that the stressed and unstressed sounds will fall into the rhythmical pattern that has been chosen. In the example above, each line consists of four feet. Each foot is made up of two unstressed sounds and one stressed sound—in that order. (For example, "'Twas the night" is one foot.) This example is rhymed, but metrical verse can also be unrhymed. If a poem has no regular pattern or rhythm, it is called *free verse*. Free verse does not have to rhyme.

The three major types of poetry are narrative, lyric, and dramatic. *Narrative poetry* tells a story. It includes *epic* poems, which are long tales, usually drawn from history, legend, or myth, about some heroic deed. The *ballad* is another sort of narrative poem. It is shorter and is often sung. *Lyric poetry* tells of the poet's own feelings and thoughts. Lyric poems were once sung to the musical accompaniment of a stringed instrument called the lyre, after which the poetry was named. Lyric poems include sonnets, odes, and elegies. A sonnet is a poem of 14 lines with a specific rhyming pattern. (One line must always rhyme with a certain other line, and so forth.) An ode is written in praise of something, such as a glowing sunset or a beautiful old vase. An elegy is a sad poem written in memory of someone who has died. Dramatic poetry has characters who tell a story through dialogue, just as a play does. Some plays, such as those of Shakespeare are written almost entirely in verse.

Poetry has been enjoyed all over the world for thousands of years. Over 700 years ago, the Japanese began writing an especially delightful form of poetry called *haiku*. A Japanese haiku has only three lines consisting of, usually, 17 syllables. The first line has 5 syllables, the second line 7, and the third line 5. Haiku have become very popular with American poets. They are not so strict about syllable length, as the examples here show. Here are some typical haiku by Elizabeth Searle Lamb.

In the hot sun
still   swinging
this empty swing
There . . . a coyote
trotting along a dry wash
Not minding us.
Broken kite, sprawled
On a sand dune, its line caught
In the beach plum. . .

■ LEARN BY DOING

Haiku holds within it a whole mood or thought. It tells of one moment captured from life. When it is read, that moment comes alive again. Haiku can be fun . . . try writing one! Look around for something that pleases you. It might be the soft fur of a kitten. It could be a raindrop rolling very, very slowly, then suddenly fast, down a wet windowpane. An oily patch of water on a city street reflects all the colors of a rainbow. Look closely at the world around you, then, carefully, choose your words. ■

Poems can tell long stories or describe a single second. The love of poetry begins when a baby is charmed by a nursery rhyme. But no one ever grows too old to love the beauty that comes from a poem.

ALSO READ: LITERATURE.

POISON A poison is a substance that will kill you or make you very sick if you swallow it, breathe it, or take it into your body through your skin. Some things are poisons even in very small amounts. Alkaloids, which are in poisonous mushrooms, can kill a person if he or she eats only a very small amount. Other things are poisonous only in large amounts and are harmless or even good for you in small amounts. Small amounts of a drug that slows the heartbeat are good for a person with certain kinds of heart disease. A large amount of the same drug is poisonous, because it will stop the heart altogether.

Some things found in almost every household are poisonous if they are swallowed. Among these are lye, ammonia, bleach, and iodine.

To help a person who has taken a poison, you must do three things, and do them quickly:
1. CALL A DOCTOR.
2. GIVE AN ANTIDOTE.
3. KEEP THE POISONED PERSON WARM.

When you call the doctor, tell him or her exactly what poison has been taken. Follow the doctor's advice. Don't try to take the poisoned person to the doctor instead of calling. You may not have time. If you cannot talk to a doctor immediately, call a *poison control center*. Many states have such places that you can phone to find out what to do about poisoning. The public health department of your town can give you a list of poison control centers and their phone numbers. You should have this list in your home. If you do not know what number to call, ask the telephone operator, who will connect you with the proper authority.

An *antidote* is a substance that combines chemically with the poison and stops its action. If a person has swallowed lye, antidotes are half a glass of vinegar in half a glass of water, or several glasses of lemon, orange, or

▲ *Robert Frost, celebrated American poet of modern times.*

When the famous writer Samuel Johnson was asked what poetry is, he replied: "Why, Sir, it is much easier to say what it is not. We all *know* what light is, but it is not easy to *tell* what it is."

The most deadly poison produced by any animal comes from the skin of the Koboi arrow-poison frog that lives in Colombia, South America. An ounce of the poison could kill over two million people.

POISONOUS SUBSTANCES

Some **household substances** may be poisonous if swallowed. Furniture polish, gasoline, lighter fluid, and kerosene are among these. So are lye, drain cleaner, bleach, dishwasher detergent, and toilet cleaner.

Corrosive poisons include acids and alkalis.

Irritant poisons include hydrogen sulfide and household ammonia.

Systemic poisons include antifreeze.

Poison gases include carbon monoxide, a gas given off by car exhausts, and poorly ventilated coal stoves.

Taken in excess, many **drugs and medicines** can be poisonous, including aspirin and sleeping pills.

Garden and farm **insecticides** and **weedkillers** can kill.

Snake venom is only poisonous if it gets into the blood stream through a bite (not if swallowed).

Poisonous plants include holly (berries); locoweed (leaves, flowers, nectar, and seeds); lily of the valley (all parts); hydrangea (leaves and buds); and deadly nightshade (all parts).

▲ *Poison ivy can cause skin irritation if it is touched. This is because its leaves contain a poisonous oil.*

grapefruit juice. For a "universal" antidote, good for most poisons, mix milk of magnesia, strong tea, and crumbled burned toast.

Sometimes it is best to get the poison out of a person's stomach before giving an antidote. To do this, you must make the person vomit. The easiest way is to tickle the inside of his or her upper throat with your finger. Or, dissolve a tablespoon of salt in a glassful of lukewarm water, and make the poisoned person drink four glassfuls, one right after the other. A drink that causes vomiting, such as this one, is called an *emetic*.

It is NOT always good to make a poisoned person vomit. If the person has swallowed a poison such as lye, which burned the mouth and throat, he or she should not be made to vomit it up. As it comes up, it will burn the mouth and throat a second time. In order to know whether to make a person vomit, read a chart that tells you what to do in case someone is poisoned. You should have such a chart on the wall of some room in your home. You can get a chart from the United States Public Health Service in Washington, D.C. You probably can obtain one from your town's public health service. Ask your teacher how to get one.

ALSO READ: MUSHROOM, POISONOUS PLANT.

POISONOUS PLANT A poisonous plant may be poisonous to touch, or it may be poisonous to eat. Whether a plant is poisonous for touching or for eating depends on the kind of poison it contains and where the poison is. (If the poison is right inside the plant, it will not be poisonous to touch.) How poisonous it is depends on how strong the poison is and how much poison the plant contains.

Very few plants are completely poisonous. Some plants are poisonous only in certain seasons or at certain stages of their development. The *cocklebur* is poisonous only at the seedling stage. Often only a part of a plant is poisonous. Some common foods come from plants that are partly poisonous. The leaf blades of rhubarb are poisonous and so are potato leaves.

The best-known poisonous plant is *poison ivy*. It contains an oil called *urushiol* that can irritate the skin, causing itching and blistering. Poison ivy can be recognized by its three shiny, jagged leaflets on each leaf stalk ("One, two, three, watch out for me!") and by its white berries. *Poison oak* and *poison sumac* are closely related to poison ivy and contain similar poisons. Poison oak also has three leaflets and white berries, but its leaves are shaped like oak leaves. However, poison oak is not really an oak. Poison ivy and poison oak are both vines. Poison sumac is a shrub that can grow as high as 20 feet (6 m). It has 7 to 13 leaflets and white berries.

If you should ever touch poison ivy, poison oak, or poison sumac, wash the oil off quickly with strong laundry soap or detergent. Do not use ordinary bathroom soaps. These will only spread the oil and the itching. Cover the itching skin with a lotion and try not to scratch.

The best protection against poison ivy and other plants that can irritate the skin is not to touch them. If you go walking in the woods, make sure your arms and legs are covered and

▼ *Lily of the valley is a poisonous plant. It was used as a heart drug in World War I, to revive gas victims.*

don't touch strange plants. Don't try to burn poison ivy—even the smoke is poisonous.

Plants that are poisonous to eat are more common than plants that are poisonous to the touch. Many mushrooms and green plants contain poisons that attack the nerves, muscles, blood, or organs of the body. The *fly amanita* is a pretty mushroom with a white-spotted red cap, but it contains a poison that attacks the brain. Another amanita mushroom is called *destroying angel*. Its poison attacks the liver and the kidneys, and there is no known cure for it.

Many plants that are grown because of their beauty are poisonous. The *oleander* is often planted in gardens and along roadsides. Its leaves are poisonous if swallowed or chewed. Many animals and a few children die every year from oleander poisoning. *Bloodroot, lily of the valley,* and *larkspur* are other common poisonous plants. *Deadly nightshade* is another highly poisonous plant, but also has medicinal uses as a sedative.

Many plants that are not strictly poisonous can still make you very sick. There is no rule that will tell you how to recognize all the poisonous plants that grow in woods, fields, and gardens. The best rule is never to eat, and try not to touch, any part of a plant unless you are absolutely sure it is safe to do so.

ALSO READ: PLANT, POISON.

POLAND The Baltic Sea is the northern border of Poland, a country in north central Europe. The former Soviet Union is to the east and Germany is to the west. Czechoslovakia borders Poland on the south. (See the map with the article on EUROPE.) Much of Poland lies in valleys made by rivers that flow to the sea. The main river is the Vistula. The country has many lakes and forests. The only tall mountains in Poland are the rugged Carpathians in the south.

Most people in Poland are descended from the Polians, a Slavic tribe. The Slavs were wandering tribes that lived in the forests of Eastern Europe in prehistoric times. Poland once extended from the Baltic to the Black Sea. Wars with Russia and other neighbors resulted in continual changes in Poland's boundaries. It was several times "partitioned" (divided) between its more powerful neighbors after wars. Poland once disappeared from the map of Europe altogether. After World War I, it became an independent country again. During World War II, Poland suffered from invasion and occupation by Germany and the Soviet Union. Many thousands of Polish Jews died in Nazi concentration camps. In 1945, after the war, the Russians set up a Communist government. Poland became the Polish People's Republic.

Before the destruction of much of Poland in World War II, most of the

▲ *Arum plants have a tuber at the base of the stem that contains a poisonous liquid. Among these plants are skunk cabbage and jack-in-the-pulpit.*

POLAND

Capital City: Warsaw (1,675,000 people).
Area: 120,734 square miles (312,677 sq. km).
Population: 38,320,000.
Government: People's republic.
Natural Resources: Coal, sulfur, copper, natural gas, silver, lead.
Export Products: Machinery and equipment, fuels, minerals, metals, manufactured consumer goods.
Unit of Money: Zloty.
Official Language: Polish.

▲ *The market square of Warsaw, Poland's capital. The square was rebuilt in its old style after its destruction during World War II.*

ests cover nearly one-fourth of the land and yield timber.

Warsaw is the capital of Poland. During the Middle Ages, the city of Kraków was the capital. The castle of the Polish kings still stands on a hill overlooking the city. Warsaw is an important industrial center. Poland's second city is Lodz.

Although religion was not encouraged by the Communist government, 90 percent of Poles are Roman Catholics. The people have sought greater freedoms in recent years, particularly the right to form free labor unions. The Solidarity labor union became a center of opposition to the government in the early 1980s and in 1989, free elections swept Solidarity candidates into power. Poland had a noncommunist-led government for the first time in 50 years.

people were farmers. Now only about one-fifth of the people till the land. The main products are rye, potatoes, wheat, barley, oats, sugar beets, and hogs. Although there are collective farms, owned and run by the state, many farmers own their small plots. Factories owned by the state produce machinery, fertilizers, textiles, tractors, chemicals, iron and steel products, and electronic equipment. For-

POLAR LIFE Late in 1967, Peter J. Barrett of Ohio State University was exploring Graphite Peak, a moun-

tain in Antarctica, the continent at the South Pole. He found a fossil bone. The fossil was examined by Edwin H. Colbert, of the American Museum of Natural History. He said it belonged to a *labyrinthodont*, a prehistoric animal and one of the earliest animals that lived for short periods out of water. Labyrinthodonts were animals of hot climates, so millions of years ago, Antarctica must have been closer to the equator. Scientists found many more fossils that showed Antarctica was once warm and full of living things.

This may seem strange, when you think of Antarctica's icy wastes today, but the continent still has a large animal population. The best-known land animals are penguins. Also found in the waters around Antarctica are many seals and whales. All these creatures must eat fish and other sea life because there are almost no plants at all in Antarctica. And no people live there (except scientists).

Around the North Pole lies the Arctic Ocean, which is frozen over. Also near the North Pole are some very cold areas of land: Greenland, northern North America, and the tundra of northern Russia. Here are more forms of life. There are polar bears on the ice, and seals and fishes beneath it. There are also people, the Eskimos. Tundra regions have some plant life—mosses, dwarf shrubs, some flowers, and a few stunted trees. Animals of the tundra include Arctic fox, elk (moose), and reindeer (caribou).

One bird that seems to like both polar regions is the Arctic tern. It lives and breeds in and around the Arctic during the northern summer. It then migrates to the Antarctic regions during the southern summer.

ALSO READ: ANTARCTICA, ARCTIC, BEAR, CONTINENTAL DRIFT, DEER, ESKIMO, FOSSIL, FOX, MIGRATION, NORTH POLE, PENGUIN, SEALS AND SEA LIONS, TUNDRA, WHALES AND WHALING.

▼ *Pictured below are some of the animals of the Earth's two polar regions: the Antarctic and the Arctic*

Animals of the Antarctic include
1) Emperor penguin, seen here with its chick; 2) Crabeater seal, which eats marine crustaceans; 3) Adélie penguins, which commonly huddle together for warmth; 4) Skuas, fierce birds that prey on the eggs of penguins and other birds; 5) Sheathbills, birds that feed on scraps of seaweed as well as carrion and living sea animals.

Animals of the Arctic include
6) King eider duck; 7) Ringed seal, which has similar habits to the Antarctic crabeater seal; 8) Polar bear, largest of all polar land carnivores; 9) Arctic fox, hunting birds or lemmings; 10) Little auks or dovekies, diving seabirds; 11) Razorbills, relatives of the auks and often called the "penguins of the north."

▲ *A policewoman on duty in Washington. There are some 2 law enforcement officers for every 2,000 U.S. citizens.*

▼ *A police officer stands beside his highway patrol vehicle. He will be checking to make sure no one breaks the speed limit.*

POLICE Police are uniformed men and women employed by a government to protect the lives and property of the people in a community. They try to enforce laws, prevent crimes, and keep things running smoothly. Some police officers, such as detectives, usually do not wear uniforms.

History Since early times, people have felt the need for protection and for regulation of society. This need has resulted in the development of police forces. In ancient societies, warriors acted as police and enforced rules of the tribe. The early Roman emperors appointed a special force to police the city of Rome. The French emperor, Charlemagne, organized a police force in A.D. 800.

The Anglo-Saxons (people who lived in England in early times) developed a system of protection based on groupings of families. Every hundred families elected a *reeve* as its leader and protector. The reeve of a shire, or county, became known as a *shire reeve*, which was shortened to *sheriff*. Each sheriff organized an informal police force to protect the shire. The sheriff system came to the United States with the English colonists. It was used in most American cities and towns until the 1800's.

Boston set up a small force of paid daytime police in 1838. In 1845, New York became the first American city to establish a large, day-and-night police force.

Police Organization Today, there are police departments in every city, county, and state in the United States. Each department is responsible to a certain level of government—local, state, or national—instead of taking orders from just one national office.

A small country town might have a small police department with one or two officers. A large city like New York or Los Angeles might have many thousands of police officers. Large cities are usually divided into districts, referred to as *precincts*. Each precinct has its own police station. The head of the police department in a large city is known as the Police Chief or the Police Commissioner. Officers who rank below are the Chief Inspector, deputy inspectors, captains, lieutenants, and sergeants. Non-ranking police officers are called patrol officers.

Most big city police departments have separate divisions for different kinds of police work. For example, the traffic division directs traffic and gives tickets to traffic offenders. The criminal laboratory analyzes chemical evidence. Police chemists there might test food to see if it contained poison. Detectives investigate crimes or look for clues to find a certain wanted suspect.

County police departments serve an entire county. They are usually run by a sheriff, who also operates the county jail. Every state has some type of state police or state highway patrol force. State police can operate throughout the state.

Federal police agencies try to find people who have violated federal laws. They work closely with local police departments to catch criminals. The Federal Bureau of Investigation (FBI), the Secret Service, the Internal Revenue Service, the Bureau of Customs, the Bureau of Narcotics, and the Coast Guard all have police agents.

Every country has its own type of police. Some European countries have centralized police forces. This means that local police are under the control of a national bureau.

Police Officers and Their Work If a person wants to become a police officer in the United States, he or she usually must have a high school diploma and pass a civil service test. He or she must also be in good health and have no criminal record. Most federal agencies and some local police departments today require applicants to have done some college work. Once accepted into the force, police officers enter a stiff training program. They learn what the laws are and how to give first aid. They are taught the police regulations of their city and how to use weapons.

A police officer works in shifts. He or she might work the day shift from 8 A.M. to 4 P.M., or a night shift starting at 4 P.M. and ending at midnight. A police officer begins the day with a roll call at the station house. Then, he or she receives instructions from the captain. Throughout the day, police officers report back to the

▼ *New York police try to sort out a crying mother's problem.*

station house from telephone call boxes or by means of a radio system. Through the radio system, they can be informed of crimes, accidents, or dangerous situations and go directly to the scene. Police officers in patrol cars have radios installed in their cars. While on patrol, they help people in many ways. They give directions to those who are lost. They may take someone home who is sick or has gotten hurt, or they may take that person to the hospital. Police officers direct traffic to prevent accidents, and they sometimes help children cross the street on their way home from school. Police officers look for stolen cars and watch out for fights and burglaries.

All police officers must train their minds to be alert to unusual activities. They must be able to decide quickly how to handle any type of situation. A police officer's work is very difficult and sometimes dangerous. He or she must be ready to help people at all times, even if it means risking his or her own life. Understanding between the people in a community and the police force is necessary. Police will be able to do their work best if they have the support of the people in their community.

ALSO READ: COAST GUARD, CRIME, CUSTOMS, DETECTIVE, FEDERAL BUREAU OF INVESTIGATION, FINGERPRINT, FIRE FIGHTING, GOVERNMENT, JUDO, LAW, LIE DETECTOR, SAFETY.

POLITICAL PARTY Politics includes everything from campaigning for election (your own or someone else's) to working with elected officials to make sure your interests are represented in government—on the local (city or county), state, and national levels. People have found that their views on important issues have more influence with other voters and with the government if they organize into political parties. Large numbers

▲ *Boston motorcycle police survey the scene beside their powerful and fast motorcycles.*

▲ *Horses are tried and trusty transport for the police force, as seen here in Albuquerque.*

▲ *A political cartoon makes fun of the Presidential campaign of 1912. Woodrow Wilson, who won the election, rides the Democratic donkey. William Howard Taft sits atop the Republican elephant, and Theodore Roosevelt is astride the Progressive Party's bull moose.*

▼ *In the United States, Presidential candidates are selected at political conventions. This picture shows delegates at the Democratic Convention of 1976.*

of people working for a common goal have more power than one person working on his or her own for the same goal.

Political parties nominate a set of candidates for current elections (local, state, and national) who will work for their interests if elected. Political parties write down their viewpoints and aims in a party *platform*. They make sure their views and candidates are well known and encourage voters to support them. Party members work at the polls during elections. When a party's candidate is elected, it can recommend to him or her people for certain jobs. (Those who have actively supported a candidate are more likely than others to receive job appointments when that candidate is elected.)

The United States Constitution does not require any political organizations. But political parties have existed since the beginning of the nation. People in the United States have found political parties the most effective and best organized method of seeking control of the government. There are two major parties in the United States—the Democratic and Republican parties. Some smaller parties exist, but they are not very powerful and few of their candidates are ever elected. Sometimes a third party will support the candidate of a

major party in return for the promised support of some of its goals. People are also free to run for office as independent candidates when no party backs them.

Canada also has a two-party system. Other countries, such as Britain, France, Italy, and Japan, have several powerful major parties. Some countries, such as the Soviet Union, China, and many countries in Africa and Latin America, have only one political party.

ALSO READ: CAPITALISM, COMMUNISM, DEMOCRACY, DICTATOR, ELECTION, FASCISM, PARLIAMENT, PRESIDENCY, REPUBLIC, SOCIALISM.

POLK, JAMES KNOX (1795–1849) "Fifty-four forty or fight!" was the campaign slogan of James K. Polk, who became the eleventh President of the United States. Polk was determined to obtain the entire Oregon Territory from Great Britain, up to the latitude 54 degrees, 40 minutes. He was finally forced to compromise with the British, and the boundary between the United States and Canada was set at the 49th parallel.

Polk was born in Mecklenburg County in North Carolina. He was the oldest of the ten children of a wealthy farmer. He graduated with honors from the University of North Carolina and went to Nashville, Tennessee, to study law. There Polk met former President Andrew Jackson, who encouraged him to go into politics. At the age of 28, Polk was elected to the Tennessee state legislature and, two years later, to the U.S. House of Representatives. Polk served as a representative until 1839, acting as speaker of the House after 1835. He was elected governor of Tennessee in 1839. In 1844, partly due to Jackson's influence, the Democratic party nominated Polk for President.

Polk was a "dark horse" candidate. This means that he was not well

JAMES KNOX POLK
ELEVENTH PRESIDENT   MARCH 4, 1845–MARCH 3, 1849

Born: November 2, 1795, Mecklenburg County, North Carolina
Parents: Samuel and Jane Knox Polk
Education: University of North Carolina
Religion: Presbyterian
Occupation: Lawyer
Political Party: Democratic
State Represented: Tennessee
Married: 1824 to Sarah Childress (1803–1891)
Children: None
Died: June 15, 1849, Nashville, Tennessee
Buried: State Capitol, Nashville, Tennessee

▲ *Gold was discovered in California during the administration of President Polk. Thousands of prospectors traveled west to hunt for gold in the California mountains.*

known, and his nomination had not been expected. Polk's name was not familiar to many Democrats outside of Tennessee. An amusing story is told about how one loyal party member received the news of Polk's nomination. "Hurrah," he shouted. "Hurrah for—what did you say his name was?"

Polk proved to be an efficient President, but he was not a popular one. In 1845, the United States annexed Texas, but Mexico refused to give up its claims to Texas and other territories in the Southwest. Negotiations between the United States and Mexico failed. Polk then sent U.S. troops to occupy territory in Texas and, in 1846, asked Congress to declare war on Mexico. The Mexican War (1846–1848) ended in an American victory. Mexico gave up Texas and later agreed to sell to the United States most of the territory west of Texas, including California. Also, the territory of Oregon was formed during Polk's administration.

Polk refused to be nominated for a second term. His health had suffered during his four years as President. He looked forward to retiring to Polk Place, a mansion he had bought in Nashville. He spent only a few months there before he died.

ALSO READ: JACKSON, ANDREW; MEXICAN WAR; OREGON.

POLLINATION see FLOWER, PLANT, REPRODUCTION.

POLLUTION In 1986, water used to fight a huge fire at a chemical factory in Switzerland poured into the Rhine River. The water was poisoned by the chemicals. The poison killed fish and made the water unfit to drink. The most important European river had become polluted.

This is an extreme example of pollution, but it is going on all the time. When you throw a candy wrapper on the ground, instead of putting it in a trash can, you are contributing to it. There are several forms of pollution. The main ones are:

AIR POLLUTION. Many factories pour poisonous fumes and chemicals, such as nitrogen dioxide and sulfur dioxide, into the air from their chimneys. Automobiles and airplanes release nitrogen dioxide and carbon monoxide from their exhausts. Particles in the air may keep the sun's heat from the ground or may prevent it from escaping back into space, thus heating up the Earth. This heating-up is called the "greenhouse effect."

WATER POLLUTION. Sewage and waste water from factories pour into our rivers and lakes. Water from farmland carries with it chemicals such as weedkillers and insecticides.

The temperature all around the Earth has been slowly rising during the 20th century. Scientists think this is because of the increased amount of carbon dioxide in the atmosphere. (Carbon dioxide is produced when coal and oil are burned.) This carbon dioxide traps some of the sun's heat radiation that would otherwise escape into space.

▲ Pollution is caused by uncontrolled discharge of factory waste, such as soot and smoke. Air pollution can be lessened by using different fuels or by cleaning the smoke before it leaves the factory chimney.

▼ This Persian painting, dated 1529, shows a game of polo. The match is one between the Queen of Armenia and the King of Persia— showing that women as well as men played polo at this time.

SOIL POLLUTION is produced by dumping farm and industrial waste, and by fertilizers, weedkillers, and insecticides. Solid waste matter like a candy wrapper that takes a long time to decay, also causes pollution.

NOISE is also a form of pollution —from airplanes, traffic, even radios!

We can all help to fight pollution by using "environment friendly" products. Some automobiles produce less exhaust and can use lead-free gas. Industries can try to cut down on fumes and farmers can use fewer damaging chemicals.

ALSO READ: AIR POLLUTION, CHEMISTRY, FERTILIZER, GREENHOUSE EFFECT, WATER POLLUTION.

POLO Polo is a game rather like field hockey but played on horseback. There are four players on a polo team. Each player rides a specially trained polo pony. Polo players usually play the game outdoors, although there are indoor polo matches, too. Three persons play on each team in an indoor polo match.

The average polo field is 300 yards (275 m) long and 200 yards (182 m) wide. *Goal posts* are set up 24 yards (7.3 m) apart at each end of the field. A goal is scored when a player knocks the polo ball between the goal posts of the opposing team. The team with the most goals wins.

A polo ball is slightly over three inches (7.6 cm) in diameter. It is usually made of solid willow root and weighs a little more than four ounces (113 g). Polo players use long-handled mallets to hit the ball back and forth. They don't strike the ball with the end of the head of the mallet, as in croquet. Instead, the players hit the ball with the side of the mallet.

The periods in polo are called *chukkers*. Each chukker lasts for 7½ minutes. There are either six or eight chukkers in a polo match.

In the United States, the number of goals a polo player is expected to score in a game is called the player's handicap. The highest handicap anyone can have is ten. In a polo game, the handicaps of each team are added up. Then the smaller rating is subtracted from the higher rating. The difference is added to the weaker team's score.

The game of polo originated in India. Indian horsemen introduced the sport to British army officers. When the officers returned home to England, they organized polo matches there. Some wealthy American sportsmen saw some polo matches in England in the 1870's. They liked the game and introduced it to the United States.

ALSO READ: SPORTS.

POLO, MARCO (about 1254–1324) The Italian adventurer, Marco Polo, made an incredible journey overland to China. He was the first to tell Europeans about the riches and the many unusual sights of the East.

Marco Polo was born in Venice. His father and uncle were wealthy merchants. They had already made one trip to Cathay (as China was then called), and on their second trip, they took the 17-year-old Marco with

▲ *Marco Polo's travels led to European trade with the East. In this painting of 1375, merchants enter Asia.*

them. After a dangerous caravan trip lasting more than three years, they reached Khanbalik (now Peking, China), the capital of the Mongol Empire. They stayed at the palace of the emperor, Kublai Khan. Marco became one of the emperor's closest friends. For the next 17 years, he traveled all over the empire and even served for a while as governor of a Chinese city. He was amazed to find in China an advanced civilization, superior to Europe's.

The Polos returned to Venice in 1295. They showed their friends the silks and jewels they had brought back. Marco dictated a long and detailed account of what he had seen in Asia. His adventures soon became known throughout Europe.

Few people believed Marco's story, and he was called the greatest liar of history. Europeans could not believe that an advanced and cultured civilization existed in China. But in later years, people began to take a real interest in Marco Polo's careful observations. Mapmakers followed his descriptions, and explorers and traders who set out to investigate for themselves discovered his travel stories were accurate.

ALSO READ: CHINA, EXPLORATION.

POLYMER see PLASTIC.

POLYNESIA Polynesia (meaning "many islands") is part of a large group of Pacific islands called Oceania. The other island groups of Oceania are Melanesia ("black islands") and Micronesia ("little islands"). The Polynesian islands are scattered over the central and southern Pacific. Most of the islands lie in small groups. The most important island groups are Samoa, Tonga, the Cook Islands, the Society Islands (including Tahiti), and the Marquesas Islands.

POLYNESIA					
Country or Territory	Status	Area in sq. mi.	Area in sq. km	Population	Capital
American Samoa	U.S. territory	76	197	42,000	Fagatogo on Tutuila
Clipperton Island	French dependency	2	5	Uninhabited	—
Cook Islands	New Zealand territory	93	241	20,000	Avarua on Rarotonga
Easter Island	Chilean dependency	64	166	1,700	Hanga Roa
Gambier Islands*	French overseas territory	36	93	515	Rikitea on Mangareva
Howland, Baker, and Jarvis Islands	U.S. possession	3	8	Uninhabited	—
Johnston Atoll	U.S. possession	1	2.5	1,007	—
Line Islands (Christmas, Palmyra, and other Islands**)	U.S. and British territory	164	425	2,300	—
Marquesas Islands*	French overseas territory	491	1,271	5,500	Atuona on Hiva Oa
Midway Islands	U.S. territory	2	5	13	—
Niue Island	New Zealand territory	100	259	2,300	Alofi
Phoenix Islands (Canton, Enderbury, and other islands**)	U.S. and British territory	10	26	250	Nabari
Pitcairn Islands	British colony	2	5	68	Adamstown
Society Islands*	French overseas territory	650	1,684	123,000	Papeete on Tahiti
Tonga	Independent (1970)	270	699	102,000	Nuku'alofa
Tuamotu Archipelago*	French overseas territory	263	681	9,000	Apataki
Tubual or Austral Islands*	French overseas territory	67	174	5,400	Mataura on Tubuai
Western Samoa	Independent (1962)	1,097	2,842	190,000	Apia
Wallis and Futura Islands	French overseas territory	106	275	15,500	Mata-Utu on Wallis

* Part of French Polynesia
** Excluding islands belonging to Kiribati

▲ *These huge stone sculptures are on Easter Island. Nobody knows who made them. Today, Polynesians live on Easter Island.*

▼ *Palm trees line the white sandy beach of this tropical Polynesian island, where a small fishing community is based.*

Many of the Polynesian islands were formed by ancient volcanoes. The volcanic islands are often rugged and mountainous. Rain clouds build up around the mountains, and the soil is usually rich and fertile. Other islands are low *atolls*. An atoll is a ring-shaped coral reef surrounding a lagoon, or shallow pond of water. A channel usually leads through the reef to the open sea. Most of these coral islands have poor soil, and the climate is dry.

The people of Polynesia are tall and graceful with light brown skins and black, wavy hair. Their language is related to the languages spoken in the other Pacific islands and in Southeast Asia. Many of the Polynesians are farmers. Coconuts are the only crop that grows well on the dry atolls. Copra (dried coconut meat from which coconut oil is made) is one of Polynesia's major exports. Farmers on the fertile volcanic islands grow crops such as yams and taros (root vegetables), bananas, sugarcane, cacao, pineapples, and vanilla. Most of the islanders keep pigs and poultry.

The Polynesians are also expert sailors and fishermen. They build strong and graceful outrigger canoes. In the past, Polynesians made long ocean voyages. The Maoris sailed across the Pacific to settle in New Zealand. Some experts believe the Polynesians may originally have come from South America. The islanders are famous for their crafts. Their traditional carved wooden war clubs and religious figures are now seen mainly in museums. But the people are still skilled at weaving baskets from the leaves of the coconut palm.

Most Polynesians are now Christian. But their ceremonial dancing and singing, still practiced on many of the islands, shows that the old Polynesian religion is not completely forgotten. The idea of *tapu* ("taboo")—that certain objects or people should not be touched—was an important part of this religion.

Easter Island in Polynesia holds one of the strangest mysteries in the Pacific. Gigantic stone heads stand on the cliffs of this island, looking out to sea. No one knows the age of the statues or who carved them.

The English explorer, Captain James Cook, visited the Polynesian islands in the 1700's. He found a people with a rich and well-organized way of life. But European traders and colonists, who flocked to Polynesia in the 1800's, brought diseases that killed large numbers of the islanders. Many of the old ways were forgotten or destroyed.

By the end of the century, most of the islands had been claimed by European countries or by the United States. Tonga and Western Samoa are independent island countries in Polynesia. Some of the Line and Phoenix islands in Polynesia are part of the independent island nation of Kiribati in Micronesia. Other Polynesian islands belong to or are controlled by France, Great Britain, Chile, New Zealand, and the United States.

Polynesians play an important part in local government on most of the islands. Visitors come from all over the world to enjoy the scenery and climate of the islands, and tourism is bringing new wealth to Polynesia.

ALSO READ: COOK, CAPTAIN JAMES; HAWAII; HEYERDAHL, THOR; MELANESIA; MICRONESIA; NEW ZEALAND; PACIFIC ISLANDS; PACIFIC OCEAN.

POMPEII Pompeii was an ancient Roman city in southern Italy. It lay at the foot of the volcano, Mount Vesuvius, on the beautiful coast of the Bay of Naples. Pompeii was a busy port and prosperous trading center. Several Roman nobles built large houses, or villas, near the city.

On the morning of August 24, A.D. 79, when the city was thronged with traders and visitors, Mount Vesuvius erupted. A black, suffocating cloud of ashes blanketed the whole area. Two days later, Pompeii and the nearby cities of Herculaneum and Stabiae lay buried under a deep layer of ashes and mud. About 2,000 people had died.

The cities remained buried, and as the years passed they were forgotten. In the 1700's, farmers digging in their land near Mount Vesuvius began to find traces of the ancient cities. Archeologists gradually uncovered almost all of Pompeii. Much of the city was found exactly as it had been on the day of the eruption. Skeletons of the people who had died in the disaster lay covered in ashes that had dried around them like plaster casts. A dog lay in one of the houses, still chained to his post. Meals, left hurriedly, still lay on the tables. The shops were filled with merchandise.

Visitors can now walk through the streets of Pompeii and into the temples, houses, and shops. They can read advertisements on the walls and admire the paintings and mosaics that decorate houses. More than half of the city has been uncovered today. Pompeii tells a fascinating story about the ancient Romans.

ALSO READ: ROME, ANCIENT; VOLCANO.

PONCE DE LEÓN, JUAN (about 1460–1521) Juan Ponce de León was one of the early explorers of the New World. He claimed the island of Puerto Rico and the land of Florida for his country, Spain.

Ponce de León was born in San Servas in the province of León, Spain. He first sailed to the New World with Christopher Columbus, in 1493. Ponce de León conquered Boriquén (now Puerto Rico) in 1508 and became the first governor of the island.

The Carib Indians on Puerto Rico told Ponce de León about a rich land called Bimini, which lay to the north. They said that Bimini contained the legendary Fountain of Youth, a magical spring that would keep a person young forever. Ponce de León sailed from Puerto Rico in 1513. His aim, according to legend, was to find the Fountain of Youth. On Easter, he reached the land that he named *La Florida*. The Spanish name for Easter is *Pascua Florida* ("flowery Easter"). He explored much of the coast of Florida and then returned to Puerto Rico.

Ponce de León returned to Florida in 1521 to set up a colony. But he was wounded in a battle with Indians. He was taken to the island of Cuba, where he died.

ALSO READ: EXPLORATION, FLORIDA, PUERTO RICO.

POND LIFE A small, still pond may look like a very quiet place. But look carefully, and you will see that it is filled with activity.

Many different kinds of plants and animals live in ponds. The mass of "green scum" you may have seen floating on a pond is really a huge colony of tiny, threadlike plants called spirogyra. These plants are part of the algae group. If you look at a drop of pond water under a microscope, you may see a number of tiny creatures. Some of them may move very fast, and other scarcely move at all. These single-celled animals are called protozoa. Protozoa, along with tiny worms and other small animals

▲ *When Mount Vesuvius erupted, the citizens of Pompeii were buried in ashes and molten lava. When this cooled and the bodies decomposed, molds of the bodies were left. Archeologists have poured plaster into the molds to make casts of the bodies of the victims.*

The Roman writer, Pliny the Younger, described what happened when Vesuvius destroyed Pompeii. Pliny saw the ground shake, the sea sucked back and then hurled forward, and great tongues of flame spurted from the black cloud that boiled up from the volcano. Ashes fell and darkness closed in.

▲ *Ponce de León, Spanish explorer of Florida.*

male flowers

female flowers

▲ *Bulrush, commonly known as cattail, is a plant that grows at the edge of ponds.*

called crustaceans, serve as food for fish and other water creatures.

Yellow perch, bass, pickerel, bream, and brook trout are common pond fish. Freshwater clams, crayfish, snails, frogs, and water snakes are also found in many ponds. Some ponds contain leeches, creatures that can cling to a body and suck blood. Leeches often attach themselves to the turtles that crawl and swim in ponds. Many forms of young and adult insects also live in and around ponds. Mosquitoes and dragonflies fly over ponds. Water beetles, mayflies, and other insects skim across pond surfaces.

On some pond surfaces there may be water lilies and water lily pads (leaves), which are rooted at the bottom of the pond. Underneath and around the water, a number of different kinds of water plants may grow. Besides providing food and oxygen, these plants offer protection and nesting places for other forms of pond life.

Many birds like to visit ponds to look for food or just to swim. Ducks, swans, and geese are often seen in

▼ *Some pond animals will live happily in a small aquarium. In a tank like this, you could keep some pond plants and animals such as water boatmen, water lice, small pond beetles, and even small fish such as stickleback. A single freshwater mussel will help to keep the water clear.*

▲ *Ponds are often rich in nutrients with plentiful plant life, which in turn provides food for insects and other small creatures, as well as for fishes.*

ponds. Herons and other fisheating birds will come to a pond for food. Small mammals, such as beavers and otters, live near ponds. Beavers store their winter food in the dams they build in ponds.

■ **LEARN BY DOING**

You can study pond life in action. Visit a pond or pond aquarium near your home. Scoop up a sample of pond water from the bottom of a pond in a large jar. Allow the mud in the jar to settle. You may see insect eggs, developing frogs (called tadpoles), water beetles, snails, tiny worms, or many other types of living things. Try this study at different times of the day and at different times of the year. Make notes and compare the kinds of things you see. You will have made a survey of pond ecology. ■

ALSO READ: ALGAE, ANIMAL DISTRIBUTION, ANIMAL HOMES, BEAVER, BIRD, CLAMS AND OYSTERS, CRUSTACEAN, DRAGONFLY, DUCKS AND GEESE, FISH, FOOD WEB, FROGS AND TOADS, INSECT, MOSQUITO, PLANT DISTRIBUTION, PROTOZOAN, SNAILS AND SLUGS, SNAKE, TERRARIUM, TURTLE.

PONTIAC (about 1720–1769)

Pontiac was a chief of the Ottawa Indian tribe who made a brave effort to stop English settlement in the region of Indiana, Ohio, and Illinois. He secretly organized an alliance of almost all the Indian tribes from Lake Superior to the Gulf of Mexico. He also allied himself with the French.

At that time, France and England were fighting to see which country would gain control of North America. Pontiac arranged to have his Indian warriors attack English forts in different places throughout the frontier on a certain day in May 1763. Pontiac led an attack on the British fort at Detroit. There, he fought the British for six months. By that time, however, the French had lost the French and Indian War.

Without French support, Pontiac was helpless against the British army. The alliance of Indian tribes came to an end. Pontiac finally agreed to a peace treaty with the British in 1765.

ALSO READ: FRENCH AND INDIAN WAR.

PONY see HORSE.

PONY EXPRESS

The "Pony Express" was the name given to the mail service that operated between Missouri and California from 1860 to 1861. Mail carriers galloped on horseback across the frontier with mail sacks strapped to their saddles. Some of the riders were killed or wounded by Indian arrows or bullets. But only one sack of mail was ever lost by the Pony Express.

The Pony Express began carrying mail between St. Joseph, Missouri, and San Francisco, California, on April 3, 1860. Riders carried the mail about 1,900 miles (3,050 km) from St. Joseph to Sacramento, California. Relay stations were set up about every 10 to 15 miles (15 to 25 km) along the way. There they could change to fresh horses. Each rider rode about 75 miles (120 km) every day. At Sacramento, the mail was loaded on boats to be taken to San Francisco.

The Pony Express route was a dangerous one. In addition to hostile Indians and bandits, riders were sometimes slowed down by snowstorms, sandstorms, and floods.

The first Pony Express trip took about 10½ days. Later trips averaged between 8 to 10 days. This was less than half as long as stagecoach mail delivery took. The fastest time ever made by Pony Express riders was 7 days and 17 hours, to deliver copies of President Lincoln's inaugural address in 1861.

The Pony Express was founded by a freight company. The company first charged five dollars for carrying each half ounce of mail, but this price was later reduced to one dollar. "Buffalo Bill" Cody, "Wild Bill" Hickok, and "Pony Bob" Haslam were among the tough and wiry Pony Express riders.

The Pony Express lasted for only about 18 months. The first coast-to-coast telegraph line was completed on October 22, 1861. This made it possible for people to flash messages across the nation in minutes. Two days after the telegraph began, the Pony Express made its last trip.

ALSO READ: BUFFALO BILL; HICKOK, WILD BILL; POSTAL SERVICE.

▲ *Pontiac, American Indian chief, confers with the council of his tribe.*

▼ *A Pony Express rider speeds past some workmen erecting a telegraph pole. The telegraph quickly replaced the Pony Express.*

▲ *A statue of Saint Peter, the first pope.*

There have been 23 popes called John. The first was pope from A.D. 523 to 526. John XXIII was pope from 1958 to 1963.

▲ *Paul VI, who was pope from 1963 to 1978.*

POPE The pope is head of the Roman Catholic Church. The word "pope" comes from the Latin word *papa*, which means "father." The pope has several other titles, including Bishop of Rome and Supreme Pontiff of the Universal Church. The pope is usually called by a first, or Christian, name that he chooses when he becomes pope. The office of pope is called the *papacy*. The pope lives in Vatican City, an independent state within Rome, Italy.

The pope is elected by a group of Roman Catholic bishops called *cardinals*. When a pope dies, cardinals from all over the world travel to Vatican City. A sacred conclave (meeting) begins from 15 to 18 days after the pope's death. The cardinals are locked inside the Vatican palace until they have chosen a new pope. The voting is conducted in secret in the Sistine Chapel. In order for a candidate to be elected pope, he must receive two-thirds plus one of the ballots cast. Any adult Roman Catholic man can be elected pope, but ever since the 1300's, every pope has been a cardinal.

The pope lives in the Vatican palace. During the summer, he may reside at Castel Gandolfo near Rome. The pope receives no salary. The Church supplies him with all his needs.

The pope has many duties. With the bishops of the world, he makes decisions and rulings about moral and religious matters affecting Roman Catholics. The pope is also the ruler of Vatican City. At one time, the popes ruled a large area of land in Italy called the Papal States. In 1870, the papal states were seized by the newly formed kingdom of Italy. In 1929, Italy and the Vatican signed a treaty and Vatican City became an independent state.

History of the Popes In the early years of Christianity, Rome was the

▲ *Pope Gregory I, called the Great, did much to spread Christianity.*

capital city of the Roman Empire. Saint Peter, the apostle of Jesus Christ, was the first bishop of the Christian Church in Rome. As written in the Bible, Jesus Christ said to Peter (whose name means "rock"), "Thou art Peter, and upon this rock I shall build my Church." Roman Catholics believe that Christ intended for Peter to be the first head of the Christian Church. After Christ's death and resurrection, Peter soon left Jerusalem for Rome. Since that time, Rome has been the traditional home of the popes.

More than 260 popes have ruled the Church since Saint Peter's time. Many have been great men. In the A.D. 400's, Leo I twice saved Rome from destruction by savage invaders. Pope Gregory XIII, in the 1500's, established the Gregorian Calendar, which is still in use today. Pope Leo XIII, in the late 1800's, spoke out in support of the working people and labor unions.

Popes in recent times have encouraged a closer understanding among various Christian churches. Pope John XXIII spoke out strongly against suffering and war. He welcomed leaders of other faiths to visit him. He was much admired throughout the world. John organized the Second Vatican Council, which met several times to find ways of modernizing the church. The council started some of the greatest changes the church has experienced in the last 400 years. After the death of John XXIII, Paul VI, elected in 1963, was the first pope to travel to many countries. He was the first to visit the Holy Land, the United States, and South America. He died in 1978, as did his successor, Pope John Paul I, who served only 34 days. Cardinal Karol Wojtyla of Poland was then chosen pope and took the name John Paul II. He became the first non-Italian pope since 1523. He, too, has traveled more widely than any previous pope.

ALSO READ: CHRISTIANITY, ITALIAN HISTORY, PROTESTANT REFORMATION, RELIGION, ROMAN CATHOLIC CHURCH, VATICAN CITY.

POPULAR MUSIC Music that many people like to listen to is called popular ("pop") music. It is the music played on jukeboxes, by disc jockeys on radio, and on pop videos. It is the "hit" that nobody had heard of yesterday, but that everybody is listening to today. By the end of the month, a new record will have replaced it in popularity. Few people can predict which pop songs will become popular. Publicity helps produce a hit song or star singers. But the music must communicate some emotion or feeling to the listeners, and singers must have some quality of voice, appearance, or personality that reaches out to people.

Popular music has always been a part of life in the United States. The early settlers sang tunes that were popular in Europe, but soon people began putting new words to the old tunes. "Yankee Doodle," which has been called America's first popular song, was a great favorite of the colo-

nial soldiers fighting in the American Revolution.

"The Star-Spangled Banner," with its patriotic words written by Francis Scott Key, was sung to a familiar tune of that time. It quickly became a popular song and was sung in the theaters, taverns, and homes. It was not long before it was adopted by the U.S. Army and Navy. President Woodrow Wilson formally declared it to be the U.S. national anthem in 1916, but Congress did not vote on it until 1931.

During the late 1800's, U.S. popular music included patriotic songs, love ballads, minstrel and vaudeville songs, and the blues or work-songs of black musicians. Stephen Foster and Daniel Emmett were popular songwriters of that time.

By the early 1900's, many publishers of popular music had their offices on 28th Street in New York City. Songwriters were kept busy composing melodies on pianos. Their instruments were not always in good tune, and many songwriters tried to quiet the sound by laying newspapers between the piano strings. Someone once remarked that these muffled pianos sounded like tin pans, and the whole street sounded like a "tin pan alley." This became the name for the popular music business.

Every music publisher sent "song pluggers" out to popularize their songs by singing them in restaurants

▲ *Pope John Paul II, the first Polish pope, blessing children at Knock Shrine during his 1980 visit to Ireland.*

▼ *At a rock concert, the songs are amplified (made louder) through a sound system. Lighting and other effects are used to heighten the excitement of the performance.*

▲ *Pop music is listened to worldwide. This popularity ensured the success of the Live Aid concerts of 1985, organized by singer Bob Geldof (center) to raise money to help famine-stricken people in Africa.*

▼ *This map of the world shows where the most densely populated areas are, in terms of numbers of people per square mile.*

and bars and convincing popular entertainers to use them. Pianists were hired by music stores to play the printed music so customers could hear it. Popular songs in the early 1900's included ragtime and jazz rhythm pieces, as well as songs from operettas and other stage performances. The invention of the phonograph, radio, and the talking movies brought music to more and more people and was important in making songs popular.

From the 1920's to about 1950, there were three main kinds of popular music: the music of dance bands and the songs from Tin Pan Alley; black popular music, often called rhythm-and-blues; and country-and-western music. The songs from musical comedies and movies were also growing in popularity.

In the 1950's, rock-and-roll became the most important popular music. It developed from mixing rhythm-and-blues and country-and-western music with the regular popular music style. Elvis Presley was the first, and perhaps greatest, star of rock-and-roll music. The rock-and-roll beat spread

from Memphis and Detroit throughout the world. Four young musicians (Ringo Starr, Paul McCartney, George Harrison, and John Lennon) from Liverpool, England, called themselves "The Beatles" and became very popular and successful in the 1960's and 1970's.

There are many styles of rock music, including hard rock, folk rock, reggae, and jazz rock. Most rock music is played on electric and electronic instruments and is amplified to make it very loud and to add special sound effects. Lasers and flashing lights are used to create exciting effects on "live" performances, but most pop music is recorded in the controlled conditions of the studio. Much of today's popular music is a mixture of several musical styles, including rock-and-roll, country-and-western, and folk.

ALSO READ: DYLAN, BOB; ELECTRONIC MUSIC; FOLK SONG; FOSTER, STEPHEN; JAZZ; MUSIC; MUSICAL COMEDY; MUSICAL INSTRUMENTS; OPERA; PRESLEY, ELVIS; RECORDING; STAR-SPANGLED BANNER; VAUDEVILLE.

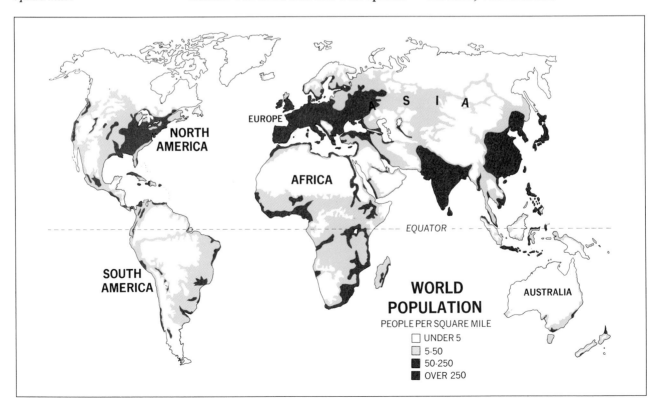

WORLD POPULATION

PEOPLE PER SQUARE MILE

☐ UNDER 5
■ 5-50
■ 50-250
■ OVER 250

POPULATION The total number of people who live in an area make up its *population*. The word comes from the Latin word for "people." To plan for the future, governments of cities and countries need to know how many persons they govern. Nearly all countries of the world regularly count the number of people living in them. This population count is called a *census*. Most countries take a census every ten years. The United States took its last census in 1990. Highly developed, industrialized countries can provide accurate figures. Underdeveloped and undeveloped countries may produce less accurate population figures.

A census tells more than just the number of people living in a particular place. People are asked certain questions, so the census can show, for example, how much money people make, where they live, and how they live. Census figures can be understood only when a person knows how they were determined. The population of a city can vary greatly, depending on whether the number of people in the central city or in the entire metropolitan (urban) area are counted. For example, according to the U.S. 1980 census 562,994 people lived in the central city of Boston. But 2,678,473 people lived in Boston's metropolitan area.

This encyclopedia includes population figures put together by the United Nations. The estimated population of the world is now more than five billion people, according to the United Nations. More than half of these people live in Asia. The world's population is growing faster than ever before in history. Many hundreds of years passed before it reached one billion people in 1840. Only 90 years later, in 1930, it had grown to two billion people. That number doubled again by 1975. Scientists predict that by the year 2000 the Earth will have more than ten billion people. Such

UNITED STATES POPULATION GROWTH 1630 TO 1980, AND PROJECTED TO 2000			
1620	2,500*	1880	50,155,783
1700	275,000*	1890	62,947,714
1740	890,000*	1900	75,994,575
1750	1,207,000*	1910	91,972,266
1760	1,610,000*	1920	105,710,620
1770	2,205,000*	1930	122,775,046
1780	2,781,000*	1940	131,669,275
1790	3,929,214	1950	151,325,798
1800	5,308,483	1960	179,323,175
1810	7,239,881	1970	203,235,298
1820	9,638,453	1980	226,504,825
1830	12,866,020	—	—
1840	17,069,453	1985	c. 232,880,000
1850	23,191,876	1991	c. 252,640,000
1860	32,443,321	2000	c. 260,378,000
1870	39,818,449		

WORLD POPULATION GROWTH 10,000 B.C. TO 1980, AND PROJECTED TO 2000			
10,000 B.C.	10,000,000	1850	1,130,000,000
A.D. 1	300,000,000	1900	1,600,000,000
1600	500,000,000	1950	2,510,000,000
1700	625,000,000	1980	4,225,000,000
1800	910,000,000	2000	c. 6,200,000,000

* estimated colonial population	c. approximate figure

rapid population growth is called a *population explosion*.

Will there be enough food to feed everybody? Some scientists are worried that there will not. Why are there so many more people? One reason is that people now know much more about health care. People live longer, and fewer persons die of disease. Many more babies now live to become adults.

Population figures change because of *migration*. Migration is a shift in population caused by people moving from one place to another. The U.S.

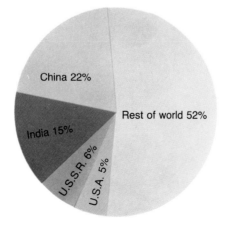

This pie chart shows that China has just over one-fifth (22%) of the world's population. The United States has one-twentieth (5%).

China 22%

Rest of world 52%

India 15%

U.S.S.R. 6%

U.S.A. 5%

The population of western Europe is decreasing quite rapidly. It has been calculated that there will be 25 million fewer people in western Europe by the year 2050 if the present birth rate continues.

1980 census showed that the fastest growing states in population are in the South and West. Also, many people have left the larger Northern cities. And more Americans are living in suburbs, areas surrounding cities, or in rural areas.

Some people believe that the population must be kept from growing any more. They urge parents to have no more than two children. This way, the children would simply replace their parents, and population growth would stop. The idea is often referred to as ZPG, or zero population growth.

■ LEARN BY DOING

Look at some of the continent maps and state maps in this encyclopedia. Can you figure out how people were attracted to places that became population centers? ■

ALSO READ: IMMIGRATION.

PORCUPINE Porcupines are animals that are covered with sharp *quill*, which are very stiff hairs. They are rodents and have large front teeth like their relatives, the squirrel and the rat. Porcupines are divided into two main groups—Old World porcupines and New World porcupines. Old World porcupines live in the forests and grasslands of Europe, Africa, and Asia. They can run fast, but they cannot climb trees. New World porcupines live in forests in North and South America. They are slow moving, but are good tree climbers. Both types of porcupines are plant-eaters. They mate in the fall, and the female usually bears one young in the spring.

A porcupine's quills grow out of its back, sides, and tail. When a porcupine becomes angry, it raises its quills and moves backward toward its enemy. The quills can become painfully embedded in the enemy's flesh and are very difficult to pull out because they have hooked ends. It is not true that porcupines can shoot their quills like spears. A porcupine's quills come out very easily, especially when the animal shakes its body.

The Canadian porcupine is a common New World porcupine. It grows about 30 inches (76 cm) long and has brownish hair. Porcupines that live in Central and South America have long, thin tails like monkeys. They use their tails to hold onto the branches of the trees they live in.

ALSO READ: ANIMAL, ANIMAL DEFENSES, RODENT.

PORPOISE see DOLPHINS AND PORPOISES.

PORTER, WILLIAM see HENRY, O.

PORTRAIT A portrait is a work of art showing us how a person looks. It is usually a painting, but sculptors and photographers do portraits, too. If the person doing the portrait is a true artist, he or she shows us not only how the *subject* (person being portrayed) looks, but something about the subject—what the person's occupation, life style, or character is.

Many ancient cultures—the Egyptians, the Greeks, the Romans, for example—used portraits. The artists often did not flatter their subjects, so that we can read the character of a Roman emperor in his *bust* (sculptured head). Medieval people cared

▼ *The North African crested porcupine eats roots, leaves, and bark. It rattles its quills to warn off an enemy and, if attacked, rushes backward to stick the quills into the enemy's skin.*

less about portraits, but by 1500, they were fashionable again. Here is a portrait of Sir Thomas More, an English official of the early 1500's. With the chain of his office (as Chancellor of England) around his neck, he looks like a person who has great decisions to make. The folded paper in his hand is probably some order that he has just written.

The More portrait is a posed one—that is, the artist has shown the subject sitting very still. Also, the artist has given great attention to the fur and the velvet of the clothing and has taken great care with all the details. There are no strong shadows. Everything is lighted. Later portrait painters often attempted to show their subjects as if caught in action. Thomas Eakins, an American of about 100 years ago, would paint a surgeon operating, a sportsman rowing a boat, a woman singing, or a man pausing to think about something that has just been said. To concentrate attention more on the subject, such a painter might put the head in strong light,

▲ Sir Thomas More *by Hans Holbein the Younger, a portrait painted in 1527.*

leaving everything else in shadow.

Look at the many pictures of people in this encyclopedia, and you will see the ways in which someone can be portrayed.

ALSO READ: DUTCH AND FLEMISH ART; GAINSBOROUGH, THOMAS; HALS, FRANS; HOLBEIN THE YOUNGER; LEONARDO DA VINCI; REMBRANDT VAN RIJN; REYNOLDS, JOSHUA; ROMAN ART; RUBENS, PETER PAUL; RUSHMORE, MOUNT; SCULPTURE; TITIAN; TOULOUSE-LAUTREC, HENRI DE; VELÁZQUEZ, DIEGO.

▼ Eva Gonzales *by the French artist Edouard Manet. He has used her dress as a contrast to the dark background of the painting.*

PORTUGAL The small country of Portugal was once the center of a powerful and wealthy empire. Adven-

PORTUGAL

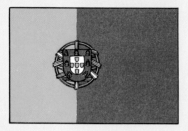

Capital City: Lisbon (860,000 people).
Area: 35,556 square miles (92,082 sq. km).
Population: 10,600,000.
Government: Republic.
Natural Resources: Tungsten, iron ore, uranium ore, marble.
Export Products: Cotton, textiles, cork and cork products, canned fish, wine, timber, resin.
Unit of Money: Escudo.
Official Language: Portugese.

▲ *The Portuguese are a seafaring people for whom fishing is an important activity. Here, a fisherman mends his nets on the shore.*

turous Portuguese explored the seas and established colonies in America, Asia, and Africa. Prince Henry the Navigator studied charts and started Portuguese seafarers on voyages of discovery in the 1400's. The work of Prince Henry's sea captains and their successors led to a planned system of exploration. Bartholomeu Dias, Vasco da Gama, and Ferdinand Magellan were some of the explorers. Portuguese ships brought home the treasures of distant lands. In the 1700's and 1800's, Portugal's empire included colonies in Africa, Asia, and South America. Today, these colonies are independent nations. Portugal has one remaining overseas territory, the tiny enclave of Macao on China's south coast (to be returned in 1999).

Portugal is on the western part of the Iberian Peninsula, which it shares with Spain. Spain borders Portugal on the north and east, and the Atlantic Ocean is on the south and west. Portugal includes two island groups in the North Atlantic, the Azores and the Madeiras. (See the map with the article on SPAIN.)

The Portuguese have always turned to the sea for food and transportation. Their small country has about 400 miles (650 km) of coast along the Atlantic. Important ports and many small fishing villages lie on this coast. Fishermen go out after cod, sardines, and anchovies.

The largest port is Lisbon, the cap-ital city. It lies on the north bank of the mouth of the Tagus River. A Moorish castle, built in the A.D. 900's, overlooks the old part of town where streets are narrow and winding. Some streets are so steep that people ride up and down in cable cars. Lisbon was rebuilt following an earthquake in 1755, which killed many people and almost destroyed the city.

The land north of the Tagus is mountainous. Dark forests of pine and oak cover the rocky hills. Rivers have cut deep valleys into the mountains. Oporto (or Porto), Portugal's second largest city, lies along the Douro river. The hills around Oporto produce grapes that are made into port wine. Coimbra is Portugal's university city. Portuguese industry produces textiles, metal products, paper, and electronic equipment.

Rolling plains lie south of the Tagus River. Olive trees and cork oaks grow here. Portugal is the largest cork producer in the world. The cork grows as bark on these oaks. Workers peel the bark off the oaks in long strips. The plains also produce wheat, rye, and citrus fruits. Farmers work their small plots with oxen and mules.

The Algarve, a resort section of beautiful beaches on the southern coast, is enjoyed by many tourists. The city of Estoril near Lisbon is also a beach resort. Entertainers in cafes often sing the *fado*, a song that tells a sad story. The people of Portugal work hard, but they also celebrate festivals with parades and fireworks.

The Portuguese are descended from the Lusitanians, Romans, and Arabs who in turn ruled the land. In the 1100's, Portugal became an independent kingdom. Before that time, its history was tied with that of Spain as a part of the Iberian Peninsula. The Portuguese language is spoken by more than 145 million people in various parts of the world.

Since 1910, Portugal has been a republic. For more than 30 years, however, the people lived under the dictatorial rule of António Salazar. The Portuguese had few rights then. Salazar's secret police crushed all political opposition. In 1968, Salazar suffered a stroke, and he died two years later. Marcelo Caetano, Portugal's new ruler, was less of a dictator.

In 1974, a leftist military group overthrew Caetano and made many reforms. The secret police was abolished, and rights were restored to the people. Political parties, including the Communist and socialist parties, were allowed in the country. Free elections have been held in Portugal since 1976. In 1986, the country became a member of the European Community.

ALSO READ: BRAZIL; DIAS, BARTHO-LOMEU; GAMA, VASCO DA; MACAO; MAGELLAN, FERDINAND.

▼ *Gathering cork from cork trees. Portugal is the world's main source of cork.*

PORTUGUESE see ROMANCE LANGUAGES.

POSTAL SERVICE When you mail a letter or a package, it goes on a very complicated journey. It starts with the mail carrier who collects your letter from the mailbox, and ends with the mail carrier who delivers it.

Types of Mail The United States Postal Service divides mail into four classes. *First-class* mail includes letters, postcards, and sealed correspondence that is at least partly in writing. *Second-class* mail includes newspapers and magazines. *Third-class* mail includes printed material and packages that weigh less than a pound. *Fourth-class* mail (also called *parcel post*) is for packages that weigh more than a pound.

At the post office, all mail is bundled or placed in special trays and then packed in mailbags. Most mail is transported by truck or airplane. A few trains and ships carry mail. Almost all first-class mail going more than 100 miles (161 km) is carried by airplane. If you want your letter to arrive very quickly, you send it by *express mail*. Often it will be delivered to its exact destination the next day. If you send it by *special delivery*, it will be sent as quickly as possible. You can also send a letter by *certified mail*. The receiver signs a receipt for your

Stanley Gibbons

▲ *This is the world's first adhesive ("stick-on") postage stamp: the British penny black of 1840.*

Balloon mail floated over the heads of German soldiers during the siege of Paris in 1870–1871, keeping the city in touch with the rest of France. The first balloon mail stamp was issued in Tennessee in 1877.

▼ *A selection of mailboxes from four different countries.*

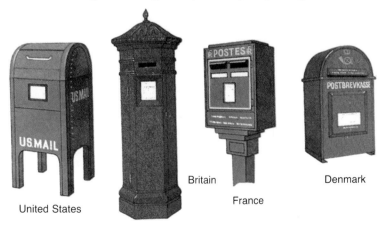

United States

Britain

France

Denmark

There was a postal service in ancient Persia in 500 B.C., where runners carried messages for the king and government officials. The Greek historian Herodotus wrote: "Neither snow nor rain nor heat nor gloom of night stays these couriers from the swift completion of their appointed rounds." These words can be seen today, carved above the entrance to the General Post Office in New York City.

Letters arriving at a modern postal sorting office are stamped with an address code in the form of patterns marked in invisible ink. The ink contains phosphors. The phosphors show up under ultraviolet light and can be "seen" by a sorting machine that directs the letters to appropriate delivery piles.

letter, and the receipt is sent back to you. This "certifies" that the letter was received, and by the proper person. *Registered mail* also uses the receipt system, but it is carried under special protection. Registered mail is most often used when mailing money (checks) or very valuable items.

All mail must be marked clearly with both the sender's and receiver's address. The ZIP Code number is very important. By reading the ZIP Code number, post office workers sort letters and get them to their destinations quickly. All mail must include the correct amount of postage (usually in stamps). Special instructions (such as "special delivery") must be written on the envelope or wrapper.

Postage   Postage is usually attached to mail as stamps that you can buy at a post office or from automatic stamp machines in some stores. Stamps have different values, and special stamps are printed for overseas airmail and special delivery. The U.S. Postal Service sells many special-issue stamps every year. These stamps are printed to honor particular people or events. You can buy postcards and envelopes with the postage already printed on them. Large companies with much correspondence use *postage meters* to stamp and cancel their own mail. A

company must get a special permit to use a postage meter. Businesses that send out a great number of identical items, such as catalogs or newsletters, all on the same day may pay an annual fee for a bulk-rate permit stamp. Companies that do business by mail often send *business reply envelopes* to their customers. The company pays for the postage on those envelopes so that customers can send their orders back free of postage charges.

Handling of Mail   After you drop a letter into the mailbox, postal workers collect it and take it by truck to the post office in your area. Along *rural routes* (postal routes out in the country), the postal officials pick up mail from the same boxes into which they put the mail they deliver. At the post office, the mail is first sorted according to class and size and whether it requires special handling. The mail is then *canceled*. Stamps are marked so they cannot be reused, and the *postmark* (post office name and date) is stamped on the envelope. Next, the mail is sorted by destination. This is where the ZIP Code speeds things up. ZIP Code numbers indicate the post offices to which a letter must travel in order to reach its destination. The first numeral of a ZIP Code number tells you the *regional post office*. The next two numbers tell you the *city* or *county post office*. The last two numbers tell you the *zone*, or local area within a city or county. The ZIP Code number 60614 immediately tells a postal worker that the letter will go to the Chicago Regional Post Office (6), the post office of the city of Chicago (06), zone 14.

Big-city post offices have machines that can automatically cancel and sort letters according to ZIP Code. In smaller post offices, much of the canceling and sorting is still done by hand. The amount of automatic equipment depends on the amount of mail each post office handles.

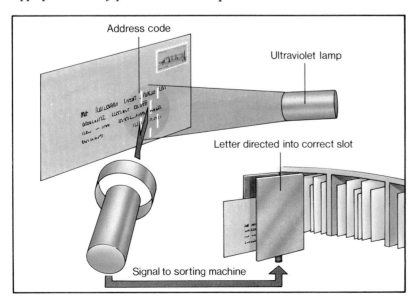

Address code

Ultraviolet lamp

Letter directed into correct slot

Signal to sorting machine

▲ *Nearly 50 mail boxes are nailed to this wooden fence in a remote country area. This is the pick-up point for many homes.*

Some people rent post office boxes. These boxes are located in a post office building. Each is numbered and mail is delivered there. Travelers often have their mail sent to *general delivery* at a post office in a particular city. The post office holds the mail until the traveler comes to pick it up. Letters without stamps or without enough postage will not be delivered and will be returned to the sender. Also, if the mail is addressed incorrectly or if the receiver cannot be found, the mail is returned to the sender. If the receiver has moved and left a *forwarding address*, the mail is sent on to the new address. If the address of the sender was not included, mail cannot be returned to him or her and it goes to the *dead-letter office* where it is eventually destroyed. Dead-letter packages are sold at public auction every few years.

History of Postal Systems Postal systems first began as messenger ser-

vices. One messenger would start out, run a certain distance, and give the letter to a second messenger. The second person would run to a third messenger, and so on. The ancient Assyrians, Persians, Greeks, and Romans all had such systems.

The Romans later set up offices and inns along post roads where messengers could rest and get fresh horses. These places were marked by special posts at the roadside—from which comes the term "post office."

During the Middle Ages, postal systems were patterned on the Roman model. When Marco Polo traveled to China in the 1200's, he discovered that the Chinese had a very advanced postal system. As trade in Europe increased, people needed regular, scheduled messenger services. Post offices were set up in towns and people brought their letters in to be mailed. They paid the postmasters a fee, and the postmasters wrote their names on the envelopes to show that postage was paid.

In 1840, the British government began issuing postage stamps. To mail a letter, people bought stamps in advance and stuck them on their letters in place of the postmaster's signature.

The first post office in the United States was established in Boston in 1639. A man named Richard Fairbanks was given permission to set up a post office in his house. All letters to Boston were sent to the Fairbanks house where Bostonians came to pick up and send out mail. For every letter he received or delivered, Mr. Fair-

▲ *These local stamps were issued in the United States between 1840 and 1866. At this time, some stamps were issued in competition with the official post office, bearing the name of the company issuing them.*

▼ *The first regular airmail service in the United States began in May 1918. For several years, the Army flew mail for the postal service.*

▲ *The United States Post Office also provides many drive-in postal facilities, such as seen here in Arizona. You don't have to leave your vehicle!*

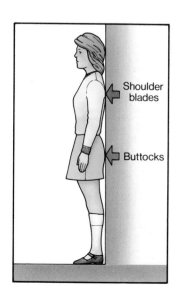

Shoulder blades

Buttocks

banks got one penny. In 1691, the first American postal service was set up by Andrew Hamilton. Letters were carried by mail carriers on horseback between Boston, New York, Philadelphia, and Virginia.

In 1775, the Continental Congress established the first U.S. government postal system. Benjamin Franklin was appointed postmaster general for the country.

International Mail The Universal Postal Union is an organization of the United Nations that regulates mail service between countries. It has representatives from about 150 countries who set up rules concerning international postage rates, delivery procedures, and weights and sizes of international mail. The Union helps new nations set up postal systems, and it handles money matters that arise from international postage rates and services.

ALSO READ: FRANKLIN, BENJAMIN; PONY EXPRESS; UNITED NATIONS.

POSTURE As you sit reading this article, you are probably not thinking about your posture, or the position of your body. But it is important to develop good posture control without even having to think about it.

Good posture refers to the way a normal, healthy person stands, sits, and moves. Posture cannot be defined in an exact way. It is the result of good physical and mental health. A person with a good posture will usually stand with the head held high and the body held comfortably straight, but not rigid.

A good sitting position is one in which the back is held comfortably straight. It is easier to sit in a good position in a chair that is at a comfortable level, so that both feet can rest on the floor.

Most people develop their posture during childhood. Physical or emotional problems during this period can cause poor posture. For example, a person who cannot see well may develop the habit of thrusting the head forward to see better. Eventually, he or she will always stand or sit with the head pushed forward.

■ **LEARN BY DOING**

You can test your standing posture by standing against a wall in your usual position. Your shoulder blades and buttocks should touch the wall. If they do not, your posture may need correction. Ask your gym teacher or family doctor to teach you some exercises that will strengthen your muscles and improve your posture. ■

ALSO READ: EXERCISE, HEALTH.

POTTER, BEATRIX (1866–1943) Beatrix Potter was the author of *The Tale of Peter Rabbit*. The story was begun in the 1890's in letters to the sick child of a friend. When Potter began publishing her stories, she illustrated them herself with delicate drawings in soft, pale colors.

Beatrix Potter was born in London, England, and was educated by a governess. She had a pet rabbit, which was later the inspiration for the story about Peter Rabbit. Several generations of children have been delighted by the story of the adventurous rabbit named Peter that broke into Mr. MacGregor's cabbage patch and barely managed to get home with all his fur. Beatrix Potter also wrote other favorite stories, such as *The Tale of Jemima Puddle-Duck*, *The Tale of Mr. Jeremy Fisher* (a frog), *The Tale of Two Bad Mice*, and *The Tale of Benjamin Bunny*.

If you check one of these books out of your school library, you may find that you enjoy it as much as your parents and grandparents did! Beatrix Potter loved small animals and lovely scenery and enjoyed drawing them. Over the years, her charming, humorous little tales have become familiar throughout most of the world. Beatrix Potter's stories have been translated into many languages. They have even been made into a ballet, created by the British Royal Ballet Company, and filmed as a movie.

ALSO READ: CHILDREN'S LITERATURE.

▼ *"The Mouse Waltz," from the movie of the ballet based on Beatrix Potter's tales.*

THE TALE OF JEMIMA PUDDLE-DUCK

BY BEATRIX POTTER

F. WARNE & Co

▲ *The British writer, Beatrix Potter, was also a talented illustrator. The cover picture (above) and illustration (below) show how well she could paint the animal characters she created.*

POTTERY AND CHINA Objects made from baked clay are called *ceramics*. The pottery maker, or *potter*, mixes clay with water to make it soft. Next he or she shapes the clay into an object and *fires* it by putting it in very high heat. Firing changes the clay, making it stiff and hard so water will not affect it. If you put water in an unfired pot, the clay will become soft and the pot will lose its shape.

Kinds of Ceramics Ceramics made of fired clay are called *earthenware*. In ancient times, earthenware was fired by baking the shaped clay over hot coals for a long time. Today, earthenware is usually fired in a special oven, called a *kiln*, that can produce very high temperatures. Fired earthenware is *porous*—full of tiny holes,

POTTERY AND CHINA

▶ *Firing clay pots in a kiln in Mesopotamia, about 5000 B.C. The pots were stacked on a raised floor with holes in it, while a slow fire burned underneath.*

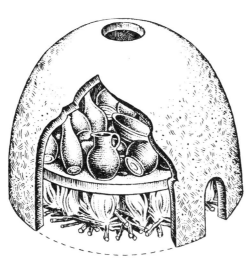

▲ *A piece of pottery from ancient Persia (now Iran) dating back to about 1000 B.C. It is brightly decorated with enamel paint.*

▲ *Greek pots are prized for their beauty and are often decorated with scenes from the Greek myths. This kind of pot, made between 600 and 530 B.C., is decorated with black figures.*

called pores. These pores allow liquids to leak slowly through the fired clay. To keep it from leaking, earthenware is usually *glazed* (covered with a thin layer of glass). Glazes can be of different colors, which add a touch of decoration to the clay. However, earthenware will crack if used over a fire for cooking.

Stoneware is a type of ceramic made with a mixture of clay and crushed rock. When stoneware is fired under very intense heat, the crushed rock melts, filling the pores in the clay. For this reason, stoneware will not leak and does not have to be glazed in order to hold liquids. Stoneware can be used for baking.

The ceramic called *porcelain* was first invented by the Chinese during the Tang Dynasty (A.D. 618–906). Porcelain is made of a white clay mixed with powdered rock. This is fired at temperatures hot enough to melt iron—about 1,560° F (850°C). Porcelain is translucent (light can be seen through it) and extremely hard. When porcelain first came to Europe from China in the 1400's, it was called "China ware." The name became popular, and now the term "china" is used for all fine dishes and porcelain objects.

In the 1500's, craftworkers working for the Medici family in Florence, Italy, tried to imitate the Chinese porcelain. They mixed ground-up glass with clay, thinking that glass

was what made the Chinese porcelain translucent. In firing, the melted glass caused bubbles and cracks to form. The pottery often lost its shape or became thick and heavy, depending on the amount of glass used. Eventually the Italian potters succeeded in making porcelain with glass, but it was not hard like the Chinese type. Porcelain made with ground glass is called soft porcelain, or Medici porcelain. Chinese porcelain, made with powdered rock, is called hard porcelain.

The Making of Ceramics Ceramics were made by all ancient peoples. The earliest known ceramics are about 10,000 years old and come from the Middle East. Before pottery was invented, grain was kept in baskets and liquids were kept in bags made of

▼ *An Egyptian making a pot by hand, in much the same way as his ancestors did 2,000 years ago. The wheel that supports the pot is spun by his feet.*

▲ *Chinese porcelain was so hard and durable that it could even be used to decorate outdoor structures such as this* Wall of the Spirits *in Peking, China.*

animal skins. Baskets were smeared with clay on the inside to keep grains from dropping through the holes in the weaving. When the basket wore out, the lining of dried clay was left. This was the first pottery.

Since these clay pots were only dried and not fired, liquids made them lose their shape. No one knows how or when firing was invented, but ancient people discovered that if a clay pot was baked in a fire, liquids could no longer harm it. People made pots by lining baskets with soft clay and putting them on a fire. When the baskets burned away, people had fired clay pots with basket-weave designs on their surfaces.

This method of shaping pots took a long time because a new basket had to be woven for every pot. A quicker method was to form the moist clay into long rolls and wind them around and around into the shape of a jar or bowl. The outside surface was then scraped smooth, a design was cut into it, and the pot was then fired.

About 3000 B.C., the *potter's wheel* was invented. A ball of moist clay was placed on the center of the wheel. As the wheel spun around, the potter shaped the clay with the fingers. Early potters needed an assistant to turn the wheel. Later, a kick wheel was added so that the potter could use a foot to turn the wheel. Modern potter's

wheels are electrically operated. Making pottery on a wheel is called "throwing a pot." Wheel-made pottery is always curved or round. Other shapes are formed with the hands or with molds.

Different kinds of clay turn different colors when fired—red, yellow, deep brown, black, off-white, or tan. Potters often dip a pot into liquid clay (called slip) of a different color. After the pot is fired, the potter can scratch through the thin layer of slip to expose the original color of the pot and create a two-color design.

The earliest glazed pottery has been found in the Middle East. The ancient Egyptians used many colors of glaze, especially a deep, bright blue. The Persians worked with special plants, called enamels, that could be used on glaze. Enamels were made of ground glass and produced brilliant colors. People living in the Mesopotamian region developed tin-enamel glaze. A tin mixture was added to clear glaze, producing a milky white color. This white glaze provided a good background to paint on. Tin-enamel glazing became very popular and has been used by people around the world.

The ancient Greeks developed a way of decorating pottery with slip instead of glaze. Greek potters usually used red clay to shape their pottery. Then they used black slip to paint figures and designs on the surface. These are called black-figure vases. Red-figure vases were made by painting the background with black slip and leaving the figures and designs in red. After the slip was painted on and fired, the pottery was polished. Greek craftworkers developed very complicated and delicate designs, often portraying the deeds of their gods and goddesses.

Chinese potters made earthenware, stoneware, and all kinds of glazes and enamels. They also used a process called underglazing, painting with colored glazes on the surface of a pot

▲ *A wine pot made of porcelain, made in China during the Sung dynasty (A.D. 960–1279). The pot sits in a warming bowl shaped like a lotus flower.*

▲ *The city of Delft in the Netherlands has been a pottery center for several centuries. This piece of Delftware shows Chinese influence in its decoration.*

before adding a second coating of glaze. The Chinese often carved their pottery to form raised and lowered areas on the surface.

Until the 1700's, the Chinese were the only people who knew how to make hard porcelain. In 1708, Johann Friedrich Böttger in Dresden, Germany, succeeded in making the first European porcelain.

Ceramics of many kinds have been made in Europe. Beginning in the 1400's, Italian potters made an earthenware with tin-enamel glaze called *majolica*. Majolica ware was colorfully decorated with copies of famous paintings as well as scenes from history and mythology. In France and Germany, tin-enamel ware was called *faïence* because it was first brought to those countries from potteries in Faenza, Italy. Dutch tin-enamel ware is called *delftware* because most of it was made in the town of Delft. Delftware potters copied Chinese designs.

Perhaps the best-known European maker of stoneware was Josiah Wedgwood of England. He first developed a cream-colored earthenware with transparent glaze that was very strong. It looked like porcelain but was much cheaper and therefore very popular. Wedgwood copied the shapes of ancient Greek pottery in colored stoneware of blue, green, pink, white, and black. He decorated his pottery with a white stone called *jasper*, and this Wedgwood style has since been widely imitated. Wedgwood was also the first person to mass-produce pottery.

Pottery making was practiced by the early European settlers in North America. Today, the Pueblo Indians are renowned for their pottery. Other modern-day craftworkers enjoy making ceramics by hand. They are creating individual pieces of pottery just as painters create individual works of art. Generally, however, most pottery today is mass-produced in factories. It can be shaped, fired, and decorated quickly and cheaply on an assembly line. Mass-produced decorations are usually applied with transfers, printed papers whose designs are fixed to the piece by firing.

▼ *Many potters use a wheel that is powered by a foot treadle. They control the wheel with one foot, while shaping the pot between thumb and fingers.*

Pot

Wheel

Bowl

Flywheel

Cam

Foot treadle

▲ *An elaborate porcelain vase from the Sèvres factory in France, made in about 1785. Sèvres porcelain is richly colored and gilded.*

■ LEARN BY DOING

If you would like to try making pottery, you can begin by molding bowls and other simple objects by hand. You can buy modeling clay that will be easy to work and will harden on its own, without having to be fired in a kiln. Then you can go on to more advanced pottery, by joining a class. Your school, community center, or a local art museum may have a kiln and potter's wheel you can use—or they can tell you where the equipment is available. Many community centers offer free classes in ceramic making for young people. ■